Monetizing Innovation

How Smart Companies Design the Product around the Price

Madhavan Ramanujam
and
Georg Tacke

WILEY

Cover design: Wiley

Published by John Wiley & Sons, Inc., Hoboken, New Jersey.
Published simultaneously in Canada.

For general information about our other products and services, please contact our Customer Care Department within the United States at (800) 762-2974, outside the United States at (317) 572-3993, or fax (317) 572-4002.

Wiley publishes in a variety of print and electronic formats and by print-on-demand. Some material included with standard print versions of this book may not be included in e-books or in print-on-demand. If this book refers to media such as a CD or DVD that is not included in the version you purchased, you may download this material at http://booksupport.wiley.com. For more information about Wiley products, visit www.wiley.com.

Library of Congress Cataloging-in-Publication Data:

Names: Ramanujam, Madhavan, author. | Tacke, Georg, author.
Title: Monetizing innovation : how smart companies design the product around the price / Madhavan Ramanujam, Georg Tacke.
Description: Hoboken : Wiley, 2016. | Includes index.
Identifiers: LCCN 2016004213 | ISBN 9781119240860 (hardback) | ISBN 9781119240884 (ebk) | ISBN 9781119240877 (ebk)
Subjects: LCSH: New products–Marketing. | Pricing. | BISAC: BUSINESS & ECONOMICS / Marketing / General.
Classification: LCC HF5415.153 .R356 2016 | DDC 658.5/752–dc23 LC record available at http://lccn.loc.gov/2016004213

Printed in the United States of America

10 9 8 7 6 5 4 3 2 1

Praise for *Monetizing Innovation*

"Too many startups focus on product engineering, ignore the customer, and end up failing. We launched last year using the approach in this book, and it led to twice the targeted revenue growth and made the difference between the success and failure of our company. Starting with the customer, market, and price is the only approach for product success."
— Spenser Skates, co-founder and CEO, Amplitude Analytic

"This book is a very practical guide to the difficult decisions that have to be made during the product development process. It's a must-read for anyone responsible for product development."
— Mark James, senior vice president of global pricing and product, DHL Express

"Many savvy marketers have adopted the important paradigm shift in pricing—moving from cost-based pricing to customer value-in-use pricing. The authors of *Monetizing Innovation* persuasively explain the next, equally important, paradigm shift: moving value-in-use thinking from the end of the new product development process to the beginning. Companies that apply this wisdom will see a vast improvement in their ability to identify and capitalize on key market opportunities."
— Robert Dolan, Baker Foundation professor, Harvard Business School

"Madhavan Ramanujam and Georg Tacke use their decades of experience working with companies across the globe to identify the best ways for organizations to innovate profitably. Their book explains how to shift focus—from the product to the customer, from internal concerns to external needs, and from company costs to buyer willingness to pay. Also, and maybe even more importantly, they tell you what not to do with your company's new ideas—to help you avoid product failures."
— Kevin Mitchell, president, The Professional Pricing Society, Inc.

"Coupling customer-driven engagement with up-front pricing strategies enables innovators to avoid failure. *Monetizing Innovation* provides an insightful and pragmatic strategy for innovation and pricing."
— Cary Burch, chief innovation officer, Thomson Reuters

"Way too many R&D teams dedicate their lives to the development of poor product ideas. *Monetizing Innovation* offers game-changing concepts that help create winning products and optimize product margins. It will also make the lives of product development teams more meaningful and fun!"

—Ralf Drews, chairman of the board and CEO, Greif Velox Maschinenfabrik; former CEO, Dräger Safety

"I have had the pleasure of working closely with Madhavan over the years and his work has made a significant impact on companies I am involved with. His book challenges existing thinking that puts pricing at the very end of the innovation cycle and presents a fresh alternative that is realistic to implement. It is a must-read for entrepreneurs and executive management."

—Greg Waldorf, CEO, Invoice2go; board member, Zillow

"Understanding and anticipating what customers value is more critical than ever in this Information Age and the authors' 'nine steps' provide a methodology that can be applied to any industry."

—Nigel Lewis, vice president of aftermarket solutions, Caterpillar

"Pricing power is one of the best predictors of stock price performance over the long run. With *Monetizing Innovation,* Madhavan and Georg address how important it is for pricing to go hand-in-hand with product innovation and design. Not only is the book full of insight and useful information, it dismisses some common fallacies."

—Chet Kapoor, managing partner, Tenzing Global; board member, BrightCove

"When it comes to understanding pricing and monetization, the team at Simon-Kucher is second to none. Any entrepreneur looking to refine their value proposition and pricing strategy should read this book."

—Sheila Lirio Marcelo, founder, chairwoman, and CEO, Care.com

"*Monetizing Innovation* bridges that chasm between mediocre product innovation and trailblazing business transformation. Now product, marketing, and finance teams can all point to a single source of truth—which provides invaluable insights, skills, and ideas to boost product ROI."

—Duncan Robertson, partner, Paxion Capital Partners; former CFO, OpenTable

"Solid price thinking and research used to be one of the few dependable and repeatable secret weapons skilled and experienced entrepreneurs could count on for giving them meaningful customer traction and a cash flow advantage over the newbies and incumbents. With Madhavan and Georg's excellent new book, *Monetizing Innovation*, it is now clearly no longer a secret."

—Allan Pedersen, CEO, Zensur.io; managing partner, Triple P Capital

"*Monetizing Innovation* is very relevant in any global context, especially India, where product innovation is just taking off. However, due to the nascent market, companies are struggling to justify investing in high-risk projects since they may or may not yield long-term returns. This book gives them the blueprint they need to remain competitive."

—Aditya Singh, associate vice president of product, Flipkart

"Innovations can achieve true economic success only when your customers find real benefit from your idea and are, more importantly, willing to pay for it. *Monetizing Innovation* provides the necessary frameworks and checklists to ensure that your ideas can truly achieve such success."

—Lothar Kriszun, speaker of the Group Executive Board, CLAAS

For Hema and Ulrike

CONTENTS

Foreword   *xi*

Acknowledgments   *xiii*

PART ONE: THE MONETIZING INNOVATION PROBLEM   1

Chapter 1   How Innovators Leave Billions on the Table: A
                Tale of Two Cars   3

Chapter 2   Feature Shocks, Minivations, Hidden Gems, and
                Undeads: The Four Flavors of Monetizing
                Innovation Failure   15

Chapter 3   Why Good People Get It Wrong   33

PART TWO: NINE SURPRISING RULES FOR SUCCESSFUL
MONETIZATION   37

Chapter 4   Have the "Willingness-to-Pay" Talk Early: You
                Can't Prioritize without It   39

Chapter 5   Don't Default to a One-Size-Fits-All Solution:
                Like It or Not, Your Customers *Are* Different   53

Chapter 6   When Designing Products, Configuration and
                Bundling is More Science Than Art   63

Chapter 7   Go beyond the Price Point: Five Powerful
                Monetization Models   79

Chapter 8   Price Low for Market Share or High for Premium
                Branding? Pick the Winning Pricing Strategy   97

Chapter 9   From Hoping to Knowing: Build an Outside-In
Business Case   111

Chapter 10   The Innovation Won't Speak for Itself: You Must
Communicate the Value   121

Chapter 11   Use Behavioral Pricing Tactics to Persuade and
Sell: Sometimes Your Customers Will Behave
Irrationally   135

Chapter 12   Maintain Your Price Integrity: Avoid Knee-Jerk
Repricing   149

PART THREE: SUCCESS STORIES AND IMPLEMENTATION   **161**

Chapter 13   Learning from the Best: Successful Innovations
Designed around the Price   163

  *The Porsche Story—Veering Off the Sports Car Track to
    Create Two Winning Vehicles*   164
  *LinkedIn—Monetizing the World's Largest Professional
    Network*   170
  *Dräger—Collecting the Specs for Successful Industrial
    Products before Engineering*   174
  *Uber—Monetizing a Disruptive Innovation through
    Innovative Price Models*   182
  *Swarovski—The Payoff from Crystal-Clear Ideas on
    What Consumers Will Pay*   188
  Optimizely—How to Price Breakthrough Innovation   194
  *Innovative Pharma—How a Customer Value Driven
    R&D Approach Boosts Success*   200

Chapter 14   Implementing the "Designing the Product
around the Price" Innovation Process   207

Notes   219

Index   227

FOREWORD

Innovation is my family business. My grandfather was a master electrician, master machinist, and inventor who came up with a new kind of fire alarm. My father is a physicist who worked day and night at the massive Bell Laboratories research and development facility in Murray Hill, New Jersey, which now has his picture at the door.

Growing up as a Bell Labs kid, I often wondered why these scientists, the smartest guys in the room for sure, were working in what looked and smelled an awful lot like a dungeon. Why weren't they rich and powerful? Of course, it may be that money and success weren't their goals, or there may be truth in the saying: *Good at chess is bad at life.*

But let me put it another way: Why don't all innovations become successful products? Why do so many fail?

This book has the answer.

Consider the way most companies turn ideas into products and services. They start by analyzing costs, a whole constellation of them: headcount, material inputs, machinery, tech requirements, infrastructure support, and on and on. They subtract these expenses from estimated revenues and out pops the expected profit. On that basis, the company places its bets.

But hold on: where did the revenue number come from? There was no careful scrutiny of detailed inputs. Generally, there was nothing more than an educated guess. That's a wild asymmetry of precision. It's even more reckless when you consider that the two elements—revenue and expense—are equally important in determining viability.

But it's much worse than that. With few exceptions, companies do not examine which features are important to the customer, and which are only important to the inventor. They do not know whether the customer wants one flavor, or a choice of many. They do not know if the customer will pay, wants to pay once, or will subscribe.

This is unfair to the innovator. The innovation team should know whether they are wasting their long nights on a concept that will go nowhere. They should know—as is often the case—when a change to the vision could dramatically increase its appeal. But that requires knowledge companies just don't have.

For the CEO, the executive team, and the R&D chief, this book lays out a battle-tested plan for getting back in control. It is based on the work that Simon-Kucher & Partners has done for hundreds of businesses, including my own. It's a straightforward plan, but not a simple one. Much of it counters the prevailing wisdom. There is no "move fast and break things," but there is a lot of "look before you leap."

It may be my bias, but I read it as a love letter to inventors—tough love in spots, but love nonetheless. Those scientists back at Bell Labs with Far Side cartoons taped to every door, the hard-working garage visionaries, the men and women of R&D teams everywhere, they all want the same thing. They want their ideas to come to life. They don't want them to die ignominious deaths on some back shelf.

And for my fellow corporate executives, this is a manifesto. I know of no other book that makes such a clear case for ensuring great new ideas will succeed, or that so clearly explains why we're wasting billions of dollars right now. Ironically, given the title, *Monetizing Innovation* isn't all about the money. Instead, as the authors would say, it's about going from "hoping" to "knowing." It's about taking control of your company's future.

—Eddie Hartman
Co-Founder and Chief Product Officer of
LegalZoom
January 2016

ACKNOWLEDGMENTS

J ust like the new product initiatives we describe in *Monetizing Innovation,* a book itself is the work of many people who play essential roles.

We start with those who allowed us to tell their stories in detail. In alphabetical order they are: Ralf Drews (former CEO of Dräger Safety), Andrew Freed and Josh Gold of LinkedIn, Bill Gurley of Benchmark Capital, Vishaal Jayaswal of Cox Automotive, Christoph Kargruber of Swarovski, Don MacAskill of SmugMug, and Dan Siroker of Optimizely.

Eddie Hartman (co-founder and chief product officer at LegalZoom) and Matt Johnson (a managing partner at Simon-Kucher & Partners) spent countless hours with us reviewing and debating ideas and giving insightful feedback that made our ideas better and more persuasive. We also owe a big special thanks to Cary Burch of Thomson Reuters, Chet Kapoor of Tenzing Global, and John Cline of Western Union for reviewing book drafts and providing invaluable feedback along the way.

Colleagues of ours at Simon-Kucher played the invaluable role of pushing our thinking. Sara Yamamoto helped shape ideas, reviewed chapter drafts, and served as our go-to person and internal editor. Hermann Simon, one of the founders of our firm and a serial book author himself, reviewed our content and provided great feedback as well. Charlie Sun and Justin Roman helped write several case examples and we thank them for their input and dedication. A number of partners and directors at our firm pointed us to examples that you'll read in the pages ahead and opened doors to their executive suites: Philipp Biermann, Gunnar Clausen, Dirk Schmidt-Gallas, Josee Hulshof, Klaus Hilleke, Dirk Kars, Nick Keppeler, Joerg Kruetten, Susan Lee, Rainer Meckes, Nina Scharwenka, Christian Schuler, Ekkehard Stadie, André Weber, and Antoine Weill. Thank you for helping us build the foundation of evidence upon which the book's insights are based. In addition, former Simon-Kucher colleagues Andrew Conrad, Frank Luby, Anya Rasulova, and Kate Woodward were big contributors to early drafts of the book. We thank you very much for your contributions. Finally we wish to thank Petra Dietz from our graphics department for helping with the numerous figures and charts.

We were truly blessed to have an all-star team of reviewers. They were (in alphabetical order): Andreas Altemark, Cary Burch, Robert Dolan, Ralf Drews, Bill Gurley, Stefan Jacoby, Mark James, Vishaal Jayaswal, Chet Kapoor, Christoph Kargruber, Philp Kotler, Nigel Lewis, Sheila Marcelo, Kevin Mitchell, Jens Müller, Marta Navarro, Mike Noonen, Stefan Paul, Allan Pedersen, Duncan Robertson, Hilary Schneider, Aditya Singh, Dan Siroker, Spenser Skates, Leela Srinivasan, and Greg Waldorf. Thank you so much for your support!

We wish to thank Richard Narramore, our editor at John Wiley & Sons, who saw the potential in our early manuscript and helped sculpt it into the book it is now. The book that is now in your hands wouldn't exist without the invaluable help of Bloom Group LLC. Thank you, Bloom Group team members Bob Buday, David Rosenbaum, and Laurie McLaughlin, for getting our thoughts into prose.

We must thank, and thank again, our family members for their nonstop encouragement and understanding. Our wives Hema and Ulrike offered us unwavering support and encouragement and served as an excellent sounding board for ideas. Finally, we also wish to thank our parents and siblings. This book wouldn't have been possible without their support.

—Madhavan and Georg
March 2016

Part One

The Monetizing Innovation Problem

CHAPTER 1

How Innovators Leave Billions on the Table

A Tale of Two Cars

L et's begin with a story about two new cars launched by two well-known, established car companies. One launch went very, very well; the other went very, very wrong.

The first car in our story was launched by Porsche, a relatively small player in the multi-trillion dollar global automotive industry,[1] renowned for its 911 sports car that will take you down the road at nearly 200 mph.

In the early 1990s, Porsche was speeding off a financial cliff—if not at 200 mph, then pretty rapidly. Annual sales were a third of what they had been in the 1980s. The company's manufacturing processes were inefficient and defective. The new CEO, Wendelin Wiedeking, at 41 years old the youngest of a new generation of German auto manufacturing executives, decided to institute Japanese-style manufacturing techniques and quality improvements. Costs fell and sales rose, and the company was able to avoid disaster.

The new CEO had bought Porsche some time. He knew the company needed a fundamental change—something different, something new. It needed, as most companies eventually do, to innovate—or risk losing everything. It needed a new car.

In the second half of the 1990s, the company began planning an automobile that was far outside the sports car niche it had focused on successfully for 50 years. Porsche decided to make a sport-utility vehicle—an SUV—a family car associated not with racing's checkered flags but with soccer moms and soccer dads slumped behind the wheel mournfully recalling their lost youth.

Porsche called its new car the Cayenne.

A Porsche SUV? It didn't make sense. The Porsche brand was about speed and power, daring and engineering, not about loading up the family car with groceries and taking Emily, Mike, and their little friends to their Saturday games. What did Porsche know about SUVs? It had never built one before.

But Porsche had done its homework. Specifically, it had designed and built the product—the Cayenne—around the price.

When most people hear the word "price," they think of a number. That's a *price point*. When we use the term price, we are trying to get at something more fundamental. We want to understand the *perceived value* that the innovation holds for the customer. How much is the customer willing to pay for that value? What would the demand be? Seen in this light, price is both an indication of what customers value and a measure of how much they are willing to pay for that value.

Porsche understood all this when it set about creating the Cayenne. Porsche's top executives knew they had a bold, perhaps even revolutionary, concept. They also knew the car would be a tremendous risk. They instructed their product team to rigorously determine what the customer wanted in a Porsche SUV and, importantly, how much they were willing to pay. The message was clear: If the customer was not willing to pay a price that would ensure success, Porsche would walk away from the Cayenne.

Long before the first concept car rolled out of the Engineering Group center in Weissach, the product team conducted an extensive set of surveys with potential customers, gauging the appetite for a Porsche SUV and evaluating prices to find an acceptable range. They were pleased to find that customers were enthusiastic. Analysis showed that customers were willing to pay more for a Porsche SUV than they would for comparable vehicles from other manufacturers. The potential for a hit was there.

This meant that Porsche could invest in building its SUV.

But what exactly should it build? Porsche wasn't about to risk creating a car with a bloated design. Every single feature stood trial before the customer.

Target customers wanted and were willing to pay for a high—and in this vehicle category, unknown—level of sportiness. They expressed an interest in a powerful engine and a handling performance close to a sports car (despite the size of an SUV). Porsche's famous manual six-speed racing transmission was not on the wish list. Out it went. But the voice of the customer convinced the Porsche engineers to include large cup holders, something Porsche was not used to. At every turn, the product team removed features the customers did not value—even if the engineers loved them—and replaced those with features customers were actually willing to pay for.

Porsche's masterstroke was thinking about monetization long before product development for the SUV was in full speed, then designing a car with the value and features customers wanted the most, around a price that made sense. The result was total corporate alignment: Porsche knew it had a winner, and had the confidence to invest accordingly.

Over time the Cayenne enabled Porsche to generate the highest profits per car in the industry—the whole automotive industry. Ten years after it hit the market in 2003, Porsche was selling about 100,000 Cayennes annually, almost five times as many as it did in the launch year. Today, the Cayenne accounts for about half the company's total profit, with the venerable 911 generating a third.[2] What's more, the Cayenne enabled Porsche to pay down a suffocating level of debt and increase its cash reserves.

By any and all measures, the Cayenne was a roaring success.

Why did Porsche succeed? It wasn't the company's engineering prowess, although the Cayenne drives quite nicely. And it wasn't a technological breakthrough that enabled Porsche to manufacture SUVs more efficiently or make consumer hearts beat faster. Porsche succeeded by designing the product around the price. This is what smart companies do.

Now, we turn to the second car in our tale. This car comes from Fiat Chrysler, a company that has six times the revenue of Porsche. In 2009, the massive automaker began working to bring something new into the world: a reimagining of the classic 1970s Dodge Dart.

The new Dodge Dart was a crucial entry in a crucial market segment for Fiat Chrysler: compact cars. Fiat Chrysler needed the Dart badly to make the company competitive in the category, a segment in which it had struggled for years. Compacts account for one in every six vehicles sold in America. Every major automaker must succeed in the compact market, explained Fiat Chrysler CEO Sergio Marchionne in a March 2012 interview on *60 Minutes*. Any carmaker unable to succeed in the category was "doomed," he said.[3]

Marchionne didn't mince words within the company about the importance of the Dart. He told employees just what was riding on the car. "Our future hangs on how well we do here," he told workers in a 2012 visit to the car's Belvidere, Illinois, plant. He backed up his words with money, committing hundreds of millions of dollars to turn a very successful Fiat model (the Alfa Romeo Giulietta) into a Dodge Dart.

"Of all the cars I can get wrong," Marchionne said, "it ain't this one."

Both cars were equally critical to their companies' futures. However, Fiat Chrysler's approach to developing the Dart was radically different from Porsche's Cayenne. Rather than starting with a hard look at the customer, Fiat Chrysler took a hard look at the product.

As it documented in a 90-second TV commercial to market the car,[4] Fiat Chrysler's product development process was to design it, build it, rethink it, design it, build it, rethink it—until the engineering team, in its exclusive opinion, felt the car was ready to go. In fact, the advertisement announced proudly that the company was "kicking the finance guys" out of the development process. Money was not going to be an issue. The company would build prototype after prototype to get it right. The executive team "suits" would only interfere with designing the Dart. This car would be built to perfection, the commercial suggested.

"Perfection" as defined by Fiat Chrysler, not the customer.

Then a price was slapped on, and Dodge took it to customers to try to sell it.

Market performance was a disaster. In 2012, the year it launched, the Dart sold about 25,000 units[5]—a quarter of the total predicted by market analysts and a number that caused Dow Jones's MarketWatch to call the Dart the year's second biggest new product flop. The number one spot was given to Apple's buggy iPhone mapping software. That's right: The Dart was "Apple Maps bad."

Since then, the Dart has failed to lure most compact car buyers away from the two segment leaders, Toyota's Corolla and Honda's Civic, or even from Chevrolet's Cruze and Ford's Focus. By the end of 2014, sales were so disappointing that the company had to issue temporary layoffs at its Belvidere plant. Ironically, these were the same workers who two years earlier had heard Marchionne say that Dart was the one car the company couldn't afford to get wrong. In the first nine months of 2015, Dart sales were only a seventh of the combined sales of the two compact segment leaders.[6]

Fiat Chrysler couldn't afford to get the Dart wrong, but it did.

The reason Porsche succeeded with the Cayenne and the reason Fiat Chrysler bombed with the Dart are the same reasons product innovations have succeeded or failed at so many companies in so many industries over the last 30 years: *Porsche placed customer needs, value, willingness to pay, and pricing in the driver's seat when it developed the Cayenne; Fiat Chrysler stuffed them in the trunk.*

This story is less about the cars than about the two different modes of thinking that went into launching them, and why one way produced a success that helped put its company on an accelerated growth path while the other produced a flop that led to layoffs.

Porsche designed its new car around the price—what the customer valued and wanted to buy; Fiat Chrysler did not.

This story illustrates the main theme of this book: How companies bringing something new into the world can leverage the science of monetizing innovation, increase the chances that their new offerings will succeed, and produce results that can be magical. The odds against successful innovation are always high. But, as you read, you'll learn how a focus on monetizing innovation can substantially increase your chances of financial success.

Unhappily, more new products in every industry go the way of the Dart, and far too few enjoy the success of the Cayenne. We see it all the time. But every company has a chance to create Cayennes and reduce the risk of Darts. The key is to rigorously determine the market for a new product long before the products are built, and making sure the market is willing to pay for that product before embarking on a long journey of productizing the innovation.

Why the Majority of New Products Fail

Each year, more and more of us find ourselves in Porsche's position. Success is defined by bringing new products to market, expanding our reach. The pace of change is accelerating worldwide. For many of us, innovation is no longer a question of prioritization or investment; it's a question of survival.

Yet the failure rate for innovation is shockingly high. Nearly three out of four new products or services miss their revenue and profit goals. Many of those crash and burn entirely, and some take their companies with them.

It doesn't have to be that way.

That's what this book is about. For 30 years, we have helped companies develop strategies for successful innovation—including the launch of the Porsche Cayenne that we described. During that time, we have uncovered the patterns of failure that doom so many innovations. More important, we have forged, and empirically validated, a framework that has helped innovative companies ranging from startups to global brands to meet or exceed their goals.

New products fail for many reasons. But the root of all innovation evil—what billionaire entrepreneur Elon Musk would call the set of "first principles"—is the failure to put the customer's willingness to pay for a new product at the very core of product design. Most companies postpone marketing and pricing decisions to the very end, when they've already developed their new products. They embark on the long and costly journey of product development *hoping* they'll make money on their innovations, but not at all *knowing* if they will.

Price is more than just a dollar figure; it is an indication of what the customer wants—and how much they want it. It is the single most critical factor in determining whether a product makes money, yet it is an afterthought, a last-minute consideration made after a product is developed. It is so much of an afterthought that companies frequently call us and say, "We built a product—oops, now we need your help in pricing it."

To boil it down, these companies conduct product development this way: They design, then build, then market, then price. What we will teach you in this book is to flip that process on its head: Market and price, then design, then build. In other words, design the product around the price.

Think back to the last business case you or your colleagues were asked to write for a new product. How did you arrive at your prices? Did you compare your product to other products in the marketplace, or did you actually ask customers what they'd pay for it? Did you know in advance what would happen if you increased your price by, say, 20 percent—that is, how that would likely affect demand and thus volume?

If you are like thousands of companies that we've worked with over the years, you probably did not. Every one of them claims to have made an airtight business case to top management that vouches for their new product. But in only about 5 percent of those business cases can you find information on how much customers will pay for the product. This means their revenue estimates are, at best, a guess. When you think about it, that's stunning. The business case gives them a level of confidence they should *not* have. It leads them down the path to failure.

The most successful product innovators we know start by determining what the customer values and what they are willing to pay, and then they design the products around these inputs and have a clear monetization strategy that they follow through with. That's what LinkedIn did before it launched its Talent Solutions service for job recruiters, which now drives the lion's share of the social networking site's revenue and profits. That's what Porsche did with the Cayenne, and what Fiat Chrysler failed to do with the Dart. That's what a large, global pharmaceutical company has done with new products since the turn of the millennium, which has helped the company grow enormously over the last 20 years. That's what crystal maker Swarovski has done in developing new offerings for consumers, and for companies that embed its crystals in their products, to great financial success. That's what Dräger, a manufacturer of gas detection equipment, did in creating a hit new product that protects miners and other underground workers from gas leaks—a product whose sales were 250 percent higher than expected. That's what a six-year-old software-as-a-service firm called Optimizely did in creating a software to help companies improve their websites' abilities to sell their offerings, a software that has been used by thousands of customers. And that's what Uber has done in shaking up the world of public transportation, while watching its private valuation soar toward $60 billion at the end of 2015. We'll tell you much more about how LinkedIn, Porsche, Swarovski, Dräger, Optimizely, Uber, and an innovative pharma profited from designing and developing products around the price in Chapter 13.

This is the model that forward-looking, highly successful product innovators use—companies whose principles for monetizing innovations we will deconstruct in this book.

Successful Innovation Matters More Than Ever

Succeeding at product innovation is difficult, and it always has been. Every other year, Simon-Kucher & Partners conducts the world's largest survey on the state of pricing. Our 2014 report polled executives in 1,615 companies across the United States, Japan, Germany, and 37 other countries. The primary focus of the survey was to measure how well companies were monetizing their innovations across industries and geographies. The disappointing findings were reported in *Harvard Business Review*: 72 percent of new products introduced over the last five years failed—either to meet their revenue and profit goals, or failed entirely. These figures applied equally to startups and large businesses in every industry surveyed.[7]

Numerous other studies over the last decade have said your chances of developing a successful innovation are not even as good as winning a coin flip. For example:

- 65 percent of new products fail, according to the Product Development and Management Association. That rate of failure cost U.S. companies $260 billion in 2010, according to researchers at the University of Texas at Austin.[8]
- 75 percent of venture capital–funded startups fail, according to a Harvard Business School study of 2,000 companies between 2004 and 2010.[9]

These numbers show something is very wrong with the way companies bring new concepts to market. No one is immune. As painful as it is to consider, the odds are stacked against all of us.

Yet succeeding at innovating has never been more important than it is now. In the 2014 Simon-Kucher & Partners study, 83 percent of companies reported facing increasing downward pricing pressures. Most companies planned to innovate their way out of this dilemma: New products, new services, and new paths to growth. But innovators face an uphill climb for four primary reasons:

1. Traditional Research and Development (R&D) is becoming more expensive, not less. Costs are going up rapidly, without being offset by price increases.

2. Disruptive innovation now comes from smaller and smaller companies, with lighter and lighter capital requirements, meaning they can be nimbler than your firm and take bigger risks.

3. Product innovation is no longer the preserve of the Western world, as evidenced by the United States and Europe's declining shares of global R&D spending, and the growing share of China and other Asian countries. In fact, China is predicted to eclipse the United States in R&D spending by 2020.[10]

4. The rate of innovation is accelerating. A key signpost: Annual global patent applications leaped 2.5 times from 1995 to 2013, and in 2014 set a record for the number of patents filed internationally.[11]

Those statistics are harrowing. But with a 72 percent global new-product failure rate, you can take comfort knowing that if you are facing problems successfully launching innovations, you are not alone.

The Good News: Monetizing Innovation Failures Come in Only Four Varieties

This book is the product of the lessons that Simon-Kucher & Partners has learned over the last 30 years while becoming the world's largest pricing and monetization consulting firm, one with more than 900 employees in 32 offices around the world. Globally, we've conducted more than 10,000 projects for large multinationals, mid-size companies as well as start-ups across industries. We've seen what works and what doesn't, what succeeds and what fails in product innovation.

We've found recurring patterns in new product monetization failure. While you might think many types of flaws can cause products to flop in the marketplace, we actually have found that monetizing failures fall into only four categories:

1. Feature shock: cramming too many features into one product—sometimes even unwanted features—creates a product that does not fully resonate with customers and is often overpriced.

2. Minivation: an innovation that, despite being the right product for the right market, is priced too low to achieve its full revenue potential.

3. Hidden gem: a potential blockbuster product that is never properly brought to market, generally because it falls outside of the core business.

4. Undead: an innovation that customers don't want but has nevertheless been brought to market, either because it was the wrong answer to the right question, or an answer to a question no one was asking.

The fact that new product monetization failures come in only four varieties should give you comfort. Imagine having to do postmortems that could point to dozens or hundreds of factors!

You *Can* Avoid Failure—but Only If You Play by Different Rules

Our experience allowed us not only to diagnose these monetization failure modes but to cure them—or even better, avoid them altogether. In this book, we have boiled these secrets down into the following nine new rules for innovation success. The rules are contrary to what most executives have learned about product development:

1. Have the "willingness to pay" talk with customers early in the product development process. If you don't do it early, you won't be able to prioritize the product features you develop, and you won't know whether you're building something customers will pay for until it's in the marketplace.

2. Don't force a one-size-fits-all solution. Whether you like it or not, your customers are different, so customer segmentation is crucial. But segmentation based on demographics—the primary way companies group their customers—is misleading. You should build segments based on differences in your customers' willingness to pay for your new product.

3. Product configuration and bundling is more science than art. You need to build them carefully and match them with your most meaningful segments.

4. Choose the right pricing and revenue models, because *how* you charge is often more important than *how much* you charge.

5. Develop your pricing strategy. Create a plan that looks a few steps ahead, allowing you to maximize gains in the short and long term.

6. Draft your business case using customer willingness-to-pay data, and establish links between price, value, volume, and cost. Without this, your business case will tell you only what you want to hear, which may be far afield from market realities.
7. Communicate the value of your offering clearly and compellingly; otherwise you will not get customers to pay full measure.
8. Understand your customers' irrational sides, because whether you sell to other businesses or to consumers, your customers are people. You should take into account their full psyches, including their emotions, in making purchase decisions.
9. Maintain your pricing integrity. Control discounting tightly. If demand for your new product is below expectations, only use price cuts as a last resort, after all other measures have been exhausted.

We don't want to suggest this is easy. Real change never is. Some chapters will teach you tactics that will ratchet up your odds of success all by themselves. But the power of our nine-rule approach lies in how each rule reinforces the one before it. It is an integrated framework, meaning that the true potential of our approach, the real game changer, can only be realized if you commit, body and soul. To further enable the change we have created a website (http://www.monetizinginnovation.com) that provides additional material and diagnostic tools.

No matter who you are, where you are, what you make, or what service you provide, the stakes for new products and services are much higher than ever before. In the pages that follow, we'll give you the insights you need to dramatically improve the odds of new-product success—techniques that will help your new product avoid becoming one of the four Monetizing Innovation failure types and instead fit into a fifth category: the Big Success.

CHAPTER 2

Feature Shocks, Minivations, Hidden Gems, and Undeads

The Four Flavors of Monetizing Innovation Failure

As we mentioned at the end of the previous chapter, we have analyzed thousands of new product and service monetizing innovation failures for clients over the last 30 years, and we find they fall into four categories: *feature shocks, minivations, hidden gems,* and *undeads.* The good news is that there are only four categories! That makes it easier to avoid them.

Which of these missteps you will likely make has a lot to do with your company's culture. Companies with strong product-driven or engineering cultures tend to be the ones that develop feature shocks. Firms with a culture of playing it safe and avoiding big risks typically suffer minivations. Hidden gems most often afflict companies that coddle the core business. And undeads are born in firms whose top-down cultures discourage feedback and criticism from below.

Let's start with feature shocks, something anyone who comes from a company with a strong engineering culture will immediately recognize.

Flavor 1: Feature Shocks—When You Give Too Much and Get Too Little

Feature shocks happen when you try to cram too many features into one product, creating a confusing and often expensive mess. In a sincere effort to have it be "all things to all people," you launch a product that pleases few. The result is the product's value is less than the sum of the parts. Due to its multitude of features—none of them a standout—these products are costly to make, overengineered, hard to explain, and usually overpriced.

Feature shocks typically begin when a company has uncertain or ambitious goals. At Amazon, ambitious goals are part of the core culture. The company thinks big, from its product warehouses to its vast cloud computing data centers. Through thinking big, Amazon has reaped big rewards: In February 2016, Amazon's market capitalization was $250 billion, making it worth 18 percent more than Walmart, the world's biggest retailer by revenue.[1]

But that did not help Amazon in 2014, when it attempted to launch its own entry into the smartphone market. With the Fire Phone, Amazon bet it could compete against the reigning champions of consumer smartphones, Samsung and Apple. In the tech world, goals don't get much more ambitious. But Amazon had scored big before in consumer electronics with its innovative Kindle e-book readers and Kindle Fire tablets. Amazon has logged years of successes across product categories using its well-known "outside-in" and customer-first focus. So, Amazon skipped the low-margin marketplace of budget phones and set sail for the shores of the premium smartphone market with the Fire Phone, counting on innovative features to make a market splash akin to what Apple's automated assistant, Siri, had created. Amazon packed in a sizable 4.7-inch screen, a hefty 32 gigabytes of storage, a Bluetooth wireless capability to connect the Fire Phone with other devices, and many other bells and whistles.

In a sea of features, the most startling was "Dynamic Perspective," which was designed to give consumers three-dimensional effects on the smartphone display without having to wear 3-D glasses. To pull this off, Amazon's designers installed four camera lenses and facial recognition technology that followed your line of sight to the phone, tweaking the display to show depth. Amazon also threw in what it called "Mayday service," which promised technology support in less than a minute.

The company also touted Firefly, a shopping feature that let you point the phone's camera at a product and then took you to Amazon.com to buy it.

Amazon tried hard to generate the kind of buzz that accompanies a new iPhone release. But reviewers saw little value in the numerous features, especially dynamic perspective, which looked impressive in some smartphone games but didn't address any pressing customer needs. Making matters worse, the four lenses required to support dynamic perspective were a big drain on the phone's battery life. Critics were particularly harsh on the muddled feature set. The review from technology site Engadget was typical:

> *The Fire's defining features are fun, but I can't help but feel as though they're merely gimmicks designed by Amazon to demonstrate the company's brilliance—and at the expense of battery life, to boot. Dynamic Perspective might be useful in a few cases (games, mainly), but it won't provide the user with functionality they'd sorely miss if they went with an iPhone or flagship Android device.*
>
> *Not only is the Fire lacking in useful new features, but its high price . . . guarantee[s] its irrelevance . . . so why come out with a smartphone that isn't particularly convenient, and isn't particularly cheap? By no means is the Fire a horrible phone, but it's a forgettable one. You might want the eventual Fire Phone 2, perhaps, but for now, you're better off sticking with what you know.*[2]

Amazon launched the phone in July 2014 at $199 with a two-year AT&T phone service contract, or $649 without a contract. Initial sales lacked momentum. And when sales stalled out four months later, Amazon cut the phone's price to 99 *cents*—that's not a misprint—with the two-year contract, or $449 without a contract.

Instead of basking in an Apple-like glow, Amazon was left with a $170 million write-down, "largely attributable to unsold Fire Phone inventory," according to *Fast Company*.[3]

How does this type of mistake get made at an ultradisciplined and very successful company like Amazon? It gets made because Amazon, like countless companies that produce engineering marvels, overengineered the product. It fell in love with the phone's many features, including some that no one outside the company wanted. Amazon fell prey to the spirit of "we can add this!"

The drive to make a product that addresses too many questions often blinds innovation teams to market realities. Then the ill-advised trade-offs in product development happen, like the battery life quandary. The Fire Phone became an overengineered product bursting with non-essential features that hiked its cost for Amazon, and therefore the price for customers, and it lacked standout features. Amazon might still succeed with Fire Phone 2, but the first incarnation was a feature shock.

When you look into organizations that are susceptible to feature shocks, the warning signs are usually subtle (Figure 2.1). But they follow patterns that you will recognize if you have ever worked in such a company.

If you hear this, you are likely designing a feature shock

"But we can also add this...."

"We want to be on the safe side."

"Customers don't know what they want, so we need to decide what to build."

"One size should fit; our market is not segmented."

"Let's build it, then position it."

"Let's get something out there."

Figure 2.1   Signs of Feature Shocks

The first danger signal is that the research and development (R&D) team keeps saying "let's add this," but can't articulate the new product's value to customers. Years ago, we met with a team to develop a pricing strategy for a product meant to revolutionize testing and monitoring for a class of machinery. Intrigued, we asked why someone should buy the product. The team members looked at each other quizzically before all eyes focused on the team leader.

"This product has seven patents!" the team leader finally said, missing the point that customers couldn't have cared less about that.

We refer to such comments as "inside-out," meaning they reflect what people inside a company believe is valuable about their firm's new product. Inside-out comments like that indicate that an R&D team has fallen in love with the product but has lost sight of the customer. That may be the earliest and most reliable indication that the product you are about to launch is suffering from feature shock. Customers won't buy a product if they do not buy your story about why that product helps them. Products that are feature shocks cannot articulate a clear value proposition and tend to be a one-size-fits-all approach to customers.

When feature shocks come to market, customers' initial responses are tepid. That only increases the innovator's frustration. Customers complain the product has too many "nice to haves" and too few "gotta haves," and they conclude they don't need the product, at least at that price. And if they do like some of the "nice to haves," they can't afford them. There is no compelling value story for the customer, and too high a price for non-compelling value because the features have hiked its cost. Naturally, adoption is slower than the company expects. Indifferent, unenthusiastic word-of-mouth fails to generate follow-up sales. After Amazon launched its Fire Phone, no one talked about its dynamic perspective feature the way they had talked about the iPhone's Siri.

Once a company recognizes a feature shock problem, it often slashes the price. This is the simplest and fastest way to correct, or at least offset, an unclear value proposition. This is what Amazon did with its Fire Phone.

The allure of a lower price point is undeniable. It also is the easiest lever to pull when a new offering's sales are below expectations, whether they are consumer gadgets or sophisticated products and services sold to businesses. Salespeople can change a price in the middle of a sentence. They can offer the product as a "throw in" for a deal. They can quote the new price and represent it as a discount or an adjustment in terms and conditions.

This insidious process can escalate into a full-scale rescue attempt as the organization loses its ability to control the price or enforce any pricing restraint. In the worst cases, finance and pricing teams face customer demands for ever-higher discounts, and the price goes into a downward death spiral, leaving the company unable to slow or stop the decline. (In Chapter 12, we will discuss repair tactics other than price cutting to deal with initial sales disappointments. A quick price slash is the worst of all options.)

Clearly, lack of restraint in product development fuels feature shocks. Technology companies are most susceptible to encouraging the spirit of "let's add this." Semiconductor companies, for example, routinely produce feature shocks; it's not uncommon to have a design specification with hundreds of features.

But organizations from many other industries fall into the same feature shock trap. Take the U.S. cable TV industry. For years, cable operators offering hundreds of channels struggled with a feature shock: getting customers to select which of the numerous premium channels they wanted the most. So most cable providers created a few package solutions, each of which offered groups of premium channels. That simplified the consumer's purchase decision.

Every day, all of us run into products that are living feature shocks. The financial services industry has plenty of them—for example, retail banks whose accounts offer money transfer services, credit cards, brokerage services, foreign exchange, and more. Or go into an electronics store and have a salesperson explain to you the wonders of a top-end, high-definition TV. Then see if you can remember them all. Or go into an appliance store and let them regale you with the features of a new high-end clothes washer. If you are like the average consumer, maybe you'd end up using 20 percent of all those features.

The reason such products become feature shocks is lack of restraint by innovation teams. They couldn't help themselves, thinking up and packing in another seemingly attractive feature. Such lack of discipline produces a feature shock that then typically leads to rampant profit-destroying discounting.

You *can* avoid creating feature shocks. You will need to tailor products differently to the needs of different customer segments based on what each segment needs and what they'll pay for products that solve those needs. We'll say a lot more about this in Chapter 5.

Flavor 2: Minivations—When You Ask for Too Little, That's What You Get

No one wants to sell his or her idea short. Minivations are products that tap neither a product concept's full market potential nor its full price potential. Companies that fall into the minivation trap underexploit the market opportunity and the price they could have charged, thereby robbing themselves of profits. Minivations go down as undermonetized products cursed with a "what might have been" tag.

With minivations, failure can masquerade as success. We worked with a Silicon Valley component maker that provides internal parts for handheld digital devices. This company, fighting hard at a time of keen competitive pressure, created a next-generation product that represented not an incremental improvement, but a step change. This new generation component had no peer. The company priced the component at 85 cents—25 cents more than the previous generation component—using its traditional cost-plus pricing method.

One of the company's hardest-to-please key customers, a prominent maker of consumer electronics, said it would incorporate this next-generation component into its new premium product line. The component maker breathed a big sigh of relief and celebrated hitting its internal sales targets. The champagne corks popped. But others in the firm knew the celebration was overblown. They knew the firm could have charged its big consumer electronics customer far more for the breakthrough component. The product was indeed game-changing, but the component maker's aspirations were too small.

The cost of a lack of ambition did show up later, when the component maker commissioned an *ex post facto* analysis of its new product development process, including pricing. The analysis showed the new component enabled that key customer to charge a $50 premium over its previous version of the product, and the premium was largely attributed to functionality the new breakthrough component provided. Clearly, by charging 85 cents, the component maker was charging only a very small portion of the value premium it had generated for its customer. The *ex post facto* analysis also showed that the component manufacturer could have charged up to $5 (10 percent of the value it generated for the consumer electronics customer). Consequently, the firm left big money on the table.

The component company failed to ask this question: "What value does this component bring to our customer and its customers, and what portion of that value can we capture?" Instead, it asked, "What does this component cost to make, and what minimum margin do I need to add on top of that?"

This example shows that coasting on "business as usual" autopilot can cost plenty when you launch a new product—money that won't be available to hire new employees, fund fresh research, and support marketing efforts.

While feature shocks enter the market overfeatured and overpriced, minivations enter the market underpriced or with volume targets that are too low. They are tame, safe answers to the right question. In the case of the component manufacturer, their device was wildly underpriced. Why? Its management perpetuated the pricing practice of the past: slapping a predictable margin on top of the previous-generation product. No one challenged the established pricing practice. No one quantified the value to customers and their willingness to pay. They just didn't think big enough from a monetization perspective.

We've seen scores of minivations over the years. Here are a few of the more noteworthy ones:

- After Playmobil's 2003 launch of its Noah's Ark play set, the set sold out in two months and started selling on eBay for 33 percent higher than the original price tag. In other words, customers were hawking it for a higher price than Playmobil offered it at! Playmobil had seriously underestimated its customers' willingness to pay for this toy. (This wasn't forced scarcity, as some toy makers have planned purposefully at holiday time.) Was Noah's Ark a success or a failure masquerading as one?

- In 2008, when low-priced personal computer manufacturer Asus unveiled its "eee PC," a mini-notebook priced at €299, consumers reacted enthusiastically. Only a few days after Asus launched it in Germany, the low-cost machine almost sold out. Merchants reported demand exceeded supply by 900 percent. Asus couldn't make them fast enough and lost significant revenue once its supply ran dry. Could Asus have priced this product much higher? Definitely. The Asus product fell far short of its price potential; it was way underpriced. Asus left lots of profit on the table. They could have priced a lot higher, serviced the market that was willing to pay, and then dropped the price (after building more units) to target the mass market.

- Audi's Q7 luxury SUV launched at €55,000 in the first quarter of 2006. Demand turned out to be 80,000 units per year worldwide, but Audi's production capacity was 70,000 units. That data points to an optimal price of €58,000 (to clear 70K units), which would have meant an extra €210,000,000 *a year* for Audi on those same 70,000 units. Audi didn't exploit the pricing or volume potential. Could Audi have reaped much more profit? Certainly.

- French automotive supplier Valeo is the maker of Park Assist, a system sold by Volkswagen and other car manufacturers. Park Assist enables a driver to parallel park by simply pushing a button. Valeo was ecstatic after selling its system (which includes a few cameras, sensors, and software) to Volkswagen for about €100 per unit, a price based on adding a margin to its costs. But VW was no doubt more ecstatic, pricing Park Assist at €670 to its end customers and achieving it! Valeo didn't truly understand Park Assist's value to customers, while VW did. Valeo could have asked much more for its system.

- When telecommunication services companies moved from 3G to 4G networks, it was a step change in value for customers—they could download website pages faster on their smartphones or listen to digital music without as many bandwidth interruptions. But some telcos didn't fully monetize the new service. One of them (the United Kingdom's Hutchison/Three) even proudly states this in its advertising: "Charging extra for 4G sucks. We don't."[4] Actually, it's worse for the company *not* to monetize its speed improvement!

So how do you spot minivations in the making? (See Figure 2.2.) Your team seems comfortable checking the box and lowballing on targets. You find evidence for lack of ambition and a desire to not "overprice." When the product is out, your sales team often is the canary in the coal mine.

If you hear this, you are likely designing a minivation

"We checked all the boxes."

"I don't want to sign up for a big number."

"I don't want to over price. I would rather be conservative."

"With our margins, we don't need to worry about price."

"It's good enough."

"We need to penetrate the market."

"It hit the sales targets."

Figure 2.2   Signs of Minivations

Compared to your other products, the sales force is easily meeting its targets with your new product. Your channel partners are reaping their maximum margins. Sellouts are popping up. Fewer pricing problems are emerging. If the majority of deals are going through the pipeline without price escalations, you may have underestimated the value of your new product and underpriced it. Tracking the number of price escalations, as well as the length of the sales cycle against historical norms, will give you more hard evidence that something new is occurring.

What fuels such minivations? "Good enough" thinking is the culprit here. In larger corporations, organizational structures can reinforce a "good enough" mindset. The division of labor necessary to run a large operation means that often it's no one's job to reflect deeply on data or analyses. Barriers between work groups inhibit information sharing, making deep reflection impossible or difficult. Moving an idea along requires too many handoffs. To maintain momentum, managers prioritize getting the handoff right rather than getting the right answer.

Unlike feature shocks, minivations are difficult to guard against because they don't end in epic failures, just value-limiting ones. Although minivations do not spell catastrophe for a single product, they take a systemic toll across a company as team members tolerate too much "good enough" thinking and too *little* ambition.

Flavor 3: Hidden Gems—When You Don't Look, You're Not Going to Find Them

With a hidden gem product, a company has a brilliant, even revolutionary idea but fails to both recognize it and quantify the product's value to customers. Or the company decides it lacks the capabilities to bring the unusual idea to market. Hidden gems often end up in limbo, neither launched nor killed. They often don't make it to market, but if they do, they arrive undervalued, as freebies or deal sweeteners.

Revolutionary product ideas, by virtue of their defining originality, often may seem tangential to a company's core business. Kodak is perhaps the most famous illustration of this. Once the top name that consumers associated with photography, Kodak got clobbered in the digital camera game because it waited too long on the sidelines. The irony: In 1974, a young Kodak engineer in the company's applied research lab, Steven Sasson, had invented a hidden gem: the technology behind digital cameras.

Kodak patented the initial technology, and Sasson kept the prototype as he moved around the company. In other words, Kodak could have been the king of the digital camera market—an industry whose products are integral to hundreds of millions of smartphones, not just the point-and-shoot cameras we've all used for years. But the notion of a digital camera threatened the core business at Kodak: film. So it remained hidden for far too long.

Exactly how do hidden gems stay hidden? In Kodak's case, Sasson's bosses never got excited about it. Kodak didn't introduce its first digital camera, the DC40, until 1995, 21 years after Sasson's breakthrough, and it didn't get serious about its digital camera effort until 2001.[5]

With no foothold in that new digital world, Kodak declared bankruptcy in 2012, emerged in 2013, and as of 2015 was trying to resurrect its business largely by licensing its patents and research technologies. Banking firms now own most of the company.

None of this had to happen. None of it was preordained. Kodak had a hidden gem way back in 1974. It just couldn't bring itself to exploit it.

Kodak is hardly the only company to bury its hidden gems. We recently met a manufacturer of warehouse conveyor belts that had developed software that dramatically improved the flow of goods (within the warehouse). Because it was a hardware manufacturer, selling software was a foreign concept. So the company had given away its breakthrough software, thinking the real value was in the hard goods it made. It had squandered millions of dollars in revenue for a product—lines of code—for which it could have charged a hefty price. This was confirmed when we talked to its customers: a majority of them had a significant willingness to pay for the software (on top of the hardware).

What about examples of companies that have harnessed a hidden gem? Two prominent positive hidden gems come from the U.S. newspaper industry, a sector that has been shrinking every year as consumers get their news for free on the Internet. Those hidden gems are Autotrader.com and Cars.com, both of which provide online classified ads to help consumers buy and sell cars.

When the Web emerged in the 1990s, most newspapers paid scant attention to it, opting to continue shoring up their print franchises. But several big media companies went against the grain, deciding to fund online classified ad ventures to hedge their bets if readers someday abandoned print news for the online world. AutoTrader.com was created in 1997 by Cox Enterprises, a major media company. (We discuss the new product success of another Cox automotive business—car auctioneer Manheim—later in this book.) Cars.com was born in 1998, backed by five newspaper companies (Gannett, McClatchy, Tribune Media, A. H. Belo, and Graham Holdings).

The hidden gem problem is not as common as feature shocks or minivations. Unlike the case of the newspaper companies, the pressure required to produce hidden gems is not always there. But when it is, team members often struggle either because they can't recognize and measure hidden gems' inherent value, or they lack the competencies to bring them to market. The gem gathers dust because it is neither launched nor killed. As in the Kodak case, teams become complacent about their firm's successful, preexisting business model, and the company stagnates. The big miss here lies in failing to recognize the value and often disruptive power of the hidden gem.

Perhaps in past product-development work you've seen signs of a hidden gem in the making. (See Figure 2.3.) Customers show excitement about the concept, though they may not understand how you'll deliver it. Or the sales force is giving away a product or feature to sweeten deals.

If you hear this, you are likely missing out on a hidden gem

"We don't know what to do with this."

"This isn't business as usual for us."

"We don't have a process for that."

"We'll throw that into the deal."

"It's not in our DNA."

"This goes against our culture."

Figure 2.3   Signs of Hidden Gems

As the word "hidden" indicates, sometimes these ideas simply do not make it to the executive suite. They are stopped by midlevel executives who are either unable to see their potential or are scared of them (since they may sabotage their division or pet project or cause big political friction). A more open culture could save these ideas from being lost too early.

The most painful outcome of not recognizing your hidden gem is seeing a rival launch a version before you do.

Your company may have hidden gems lying around if you are going through one of these situations: changes in business models; a disruption in your industry; a commodity business trying to differentiate itself; a shift from offline to online business; a change from selling a product to a service; a move from analog to digital; or a move from hardware to software.

"Where does the buck stop?" becomes a tough question to answer in the case of hidden gems. Who was responsible for the big miss? Remember, recognizing the hidden gem's potential is key. But in most organizations, no one is responsible for recognizing them.

Flavor 4: Undeads—When Nobody Wants Your Product

The term "undead" historically has been used in fiction to refer to dead people who come back to life, such as vampires and zombies. Applied to monetizing innovation, an undead product is one that still exists in the marketplace, but demand is virtually nonexistent. The product, for all intents and purposes, is dead, yet it continues to "walk around" like a zombie.

How do undeads happen? They occur when a new product is the wrong answer to the right question—or an answer to a question that not enough people care about. These products emerge from organizations that struggle to separate the technically feasible from the commercially practical. Undeads hit the market with an almost audible thud and poor sales.

Undead failures teach us that some well-intentioned, marvelously engineered new products should never be brought to life. One of the most celebrated—and then reviled—was the Segway. In December 2001, after tremendous prelaunch hype, inventor Dean Kamen unveiled his vision for a breakthrough personal transporter, developed for $100 million, under the codename "Ginger." You've probably seen the Segway PT in action at a shopping mall or a tourist site, but not in many other places.

The Segway PT has covered a long distance in going from excitement to disappointment. It was supposed to change the world. At launch time, Kamen proclaimed he would sell 50,000 the first year.[6] Six years later, by the end of 2007, Kamen's company had sold about 30,000 of the scooters in total, not per year.[7] In April 2015, the company, having quietly faded from the public eye, was sold to the Chinese firm Ninebot.[8] Kamen's invention found a home with tour operators and security organizations.

Why didn't the Segway transform the world? At the top of consumers' reluctance to buy the machine was its price. Asking between $3,000 and $7,000 for a scooter, the company arguably had little hope of building a mass following. The Segway's appeal was narrow, like all undead products. Fascinating from an engineering and technology standpoint, the Segway was the wrong answer to the right question: What's the most efficient way for people to get from point A to point B? The Segway was far more expensive than a plethora of options, so it came to the market as an undead product.

Undeads are born in hugely successful companies as well. Take online search engine leader Google. In 2012, the company unveiled Google Glass, a pair of glasses with a small camera that, upon verbal command, could take pictures or record videos. The wearer could also look up at Glass and see maps and other information found on smartphones. According to Google, the consumer didn't need to touch anything to get some of the features of a smartphone. Google made the first version of Glass available to the digerati and journalists for the princely price of $1,500. The idea was that they'd fall in love with Glass and use their online pulpits to urge others to buy it. Only, it didn't happen that way. Reviewers panned it for shortcomings such as its short battery life and glitches. And the device spooked people who feared that nearby Glass wearers would record moments they'd prefer to keep private. Because of this privacy concern, a number of theaters, bars, casinos, and other public places prohibited patrons from wearing Glass.

A year later, in January 2015, Google announced the end of its Glass product.[9] Google Glass was an undead product for its initial target audience: everyday consumers using smartphones. We believe that had Google targeted commercial applications as its primary segment—surgeons and other professionals who need information rapidly while their hands are doing vital work—and focused and developed the product for the business segment, Glass might not have been born undead. For the broad consumer segment, however, Google Glass answered a question no one was asking.

By the way, technology companies like Segway and Google aren't the primary sources of undeads. They go well beyond tech. Consumer product companies collectively have hundreds of undead products they try hard to forget. Remember when Coca-Cola introduced "New Coke" in 1985? Facing pressure from Pepsi, Coke tweaked its recipe for the first time in almost a century. Consumers didn't love the new taste—and they *hated* that the old Coke had disappeared from store shelves. Within three months, the company salvaged the situation by returning the old Coke, now called Coke Classic (using the original recipe), to the shelves.[10]

In the cemetery of undead new products, New Coke has plenty of company: McDonald's Arch Deluxe burger, Microsoft's Zune music player, Harley-Davidson's brand of perfume, Procter & Gamble's Touch of Yogurt Shampoo, Rocky Mountain Sparkling Water from Coors—all of these were brought to the market as undeads.

Undeads pop up in the life sciences industry, too. Take the concept of inhaled insulin. Its inventors thought needle-phobic diabetics would embrace this breakthrough. The concept generated enormous excitement at the firm. But while it sounded like a great idea, in practice it was . . . well, impractical. A patient had to use five to ten times more inhaled insulin, and the price was three to four times the price of injected insulin. As a result, the clear majority of patients continue to inject insulin. Wrong answer for the right question.

How do such undead products make it to market? They happen when their proponents wildly overstate the customer appeal and don't segment the customer base effectively. Had these firms asked customers what they'd be willing to pay for their inventions before drafting the engineering plans, and had they identified the market size by segment and who would be willing to pay the most (and least) for it, they would have reformulated their products to meet an acceptable price. Or, finding there is no acceptable price, or that the market size is too small, they would have scrapped the product altogether before they incurred too much financial damage.

It's easy to recognize that your innovation is undead. (See Figure 2.4.) When an undead is in the making, you become delusional and detest any evidence that goes against your beliefs. You resist objectivity and keep investing time, feeling you have come too far. Once the product is in the market, your sales teams can't sell it, and it causes them to miss their

If you hear this, you are likely designing an undead

"I'm not going to be the one who says 'no'."

"Personally, I'd never buy this myself, but . . . ."

"Screw what the research says; I know this will work!"

"Let's wait for more evidence before we pull the plug."

"The train has left the station."

"We've come too far. If we kill this now. . . ."

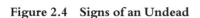

Figure 2.4   Signs of an Undead

targets—by a lot. Salespeople don't want to bring the product into conversations with customers for fear of poisoning relationships. Meanwhile, customers either say they don't want the product or say they find it intriguing, but not intriguing enough to buy. Press coverage and social media posts turn negative and sarcastic. That's what happened to Dean Kamen's Segway, which was lampooned in the hit U.S. TV cartoon show *The Simpsons* over several episodes.

While it is easy to recognize undeads, it's far more important to know what kind of organizational culture fosters them in the first place. Many of the undeads we've seen are a result of having a "yes-maybe-no" reaction to new product ideas. Every idea in such companies starts with massive excitement, and everybody says, "Yes, let's do this." However, the commitment to design and build the product comes much ahead of finding the market potential or the customer willingness to pay for such ideas.

By pushing the willingness-to-pay conversation too far out in the innovation process, these companies put themselves in a situation where saying "no" comes too late. They have already overinvested at that point. In some situations, this could get even more complex if this is the pet project of senior management and no one wants to say the idea is a bad one. In such environments, people and teams bring undeads to market. They simply have a hard time saying "no"—even if in their gut they know the new product won't fly in the marketplace. They're not asked

Failure Type	Description	Symptoms	Where does it occur?	Solutions
Feature shock	Cramming too many and sometimes wrong features into a one-size-fits-all product	• Product driven culture • Over-engineering • Unclear value-prop • Too many escalations • Difficult selling • Frequent price cuts	• Tech companies • Software/internet • Subscriptions • Financial services • Media/telco	Focus on: Chapter 4 Chapter 5 Chapter 6 Chapter 8 Chapter 12
Mini-vation	Despite being the right product for the right market, it is underpriced and does not achieve full market potential	• Lack of ambition • Low-balling targets • Minimal escalations • Few pricing problems • Fast sales cycles • Sales easily hits target	All industry verticals – tech, software/ internet, auto, financial services, chemicals, industrial, healthcare, CPG/ retail, telco, etc.	Focus on: Chapter 4 Chapter 7 Chapter 8 Chapter 9 Chapter 10 Chapter 11
Hidden gem	A blockbuster product that is never properly brought to market because it does not get recognized	• Lack of recognition • Play it safe mentality • Outside comfort zone • No one responsible for harnessing gems	Occurs whenever there is a disruption or change: in business models, channel strategy, focus change from product to services, etc.	Focus on: Chapter 4 Chapter 7 Chapter 9
Undead	Products that should have been killed - Answers to questions no one asks or the wrong answer to the right question	• Lack of objectivity • Yes-maybe-no culture • Pet projects • Very low demand • Sales struggles • Negative press	All industry verticals – tech, software/ internet, auto, financial services, chemicals, industrial, healthcare, CPG/ retail, telco, etc.	Focus on: Chapter 4 Chapter 9

Figure 2.5   Comparing the Four Types of Monetization Failures

for their opinion, and raising concern only puts their careers at risk. And so they don't speak the truth about the undead in their midst. They only execute their piece of the project as they are told. And that's how such fatally flawed products hit the market.

These Four Monetizing Innovation Failures *Can* Be Avoided

You don't want your product to fall into one of these four categories. They are entirely avoidable, but only when executive management, product development, marketing, sales, and other functions in charge of a new product understand the nine rules of monetizing innovation that we will explore in depth in Part 2 of the book. In those chapters, you will learn the process of identifying the value customers perceive for a product and its features long before that product is launched in the marketplace— in fact, long before it's built, engineered, and produced. Figure 2.5 sums up the failure categories and shows which chapters you need to pay special attention to in order to avoid each type of failure.

Bringing pricing considerations—based on real customer input— into the new product development process early is critical to avoiding disastrous feature shocks, minivations, hidden gems, and undeads.

But before we do that, we explain why the prevailing mindset of postponing monetization discussions is widespread. This is the focus of Chapter 3.

Why Good People Get It Wrong

If our product failure categories in Chapter 2 bring back painful memories, don't despair. You are in very good company. The 72 percent failure rate of innovation shows that the clear majority of new product initiatives end up as minivations, feature shocks, hidden gems, or undeads. The question, of course, is how do you prevent these from happening in your organization?

It would be easy for us to say the problem is that companies wait until the last moment in their product development process to think about monetization. Indeed, that's exactly what happened in most of the thousands of new product or service failures we have seen over the last three decades. But why is last-minute pricing so prevalent?

The reason is the reigning mindset or paradigm about monetization and product development. In that mindset, the work of monetizing a new offering is often viewed as unsavory, dirty, and detrimental to true innovation. According to this sentiment, dreaming up big, bold new product concepts should not be encumbered by asking for a price check.

If innovators are to succeed, this thinking goes, they must be given lots of runway. In the United States, the popular portrait of the innovator combines artistic spirit with the image of an underdog. Apple appealed to this in 1997 upon Steve Jobs's return to the company, using artistic icons like Miles Davis (a rebellious artist) in its Think Different campaign.

Using this mindset, asking product developers to think about pricing and willingness to pay infringes on their creativity. In coming up with the initial advertising concept in 2012 for its new Dodge Dart, the Fiat Chrysler TV ad mentioned in Chapter 1 played to this widely and deeply held mindset. "Kick out the finance guys!" the commercial proudly proclaimed. The ad played into the prevailing mindset of what happens when a firm introduces the bean counters too early into product development: Big, bold ideas become small ones that no customer will get excited about.

That's the prevailing mindset. If you dig deeper, you will see this mindset is based on five myths and misconceptions.

Myths and Misconceptions with the Prevailing Mindset

Myth #1: *If you simply build a great new product, customers will pay fair value for it.* "Build it, and they will come" is the mantra.

It is a hope-sustaining mindset for innovators who face long odds. And it warms many other hearts as well. Can we ever get enough stories about the underdogs who were told "it will never work" until it does? The books *Catch-22* and *Gone with the Wind* were rejected by dozens of publishers before achieving best-seller success. Vincent Van Gogh died in poverty, but his paintings now sell for tens of millions of dollars.

Many critics made fun of the movie *Star Wars* when it came out, as did director George Lucas's friends and fellow directors (with the singular exception of Steven Spielberg). Nonetheless, it became one of the biggest movie and merchandising blockbusters of all time. The first Harry Potter book was rejected 12 times before one publisher saw hope in J.K. Rowling's manuscript.

And like most people, Fred Smith's business plan for FedEx earned a failing grade in business school.

We all love these stories. But we love them, in part, because they are exceptions to the rule. No one talks about the 95 percent of cases where the exact opposite happened. We all love to hope. This book is about switching from *hoping* your innovations will find market success to *knowing* they will.

Myth #2: *The new product or service must be controlled entirely by the innovation team working in isolation.* These corporate "artists" need to work by themselves, sealed off from others who might pollute their ideas. Bringing in outside voices—market data, customers' perspectives, and financial considerations—risks compromising innovation, even ruining it.

Customers' perspectives? Many businesses believe, like Henry Ford did, that customers don't really know what they want, so asking them is a useless exercise. Developing a robust product first and leaving monetization to the very end of the process makes sense to these executives. After all, they're the experts; they know their customers' needs as well as (or better than) the customers themselves. Besides, innovators hear enough negative voices in their own heads. Throwing cold water on hot ideas will result in ugly compromises—or worse, nip great ideas in the bud by upsetting the geniuses building the next new thing. Or so the thinking goes.

Myth #3: *High failure rate of innovation is normal and is even necessary.* To use baseball terminology, today's businesses believe the more often you step up to the plate, the more swings you take, the better your chance of hitting a home run. Executives in established businesses believe this is how it's supposed to work; the few winners bail out the many losers. If the product fails, there will be many more after it, and some of those have to succeed.

Myth #4: *Customers must experience a new product before they can say how much they'll pay for it.* Businesses believe it defies the law of nature to determine how much customers would be willing to pay for an innovation before the innovation is complete. How could customers possibly know what they're willing to pay for something until they see it?

Myth #5: *Until the business knows precisely what it's building, it cannot possibly assess what it is worth.* Especially if the business is operating in a cost-plus environment (where it applies a percentage markup to a product's manufacturing and shipping costs to arrive at a price), it has to understand all the costs that will go into the product before deciding what to charge customers.

Embracing a New Paradigm

All of these are attractive arguments. They seem to make eminent sense. In fact, to many in the world of innovation, they seem like laws of nature. It's not surprising that they've shaped innovation practices at companies around the world for decades.

They have also played a role in the 72 percent failure rate of monetizing innovation. The point of this book is to get you to embrace a new paradigm: *Understanding if customers are willing to pay for your invention, before you commit too many resources to building and launching it, will dramatically increase your likelihood of success.*

By designing your product around a price, your innovations will stand a far greater chance of surviving and thriving. Figuring how much customers will pay for your product when it is still in the concept stage will make your innovation process far more reliable. You and your company will be far more likely to succeed.

You won't hope your product takes off in the marketplace after you launch it; you'll *know*. And you'll know this because you've designed it with features that customers got genuinely excited about when you described the benefits and because they also embraced a certain price for the product.

Those nervous, nail-biting weeks of wondering whether your new product will actually sell according to forecast will come to an end. You'll know about the market viability of your new product long before you put it out to the market. You'll have a rigorous assessment of your product's true market potential at the *front end* of innovation, not at the *back end*.

Oh, by the way: We will be sure to debunk those five myths in the rest of the chapters!

The bottom line is we will show you that putting monetization front and center in the product development process is not antithetical to innovation by any means. If you give it a try, you'll see the myths and misconceptions we have mentioned in this chapter fall away. In fact, you'll come to understand how bringing up monetization early can spur a product development organization to new heights. Eventually, you'll wonder how product development could be run any other way.

Introduction to Part 2

In the nine chapters of Part 2, we lay out the precise steps your company must take to rigorously assess the potential of your new products, as well as the path to realizing that potential: truly satisfying your customers and thus generating a big hit.

As the comedy troupe Monty Python used to say, "now for something completely different." The nine rules for monetizing innovation will be counterintuitive to what you have learned about product innovation from your professors and from your career. You won't have read about these rules in your college textbooks on innovation or in the dozens of innovation books penned by consulting firms over the last few decades.

Part Two

Nine Surprising Rules for Successful Monetization

CHAPTER 4

Have the "Willingness-to-Pay" Talk Early

You Can't Prioritize without It

O f all the chapters in this book, this one might surprise you the most. In it, we will explain why you absolutely must discuss pricing at the beginning of a new product development initiative, not at the end. As mentioned in Chapter 1, when we say *price* we mean it to be an indication of what customers *value* and a measure of how much they are *willing to pay* for that value. To build a product around a price, you must engage in deep discussions with potential customers before you design and develop it.

Your dialogue must be specifically about their willingness to pay for the product you have in mind. The term "willingness to pay" is so important for us, and our clients, we refer to it by the acronym WTP.

Before we show why having the WTP talk is so important, we'll let a real story do some explaining. It's the story of Gillette's new razor for the Indian market.

How an Early Willingness-to-Pay Talk Propelled Gillette

A unit of consumer products powerhouse Procter & Gamble, Gillette is the king of the U.S. razor blade industry. Gillette razor brands account for more than 60 percent of the $3 billion U.S. retail market for razors and blades. But in India, a market with the potential to be four times bigger than America's for shaving products, Gillette had only a 22 percent share in 2009. Why? Price. The Gillette Mach 3, a U.S. product, was 100 rupees in India, or $2.24 in U.S. currency. For the majority of the Indian market, that was much too expensive.[1]

To increase market share in India, P&G realized it had to target the mid- to lower-income segment. The P&G innovation team took a unique approach. In the company's own words, ". . . inspired laser-like focus drove inclusion of only the most important features that were meaningful for the consumer and allowed the product to be offered at an affordable price."[2]

So *before* sketching out its new product design, the Guard, Gillette spent thousands of hours interviewing people in India and other emerging markets. It observed them in their homes and on shopping trips to understand what features were *must-have*s and what features were *nice-to-have*s. From this analysis, the company determined a price that Indian consumers were willing to pay. The target price: 15 rupees for the razor, with 5 rupees for the replacement blades.

P&G designed the Guard around the price. It cut the Mach 3's 25 components down to four for the Guard, making it much simpler and cheaper to manufacture. They made the handle hollow. "I can remember talking about changes to this product that were worth a thousandth, or two thousandths of a cent," Jim Keighley, the company's associate director for product engineering, told a reporter.[3]

The results were swift and stunning. By 2012, just two years after its launch, the Guard had captured more than 60 percent of the razor category in India, nearly three times the share of Gillette's previous products and on par with its dominant share of its home U.S. market. The impact on Gillette's customer base was even more substantial, considering the total potential market in India is 400 million men, compared with an estimated 94 million in the United States.[4]

That was just the short-term impact. P&G's Alberto Carvalho pointed to the new razor's ability to carve out space in Indian men's medicine cabinets for other products from his company. "The first job is to bring more consumers into Gillette. When they start enjoying a better shave, they'll be more open to all solutions," he said.[5] P&G expects the Guard to increase the lifetime value of the company with all those Indian customers, now and going forward.

Why You Should Have the Talk Early: The Three Benefits

As the Gillette story shows, it is critical to start the conversation with customers about their willingness to pay for your product *before* you begin building it. The early WTP talk will help you in three essential ways:

1. It will tell you right away whether you have an opportunity to monetize your product—or not.
2. It will help you prioritize features and design the product with the right set of features.
3. It will enable you to avoid the four types of failures.

Early WTP talks help you avoid feature shocks by restraining you from overloading your product with unnecessary features that in turn force you to price it too high. They prevent minivations by giving you critical information on how much your customers value your product, and how much they're willing to pay for that value. That information will give you the courage *not* to price your product too low. The early WTP talk will also help you identify the hidden gems in your firm by arming you with the proof that there is indeed a market for these ideas. Your firm is far more likely to regard them seriously and invest resources to harness them. Last, the early WTP talk will save you from bringing an undead product to market. If customers tell you they're not willing to pay the price you need to make money from your product, that will save you lots of anguish later.

Let's take an example of how an early WTP talk redirected a new product in the works. We worked with a company that served as an Internet marketplace for connecting buyers and sellers. The company was already making money from the sellers and was planning to build a product to improve the buying experience and, as a consequence, charge buyers for using the service.

This was an exciting project, and the innovation team spent more than four weeks identifying "cool" features they *could* build. After numerous brainstorming, white-boarding, and Post-It notes sessions about how buyers could use the marketplace, the team showed the CEO a product with 25 features. (They had killed 30 ideas and were passionate about the 25 survivors.)

But the CEO was skeptical and asked the team: "How do you know our customers will value these specific features? How do you know which features they'll pay for, and which they'll figure they can do without?"

What followed was dead silence. Nobody could answer the questions. The entire process had been driven by inside-out thinking, and the CEO knew it. So the CEO pushed the team to prove customers would be willing to pay for the service—and would find value for each of those 25 features—before they embarked on a long journey of turning it into a product.

The innovation team recruited several hundred potential customers to validate how much they were willing to pay. First, they explained the product concept and the functionality they were planning to build. Then they tried to understand if the customers saw any value in the concept. Most important, they asked customers whether they would be willing to pay for such a product. They found customers truly valued the concept and were willing to pay anywhere from $10 to $20 for a monthly subscription fee, as shown in Figure 4.1.

The conversations demonstrated the company had a product customers were willing to pay for. Its managers were no longer operating on a wing and a prayer. Next, the innovation team dug one level deeper to find out

Figure 4.1   Distribution of Customers' Willingness to Pay

which features customers were willing to pay for. Prior to that discussion, the team believed one of the coolest features was enabling buyers to find out if one of their Facebook connections had used a seller of a product/ service they were interested in. The team thought this feature would be critical to creating trust. They were superexcited about building this and touted it as the number one feature. Certainly, consumers would be willing to pay for that and all the other features (25 in total), wouldn't they?

When the company actually validated this with customers, it turned out customers were only willing to pay for 10 of the 25 features. (These are shown in Figure 4.2.) Of those 10, the Facebook feature ranked seventh in WTP. For customers, the Facebook feature was a nice-to-have, not a must. Customers had become so used to relying on third-party reviews (common at other Internet sites), that they didn't really care much if the reviews came from their Facebook buddies.

The CEO told the R&D team to focus on the 10 features customers valued. The other 15? Forget about them.

In this way, the WTP talk allowed the company to prioritize. Equally important, the talk showed them which features customers didn't need at all. The ranking of the 10 most desired features gave the R&D and innovation team its marching orders—which features should be

Features	WTP in $
Free ground shipping	
Communicate online with seller over chat	
24x7 customer support	
Early access to special deals	
Price guarantee	
Membership sharing	
Highlight connections from Facebook	
Ability to place a video call with seller	
$10 off first purchase	
Message with friends	

Figure 4.2   Willingness to Pay for Features

developed first, second, third, and so on. In the vernacular of software development, it gave the team a product roadmap. More important, because the team focused on only the important features, they consequently built a better product experience for customers.

The WTP talk helped prevent the company from creating a feature shock.

Most companies don't do this kind of homework when they develop a new product or service. Our 2014 survey of 1,600 companies in more than 40 countries (encompassing a range of business-to-business and business-to-consumer industries) found 80 percent wait until just before their product is introduced to the marketplace to determine its price.[6] Of those 80 percent, the majority do not have the WTP conversations at all. For those that do, the conversation happens after the product is built, but by then it's too late.

All of these companies operate on the huge hope that customers will be willing to pay for their products and services, but in reality they simply don't know. No wonder the survey also indicated that 72 percent of new products are failures and don't meet their revenue or profit targets.

The smart companies, on the other hand, have the WTP conversation earlier and use this to shape the product and their own destiny.

The Information You Need from Those Early Pricing Talks

So having early pricing discussions is essential. But what kind of information are we trying to uncover?

First, you want to understand your customers' *overall* WTP for your product—the price range they would consider reasonable (if, in fact, they would pay anything at all). Then you have to ask yourself whether that price range would work for your company. It may not if you can't deliver a market-acceptable product at a price that makes you a profit.

Second, you must understand how much value customers place on each feature and what they'd be willing to pay for that value. In this step, you dig a level deeper to understand exactly which features customers value most and would thus be most willing to pay for. This step will help you create your product roadmap—what features to develop first, next, and so on. What's more, it will focus your team on the features that generate the most customer interest and help avoid a feature shock.

One Internet company found this out the hard way—*after* it had brought a new product to market. The company hosts web pages and registers domain names for small businesses. It launched a new product and wasn't getting sufficient revenue for almost a year. We investigated and diagnosed the product as a feature shock: It had 27 features, many that small businesses did not care about. We told them to whittle the product down to eight features and then *increase the price*. It worked beyond the firm's wildest dreams, boosting the sales conversion rate and revenue more than 25 percent.

This sounds counterintuitive: *Fewer* features create *more* demand? But it was true in this case. Piling too many features into the product was killing demand by hiding the features that truly mattered. The company had created something that many customers thought excessive and thus actually *reduced* their WTP. Today, the firm wishes it had known that before it launched and watched a year's revenue go *poof*.

We see this scenario over and over again: A company guesses what customers will value about its product and what they'd pay for it. Don't just hope; find out! Amazon could have found out whether customers valued the 3-D features in the Fire Phone. Validate feature value and willingness to pay, and you'll build far more successful products.

Insights, Tips, and Tricks

By now you should understand why it's essential to discuss your new product concept with customers, and ask what they'd pay for it, early in your development process. But if you are like most of our clients, you are a little nervous about discussing pricing with customers before you have a product. How does one do that?

The simplest way is to ask direct questions about the value of your product and its features, for example:

- "What do you think could be an acceptable price?"
- "What do you think would be an expensive price?"
- "What do you think would be a prohibitively expensive price?"
- "Would you buy this product at $XYZ?"

Then follow each question with the most powerful question of all: "Why?"

What your customers will tell you will be worth its weight in gold.

Direct questioning is very useful for getting to a quick ballpark range. More fundamentally, it provides a fast way to see if customers value your product and if they will pay for it—*before* you sink a lot of money into it.

More sophisticated methods for getting at pricing include simulating purchase scenarios that ask customers to pick an option. For instance, you could show a product lineup with different price points and feature combinations and then ask which ones they would choose (including not choosing any option). Again, ask "why?" Then you change the scenario (for example, the feature and price combination) and ask them to choose again.

With this technique, you are tapping into the mental models and rules people use to make choices. This will enable you to understand what aspects of your product drive the most value and how much people will pay for them.

In Figure 4.3, we detail the five methods we have found most useful that you should use when you have the conversations with your prospective customers. Your conversations will typically take one of three forms: one-on-one conversations, focus groups, or large-scale quantitative surveys.

We have conducted thousands of conversations like these for our clients over the last 30 years. Below are the 10 most important insights we have learned from them:

1. **Don't forget to tap into pockets of internal excellence:** Before you have customer conversations, form a group of internal cross-functional experts (product, sales, marketing, finance, and engineering) and conduct an expert judgment workshop. It is important to put this group through the types of questions you would ask customers. This would also serve as a pilot test before you take it to customers. Send out the questions before the meeting and ask participants to show up with answers (to avoid behavior in the room that generates biased answers). Then conduct an objective discussion of why people answered the way they did.

2. **Position customer discussions as the "value talk:"** Don't position the talk as "pricing" or "willingness to pay." Rather, frame the talk as "we want to talk about our latest innovation ideas and how we can continue to add value for you." This positioning is essential to

Method	Description	When to use
1. Direct WTP questions	First ask, "What do you think is an acceptable price?" Next ask, "What do you think is an expensive price? And finally, "What is a prohibitively expensive price?"	This is the easiest way to see if there is WTP for your product innovation. This method is powerful in the early stages of innovation. Asking enough people about their willingness to pay, helps form a range of what the market is generally willing to pay. Moreover, it will quickly show you if you are completely off track (especially when the market's willingness to pay is much less than what you expected). Bonus: You could also run a large-scale survey with this question and plot a graph similar to the one shown in Figure 4.1 earlier in this chapter. See if you have any psychological drop-off points.
2. Purchase probability questions	Show a new product concept, explain the value and benefits, attach a price to it, and then ask, "On a scale of 1 to 5, where 1 is, I would never buy this product and 5 is, I would most definitely buy this product, how would you rate this product?" If the answer is 4 or 5, you stop. If the answer is less than or equal to 3, you lower the price and ask the question again. Ask it a few times and see if people increase their rating (in which case, by reducing the price, your product becomes more attractive) or not (in which case you have a product/innovation issue and adjusting the price may not help).	This is the easiest way to see if someone would actually purchase your product if it were available. Typically, from our benchmarks, if someone says 5, the probability of them buying it is about 50 percent. If they say 4, the probability drops to 10 to 20 percent. While this varies by industry, you can make this a rule of thumb. If you ask this question in a larger group, you can quickly gauge the number of units you might actually sell. This would give you a reasonable indication of your market potential before building the product.
3. Most–least questions	Start with a finite set of features (10, for instance). Then create a subset of these features (say, six features) and ask customers to identify the feature they value most and the feature they value least. Then show them another subset from the same feature set and repeat the question. Repeat this process a few times (typically 5–7 sets) until you exhaust your combinations. This technique is also called MaxDiff.	This method is the quickest way to determine the relative priorities of features and identify the leader (most valued), fillers, and killers (least valued). More on leaders, fillers, and killers in Chapter 6. This method forces people to make trade-offs and indicate which features they do and do not value. The logic behind this method is that when given a set of features, people can easily identify the extremes (most and least). But people struggle to identify the in-betweens. Thus, by changing the subset and asking the most–least questions repeatedly, you force people to make the appropriate trade-offs. This helps to identify the relative priorities of a set of features.

Figure 4.3   Top Five Methods for Having the Willingness-to-Pay Conversation (from Easiest to Most Advanced)

Method	Description	When to use
4. Build-your-own questions	Before using this method, you need a rough idea of your customers' WTP and how much they value each feature (from using the previous three methods). Next, give customers your list of features and ask them to build their "ideal product" by selecting features they value most. The trade-off is that when they add more features, the total price should also increase. You try to see where they stop (based on their price and value expectations).	Use this method to identify what the ideal packages could look like for each customer (regarding feature and price combination). Bonus: You can also test for segments and bundles/packages. Particularly, if you have significant clusters of customers with varying degrees of features in their ideal product, you should avoid a one-size-fits-all approach and segment your customer base. At the least, since you know how many features were added to build an ideal product, you can use this information to avoid a feature shock.
5. Purchase simulations	This is the most advanced method in the list. (It is sometimes called conjoint analysis.) You provide customers with a product that has a specific feature set and price, then ask if they would buy it. Next you change the feature set and price and ask the question again. Typically, you show 5–8 such combinations and see how people react. This method is the closest to a real sales situation. Once you vary features and price systematically, you can estimate the value of the features and the WTP for each one.	This method is useful if the willingness to pay estimate for a product and its features needs to be more precise. A prerequisite to using this method: Identify a good set of features and have a good approximate understanding of the WTP. (Try a few of the other methods above before this one.) Based on the output, you can build a market-based model to estimate the purchase probability of any combination of features and price for your product. This method is very useful for performing advanced scenario modeling.

Figure 4.3   (*Continued*)

get customers in the right mindset. Start by asking customers about their pain points, and pitch your product's features and the value they would bring. Ask questions like "Do you value these products/ features?" and then ask why. Then switch gears to ask questions like "What would you consider an acceptable price?" Switching from value to price is an easier transition to make in determining customer WTP. If your product is totally new and you cannot articulate its value to customers, they really won't be able to respond well to your WTP questions. Hence, you need to focus on talking value with customers before you ask them about pricing.

3. **Valuable insights already come from the simplest questions:** Direct questions often yield important insights. Typically, we find customers would pay the acceptable price (see Figure 4.3) and love

the product. They might pay the expensive price, but they wouldn't be thrilled about it. You will likely leave them in a neutral state—neither hating nor loving your product.

4. **Make 25 percent of the questions "why" questions:** As simple as it sounds, the "why" question is the most powerful one. If someone says, "I would pay $20," ask them, "Why do you say that?" If someone says, "I don't see value in a particular feature and won't pay for it," ask them, "Why is that, and what would the product need to make it more valuable?" You may get tips that improve your product significantly. Asking why also helps create a culture that's hungry for information.

5. **Mix it up:** Don't always operate from a standard script. Sometimes allowing the conversation to be unstructured, especially for leading-edge innovations, can lead to more insightful findings. If you always stick to a structured script, you might only learn what you already know (or think you know).

6. **Be part of the action:** Don't leave the WTP conversations to your product teams alone. This is important information. Have all your key people (across product, sales, and marketing functions) sit in on focus group meetings and interviews to hear the voices of your customers. The sooner you have a cross-disciplinary team involved, the better your chances of monetizing innovation. (More on this in Chapter 14.)

7. **Avoid the "average trap:"** When you analyze the answers to your WTP questions, look at the distribution, not just the average response. The average response can be misleading. For instance, for two groups of customers, one willing to pay $20 and another willing to pay $100, if you calculated the average price they would pay, it would be $60. But that would leave money on the high side (the group that would pay $100) and make your product unafford-able to the low side (they'll only pay $20). You might be better off building the product to a $100 price point or—even better—making two versions, one at $20 (with different features or materials) and the other at $100. Either way, you must look at the distribution to arrive at the right insight, not just the averages.

8. **Don't rely only on quantitative numbers:** This is especially important if you are building a truly innovative product. You need to have the qualitative discussions (one-on-one or in focus

groups) before doing a quantitative study. Talking to your customers qualitatively first will enable you to create a more robust quantitative survey and give you a sanity check.

9. **Be precise in your language:** The questions "Would you buy this?" and "Would you buy this for $20?" are totally different. Make sure customers answer your real, underlying question.

10. **Garbage in is garbage out:** When you use the advanced methods in Figure 4.3, keep the design of your questions simple. Use your business knowledge and common sense to isolate the most important variables to test. Many companies treat this purely as a market research exercise. But that typically results in asking far too many questions or making them extremely complicated. When customers are overwhelmed, they will give you inconsistent and incoherent responses.

With the five methods for conducting the all-important WTP talk with customers and these 10 tips for using those methods, you are now ready to begin testing your product's market viability.

Summary

The most important aspect of moving to a "design the product around the price" innovation process is finding out as early as you can whether customers value your innovation and would pay for it. You can only determine customers' WTP by actually asking them—*not* by imagining what they will say.

Two pieces of information are important in this phase: customers' overall WTP for a product (the price range they have in mind) and their WTP for each feature (so you know which features matter most and which features don't matter at all).

Five types of research questions will help you get these answers: direct, purchase probability, most–least, build-your-own, and purchase simulations. Best practices in having these discussions include positioning them as "value talks" (not as pricing discussions), expecting key insights to come from the simplest questions, mixing structured with unstructured questions, and not relying solely on quantitative data.

CEO Questions

1. Does our product development team have serious pricing discussions with customers in the early stages of the new product's development process? If not, why not?
2. What data do we have to show there's a viable market that can and will pay for our new product?
3. Do we know our market's WTP range for our product concept? Do we know what price range the market considers acceptable? What's considered expensive? How did we find out?
4. Do we know what features customers truly value and are willing to pay for, and which ones they don't and won't? And have we killed or added to the features as a consequence of this data? If not, why not?
5. What are our product's differentiating features versus competitors' features? How much do customers value our features over the competition's features?

CHAPTER 5

Don't Default to a One-Size-Fits-All Solution

Like It or Not, Your Customers *Are* Different

In the previous chapter, we discussed why you need to have the value and willingness-to-pay (WTP) talk early. But not all your customers have the same WTP. We have not found a single market where customer needs are homogeneous. Yet, time and again, companies design products for the "average" customer.

The reality is your customers are different, whether you like it or not. They have very different needs, differing abilities to pay, and they vary by the degree to which they value your product's key benefits. The only way to cope with this variance is to embrace customer segmentation.

Customer segmentation is the most talked about and at the same time the most misused concept in product design. Why? A guessing game will help explain.

Here we go. Guess the identity of this person: famous Englishman, wealthy, 67 years old, married, two children, and lives in a castle. Of course, you know who we're talking about. Or do you? We'll bet 90 percent of you guessed Prince Charles. While that is absolutely correct, the description also fits Ozzy Osbourne. He's someone every baby boomer rock music fan will know from the early 1970s heavy metal band Black

Sabbath, and their children will know him as the star of the early 2000s TV reality show *The Osbournes*. Even though Prince Charles's and Ozzy's customer personas are similar based on certain characteristics, their needs and preferences undoubtedly differ.

We'll take a wild guess that these men don't dress alike or drive the same car. And their music tastes probably diverge as well. However, if you had based your product design segmentation on demographic variables—age, gender, nationality, marital status, and so forth—you would have put both Prince Charles and Ozzy in the same segment. As a result, you would have designed identical products for them. Imagine that!

Most companies tell us they have a segmentation strategy. But about half of the time they don't use it to guide product development. When they do, they generally segment in the wrong way. You see, there are many flavors of segmentation that may be good for customizing sales and marketing messages, such as persona, behavior, attitude, demographics, and more. But when it comes to innovation, there is only one right way to segment: by customers' needs, value, and their willingness to pay for a product or service that delivers that value.

Companies that fail to achieve this understanding end up putting both the Prince Charleses and the Ozzy Osbournes of the world into the same segment. Companies that get it right create products customers are willing to pay for.

A Paper Company's Segmentation Story

A paper company took this approach in developing a new offering (product plus services) for its North American customers. The company makes packaging material and is one of several such firms in the market, some of which are tiny shops while others are enormous global companies.

Historically, the paper company segmented based on customer size— small, medium, and large. But several functions, including sales and customer service, had routinely pointed out this segmentation was not actionable. For example, some of the largest customers only needed the most basic features and were willing to pay less as a consequence, while others needed fully featured offerings. To make matters worse, many small and medium-sized customers valued features such as support services that had only been offered to large customers. What's more, many customers of all sizes complained delivery was too slow and needed to be "just in time." Other customers, those with large warehouses that could stock plenty of paper, didn't care about just-in-time delivery. They could just pull it from their warehouses.

So in thinking about how to design its new product and service offering, the paper company realized it would have a failure on its hands if it continued with the status quo segmentation.

So the paper company went back to the drawing board. It needed to identify the right segments. The firm surveyed about 200 customers. (The firm used the methods we described in Figure 4.3 in Chapter 4, including most–least and purchase simulations/conjoint analysis.) The foremost goal of the validation was to answer two questions: What features and services really mattered most to customers, and what were they willing to pay for them?

You can see the results of this research in Figure 5.1.

The research showed that on average, from the customer perspective, price was the most important aspect of the paper company's offering.

Needs/ Features	All customers	Segments			
		"Want the best" (30%)*	"Want it now" (40%)	"Want product only" (10%)	"Want price only" (20%)
Price	21	12	18	26	36
Service programs	15	19	15	8	14
On-time delivery	15	14	19	10	13
Product performance (end user)	14	21	10	21	9
Product quality (converter)	13	17	10	18	10
Speed of delivery	13	8	18	10	11
Tech support	9	9	10	7	7

* Segment size (value)

Importance of needs/features in %

Figure 5.1 A Paper Company's New Segmentation

Technical service was the least important factor. However, the company was surprised to learn that customers valued service programs that increased the efficiency of their operations—so much that they were willing to pay for this feature. The firm was shocked. Before conducting the research, they regarded this feature as a cost center, not a potential source of revenue.

But the biggest insight from the research was something different: There were significant differences on what was valued across customer groups. The firm's packaging customers could be segmented in four very different ways, each with distinct needs and WTP for features that met those needs:

1. *A "want price only" segment.* These customers primarily cared about getting a low price. Tech service and delivery terms were unimportant, and they were not willing to pay extra for them. And in terms of product quality, as long as the product met their minimum requirements, they were fine.

2. *A "want it now" segment.* This group was largely interested in speedy delivery. Because their own customers often needed packaging in a rush, this segment depended on suppliers that could respond quickly, and thus they were willing to pay for fast delivery.

3. *A "want product only" segment.* This segment coveted product performance and quality above all other features. Service, delivery, and speed were least important.

4. *A "want the best" segment.* This was the least price-sensitive group, and it emphasized quality and service features. They had a high WTP because their customers demanded high quality themselves. What's more, reliability and just-in-time delivery were more important than price.

This shows how useless and misleading averages are in segmenting customers. The sales team was right: Dividing customers simply by their size didn't shed light on what they really needed from the paper company and how much they would pay to fill those needs. Before segmenting its market this way, the company didn't understand what customers really needed and what they'd pay to fill those needs. The research upended earlier assumptions. In fact, each of the four new segments had a mix of customer sizes. The sales team was right: Dividing customers simply by how big they are didn't shed real light on what they really needed from the paper company.

With this new way of segmenting its customer base, the product development team went to town. They saw new possibilities—with both product and services—to meet the needs of the four new segments. They developed solutions—products plus services—for each segment. And in constructing the portfolio of products and services for each segment, the product developers had a good idea of how much they could charge for them. They knew what customers were willing to pay. We'll say more about that in Chapter 6.

Typical Pitfalls of Segmentation

The paper company used segmentation to drive the way it designed new products based on the needs, value, and willingness to pay data. Is that what you're doing? Probably not. Most businesses do segmentation, but many are ineffective because of these three pitfalls:

1. Segmenting too late.

   Many companies start out with a one-size-fits-all approach to product development and use segmentation only to determine their marketing and sales messages. But if they don't design offerings to suit the needs of each segment, they run the risk of creating products no segment gets excited about. For example, if you have two customer segments and you design offerings for the "average" customer across both segments, you end up building a product neither group is fully happy about. You can try to repair the damage through sales and marketing segmentation fixes—essentially, tailoring messages that appeal to each segment. But it's too late by that point. You still have only one product to suit a range of diverse and sometimes incompatible customer needs.

2. Segmenting only by observable characteristics.

   Remember Prince Charles and Ozzy? The simple rule for product design is to base segmentation on your customers' needs, value, and WTP for features you are developing. Period. Revenue size (for business-to-business), age (for consumer segments), ethnic background, and other observable characteristics are often purely uncorrelated to what matters the most in product design.

3. Having too many segmentation schemes.

   Letting your managers create different segmentation methodologies for marketing, promoting, and selling the same product in addition to your product design will lead to confusion. Ideally, your company will settle on *one* segmentation scheme used by all your firm's functions so you have a unified approach to servicing your customers. Worst case, you must reduce your number of segmentation schemes. If you have more than three, you are headed for organizational confusion.

What Best-in-Class Companies Do

To do segmentation right in designing new products, remember this golden rule: *You* can *act differently*. (See Figure 5.2.)

Successful innovators build the right product for the right segment at the right price. They use segmentation as a guiding influence, starting with the R&D stages of an innovation. They constantly explore how customer needs, value, and WTP differ in the market, and how they can act differently to shape products and versions differently for different segments. If there's capacity to build only one product (for example, in a startup), the company prioritizes and builds that product for the segment with the biggest opportunity (either in terms of size or revenue potential),

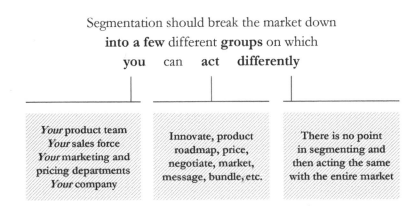

Figure 5.2   The Golden Rule of Segmentation

while creating a plan to introduce future products for other segments. In all these ways, successful companies avoid building a one-size-fits-none new product.

An excellent example of this is Garmin, the maker of global positioning system (GPS) devices that direct you on your journey, whether you're a driver, golfer, runner, hiker, or biker.

Hikers want to be safe, so they need a device to navigate the wilderness. Runners want to improve their performance, so they need to track distance, time, and speed. People driving cars want a GPS device that tells them where the traffic is. Golfers need to navigate a course in as few strokes as possible and choose the right golf club (to avoid sand and water). They need a device that tells them how far they are from the pin (so they can use the right club) and where the sand and water are.

It's hard to imagine one device (no matter how brilliantly engineered) that would please all Garmin customer segments. As a result, Garmin makes a variety of navigation devices. It could have easily created a feature shock product by designing a one-size-fits-all handheld or wearable GPS product. Instead, the company used sensible segmentation to develop multiple products. That approach makes total sense.

Consider the case of Mettler Toledo, a $2.5 billion global manufacturer of weighing instruments. The company's industrial customers need scales that can withstand high impact, large temperature fluctuations, and hazardous environments. Laboratories must have scales that are 100 percent accurate. Retailers need scales that are low-cost, capable of printing, and user-friendly. The underlying technology for weighing things is the same. But Mettler Toledo created different scales based on customer segment needs and WTP. Had it manufactured only one scale, it would have built a one-size-fits-none failure.

Segmentation gives you the power to serve customers better by catering to their specific needs. Segmenting in the early stages of your innovation process will help you build products that resonate with customers. Plus, your sales and customer support teams will know how to service them better. Fundamentally, you'll increase revenue, growth, and profits by serving multiple customer groups, and achieve broader adoption by offering products at multiple price points. Imagine the money Apple would leave on the table if it didn't offer so many models of iPhones. In only one flavor, the iconic phone would appeal to far fewer people.

Smart segmentation creates a win-win situation for your company and customers. Like the paper manufacturer we mentioned earlier in this chapter, you make it easier for your customers to find the right product, make the purchase, and get the right level of services from your company.

Insights, Tips, and Tricks

Most companies are familiar with the methodologies for segmenting customers (clustering analysis, for example). But to do segmentation along the lines we're talking about, keep in mind these five principles:

1. **Begin with customer WTP data.** In Chapter 4, we explored how to determine the WTP based on customer needs and value. By clustering individuals according to their WTP, value, and needs data, you will discover your segments—groups of people whose needs, value, and willingness to pay differ.

2. **Let common sense be your guide in using statistics.** Methods such as cluster analysis will give you many different options on how to segment with similar statistical accuracy. But choosing the most statistically significant outcome might not give you a segment strategy that will work in practice. Pressure-test your findings: Have you defined a customer group to which you can sell? Are there clear "fences" between segments—features one segment strongly wants but others don't? The acid test is asking a group of salespeople whether they can sort their clients into the segments you've come up with. Practicality and common sense are as important as statistical indicators.

3. **Fewer is more.** One important segmentation task is to decide on the number of segments. Theoretically, each customer could be one segment, which would make each segment perfectly homogeneous. The opposite extreme would be treating the whole market as one segment. The fewer segments you have, the less homogeneous and distinct they will be; the more segments, the higher the complexity. Do not underestimate the latter. Serving each new segment adds significant complexity for sales, marketing, product and service development, and other functions. Smart companies start with a few segments—three to four—and then expand gradually until they reach the optimal number.

4. **Don't try to serve every segment.** You're not obligated to serve every possible customer. The products and services you develop should match your company's overall financial and commercial goals. A segment must deliver enough customers—and enough money—to make the investment worthwhile. This part of segmentation is called market sizing. Market sizing doesn't mean simply counting the segment's customers. It means estimating how many of them you can acquire and keep, and at what prices—separating the attractive segments from those that don't make business sense.

5. **Describe the segments so you can address them.** Investigate whether each segment has observable criteria for customizing your sales and marketing messages to them. For example, if you find that your high-price segment has a disproportionate number of businesses that operate 24x7 vs. normal business hours, you can better describe your segments in your marketing. This is critical. In writing TV commercials, Internet banner ads, or any other marketing and sales messages, companies must describe their target segments as precisely as possible.

To fully monetize your innovations, you need to incorporate segmentation early in the product development process. And you should base that segmentation on customers' needs, value, and their willingness to pay for a product that delivers that value. If you do, your product development initiative will be off to an excellent start.

Summary

We have not found a single market where customer needs are homogeneous. Yet, time and again, companies design products for the "average" customer.

The message here is clear: *You need to create segments in order to design highly attractive products for each segment.* And you must base your segmentation on customers' needs, value, and WTP. This way, segmentation becomes a driver of product design and development, not an afterthought.

The following tips are among those that have helped numerous companies do segmentation right: Begin with WTP data; let

(*continued*)

(Continued)

common sense be your guide; create fewer segments, not more; don't try to serve every segment; and describe segments in detail in order to address them.

Understanding customers' needs and WTP will give you segmentation power. And segmentation power, in turn, is what gives you monetization power.

CEO Questions

1. Did we segment before we designed the product? If not, why not?
2. What were the segments? How did we get to these? Which ones would we serve initially? Do they represent a sizable market?
3. What criteria were they based on? How different are these segments in their WTP? Can we respond differently to each segment? If so, how?
4. How did we describe the segments? What observable criteria do we have in these descriptions? Do our descriptions and observable criteria on each segment pass our sales team's sniff test?
5. How many segmentation schemes do we have in our company? Can we consolidate to *one* segmentation across product, marketing, and sales?
6. Who in our company is responsible for segmentation? At what point in the innovation cycle does this person (or people) get involved?

CHAPTER 6

When Designing Products, Configuration and Bundling is More Science Than Art

S o you've segmented your customer base along the lines we laid out in Chapter 5: on their needs, the value of your offering, and their willingness to pay (WTP) for that value. Now you're ready to get down and dirty into the design of what you'll offer each customer segment— exactly what features and functions to deliver. There are two core design decisions you will need to make here. One is product configuration, and the other is bundling. This chapter will examine and illustrate these important design constructs.

But first, a clarification: Our definition of product configuration refers to the decision of which features and functionalities will be included in a product. In some industries, like software and tech, product configuration is also referred to by the term *packaging*. By bundling, we mean combining a product or service with other products and services.

Successful innovators get the product configuration and bundling decisions right from the start.

Product Configuration Done Right

Doing product configuration right means you design a product with the right features for a segment—that is, just the features customers are willing to pay for. This is a core tenet of designing new products that will succeed in the marketplace. Too many features lead to feature shock products, especially if your customers are not wild about those features. If they *are* wild about them and you didn't realize it, you design a minivation. Products with features that customers won't pay for wind up undead.

Let's illustrate how product configuration works when it's done correctly. Do you remember the paper manufacturer we discussed in the last chapter? The company had identified four distinct customer segments, which it referred to as "want price only," "want product only," "want it now," and "want the best." The firm's next task was deciding how to design offerings that best addressed each segment. The firm gave each segment the specific features it needed most—again, as determined by that segment's needs, value, and WTP. This is captured in Figure 6.1.

The Core offering became the firm's basic product, which included the core product at a very affordable price. This offering had the standard level for technology, application support, and logistics services, and no extra features. In contrast, the Product Plus and Logistics Plus offerings had additional features—according to each segment's needs, value, and WTP. For instance, the Logistics Plus offering guaranteed next-day delivery of stock products and seven-day delivery of customized products. The offering also provided priority delivery in the event of inventory or capacity issues. The Best offering combined the features of the Product Plus and Logistics Plus offerings.

In designing each offering, the company was guided by the elements customers were willing to pay for. The firm integrated product and service features into the three more expensive offerings (as compared to the "want price only" offering) because those customers indicated they would pay extra for them. The result was the firm priced its Best offering at a significant premium compared to its base offering.

By having their feature sets tailored to each segment's needs, value, and WTP, each offering finally had a distinct value proposition. The design of these products also minimized the chances they would canni- balize one another, since customers clearly saw what they gave up at the

Product	Core	Product Plus	Logistics Plus	Best
Value/ features		**Core** ⊕	**Core** ⊕	**Product Plus** ⊕
	• Standard paper quality and dimensions • Basic phone support for trouble shooting • 7-10 day delivery time	• Advanced paper quality • Customized paper dimensions • Access to lab and lab engineers for further customization • Dedicated team for trouble shooting	• Next day delivery of products on stock • <7 days delivery for all others products • Delivery guarantee (freight will be paid if late) • Priority delivery in case of capacity issues	**Logistics Plus**
Price (index)	100	115	115	125
Addressing the segment	"Want price only"	"Want product only"	"Want it now"	"Want the best"

Figure 6.1   A Segment-Based Product Offering in a Business-to-Business Market

lower price points. The way we like to put it is that the company established clear "fences" between its products. Customers only get a low price if they go without extra product or logistics services; the company can offer a low price on this product because value and costs are lower.

What we've just described may sound simple to accomplish. On the contrary, it typically is anything but. Leaving out features from a new product is extremely difficult for nearly every company in the product configuration phase of product development. It is especially hard for firms that compete on the basis of quality and like to stuff value-adding features into their new products. However, if they succumb to this temptation, they greatly risk cannibalizing the products they designed for each segment. Had the paper company's product developers felt the Core offering was far too basic and beefed it up with service and logistics features but kept the price the same, that product would have taken away customers who would have chosen the other three higher-priced offerings.

To maximize the monetization potential of new products, companies should curb their instincts to please customers by giving away value-added functionality—unless those customers will pay for it. These firms must get comfortable with the idea of giving their low-price segment only basic quality and service levels, rather than giving them everything. In other words, *product configuration requires the guts to take away features.*

Both product and service companies alike grapple with this problem of creating distinct offerings for each segment. Consider the experience of a regional European retail bank. Its executives asked us to look at the offering lineup for personal banking customers. Over time, the bank had added one new offering after the other. When we came in, the bank had 30 different account offerings. But what looked good on paper did not work at all in reality. The large number of choices made it harder for the sales force to sell them. Neither customers nor the bank's salespeople knew which offering was the best fit for a given customer. Thirty offerings was far too many.

We then interviewed a number of the bank's customers. What they wanted, and were willing to pay for, could be boiled down into three customer segments: Comfort (peace of mind was, by far, this segment's most important need, and they were willing to pay a high price for it); Direct (who preferred to do business online and rarely used the bank's offline services such as visiting the branches); and Classic (who used the branches frequently and did not trust or like its online services). With the bank team we developed three new offerings, each of which addressed those segments. (See Figure 6.2.)

The Comfort product came with all features and the highest price per month. The Direct and Classic products were offered at lower prices, but they lacked online or offline features.

So what happened after the bank shrank its thirty products to three? You might think sales plummeted because customers had far fewer choices. On the contrary, sales skyrocketed. Why? The bank had finally made each product distinct; its sales staff could articulate each product's value; and customers could easily determine which one best fit their needs. Total annual profit increased by 30 percent in the institution's personal banking services unit.

Current Account Offers

Features	Comfort	Direct	Classic
Manual transactions	free	€1.99	€0.79
SB scanner transactions	free	€1.99	€0.49
Deposits and withdrawals at counter	free	€1.99	5 free, then €0.49
Deposits and withdrawals at ATM	free	free	free
Online transfers	free	free	€0.09
Other paperless transactions	free	free	€0.49
Mobile TANs	✓	✓	✓
Debit card	✓	✓	✓
Monthly fee	**€8.90**	**€2.90**	**€2.90**

Figure 6.2   A Retail Bank's Product Configuration Decision

Bundling Done Right

Bundling helps you determine whether your products and/or services should be sold together or separately.

When done right, it can increase total profit because customers end up buying more than they would have if you hadn't bundled. Take an example many are familiar with: McDonald's and its Value Meals. With the Value Meal, McDonald's is trying to convince customers who might have skipped the soda or fries to go all in on the bundle. It's a win–win. The customer gets soda and fries for an appetizing bundle price; for its part, McDonald's realizes more revenue and profit.

You and your customers win when a good bundling decision is made. It not only boosts your revenue, it increases your customers' satisfaction because you've made the purchasing decision easier. They didn't have to choose between A or B; they got both, and generally for less than they would have paid separately for A and B.

Let's take a look at the benefits of bundling using a fun example—
pizza and breadsticks—and an actual case study on Microsoft.

THE PIZZA AND BREADSTICKS PUZZLE: TO BUNDLE OR NOT TO BUNDLE, THAT IS THE QUESTION

Up for a challenge? Let's see if you can crack this puzzle.

Question: Imagine you own a world famous pizzeria that makes delicious pizza and cheese breadsticks. You have long wondered how to price your products. You study your customers and determine that you have four types, or segments. Segment A loves pizza and will pay as much as $9 for it but is not a big fan of breadsticks (they'll only pay $1.50 for this). Segment D loves breadsticks and will pay $9 but doesn't love pizza (they will only pay $2.50). The other two segments, B and C, fall in between A and D in WTP. You also find out the size of your segments is the same—100 people in each. So your numbers are as shown in Figure 6.3.

Segment	Segment Size	WTP for Pizza	WTP for Breadsticks
A	100	$9	$1.50
B	100	$8	$5
C	100	$4.50	$8.50
D	100	$2.50	$9

Figure 6.3   Pricing of the Pizza and Breadsticks

Since you operate in a transparent world (anyone can walk into your store, and you must post your prices), you cannot charge each segment a different price for each item (that is, you cannot sell pizza to segment A for $9 and the same pizza to segment C for $4.50). You can only set one price per item or bundle. Further, assume the WTP numbers in the table are the maximum a segment would pay for each item. If you offered any segment a product priced less than or equal to the maximum WTP, they would buy that item. If it is more than the maximum, they would not.

Also assume you can sell to all 100 people in each segment, which means you have the chance to sell to 400 people in total. Your goal is to maximize revenue. So as an example, if you sell the pizza at $4.50 and the breadsticks at $5, you would make a total of $2,850, since at $4.50, segments A, B, and C will buy the pizza; at $5 for the breadsticks, segments B, C, and D would buy it. Total revenue would equal ($4.50 * 3 * 100) + ($5 * 3 * 100) = $2,850.

Now that you understand the puzzle, answer this question: What is the maximum revenue you can make? Ready, set, go.

Answer:

Most people would say the answer is $3,300. They would arrive at this by setting the pizza price at $8 (segments A and B would buy it) and the breadstick price at $8.50 (segments C and D would buy it). Total revenue = ($8 * 2 * 100) + $(8.50 * 2 * 100) = $3,300. This is the maximum revenue you can generate if you cannot bundle.

But what if you could bundle the pizza and the breadsticks? Some of you would have surely considered that option and landed at $4,200 as the answer. You could say to bundle the breadsticks and the pizza at $10.50. All four segments can afford it and would buy it. You would make a total of $10.50 * 4 * 100 = $4,200.

Congratulations if you said that! Yes, bundling directly raised your revenue from $3,300 to $4,200 (a revenue increase of 27 percent).

Are you convinced of the power of bundling? If you had racked your brain, you would have come up with $4,400 as the maximum revenue, not $4,200. Why? In this scenario, you would sell the pizza and breadstick bundle at $13; segments B and C would buy it. You would also sell the pizza and the breadsticks each at a stand-alone price of $9; segment A would buy the pizza and segment D would buy the breadsticks. Your total revenue would be ($13 * 2 * 100) + ($9 * 1 * 100) + ($9 * 1*100) = $4,400.

This is called *mixed bundling*, where you sell the products both as stand-alones and in a bundle. You generated 33 percent more revenue than selling them as stand-alones (which yields $3,300).

If you answered $4,400, give yourself a pat on the back. When we present this puzzle to executives, less than 10 percent answer $4,400.

Advance tip: Note that if you priced the stand-alone pizza and breadsticks at $9 each and the bundle at $13, it appears as if you gave a $5 discount on the bundle (compared to $18 for buying each stand-alone at $9). In reality, you didn't discount at all. You just tapped into each segment's WTP. However, you can "showcase" the bundle as if you had discounted it, which will further boost sales. If you do your math right across segments, you can often show discounting without actually discounting. How cool is that?

(*continued*)

(Continued)

The answers we discussed are summarized in Figure 6.4 for ease of comparison.

Segment	Segment Size	WTP for			Revenue		
		Pizza	Breadstick (BS)	Bundle	Pizza at $8 BS at $8.50	Bundle at $10.50	Mixed Bundling
A	100	$9	$1.50	$10.50	$800	$1,050	$900
B	100	$8	$5	$13	$800	$1,050	$1,300
C	100	$4.50	$8.50	$13	$850	$1,050	$1,300
D	100	$2.50	$9	$11.50	$850	$1,050	$900
				Total Revenue	$3,300	$4,200	$4,400

Figure 6.4   Bundling of Pizza and Breadsticks

Now let's examine an actual example in practice to illustrate the benefits of bundling: Microsoft's iconic Office software.

Microsoft Office: A Bundling Blockbuster

Microsoft is a compelling example of a company that soared thanks to bundling. When it released its Office suite of software in the 1990s, its customer base was used to paying for word processing, e-mail, spreadsheet, and presentation software applications separately. Microsoft pitched a discounted price for the bundle (as opposed to individual application prices), and it touted how convenient it was to have all the applications in the suite have a similar look and feel. The bundle helped the company cement customer loyalty and grow market share in the face of pressure from plucky, perfectly competent competitors that focused only on parts of the solution (such as Lotus 1-2-3 for spreadsheets and WordPerfect for word processing).

Over time, Microsoft developed different versions of its Office suite that varied in functionality. That let different customer segments—business, home, and education customers—find options that suited their different needs. By 2013, the Office business division was Microsoft's biggest, accounting for about a third of the company's total revenue and more than 40 percent of operating profit.[1]

That's the benefit of bundling.

Two Key Principles of Product Configuration and Bundling

When you configure and bundle your new product, you may get overwhelmed with deciding which features to include in each segment offer. In a different way, it is easy for customers to become overwhelmed trying to decide which offer is right for them. Designing your product with leader, filler, and killer features in mind will help you with that first challenge. Creating good, better, and best options will address the second.

Principle #1: Leaders, Fillers, and Killers

You should approach your product configuration decision strategically—that is, through monetization techniques—to avoid leaving money on the table. To determine what features you should bake into which product configuration, you should start by separating the must-have features from the nice-to-haves. On their own, nice-to-haves won't convince customers to buy a product.

It's equally important to think about which features might turn off customers. Critical features—what we call *leaders*—are what drive customers to buy a product. Customers have high WTP for such leader features. *Fillers* are features of moderate importance or nice-to-haves. In contrast, *killers* are features that will blow the deal if the customer is forced to pay for them.

The leader/filler/killer classification is the most important aspect of configuring your new product. We described methods for doing this in Figure 4.3 in Chapter 4. You can see the kinds of output that come from such classifications in Figure 6.5. Here, Feature 1 is a leader since the majority of customers find value in it. In contrast, Feature 11 is a killer because a significant portion of people see no value in it, and only a few

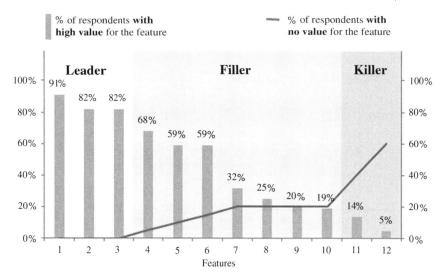

Figure 6.5   How Customers Viewed a Product's Features as Leaders/Fillers/Killers

find it valuable. A killer feature should be eliminated from the offering, but it could be sold à la carte to the few who want it.

Here's an easy way to identify killer features: Look for those that are valued by less than 20 percent of your customers *and* are not valued at all by more than 20 percent.

Sometimes, a product's features may fall into one category for a certain customer segment and another category for a different group. For example, for drivers in the frigid north, heated car seats are a leader. But in very warm or tropical climates, they are a filler (or even a killer if they add to the price of the car).

Customer segmentation is your tool for identifying these distinctions—that is, which features each segment considers to be leaders, fillers, and killers.

Principle #2: Creating Good, Better, and Best Options

The classic approach to product configuration and bundling is to create a three-tier model, sometimes referred to as *good, better, best* or G/B/B.

Typically, the good version has the most important core features, and the best has all the bells and whistles (the all-in product/bundle). You have probably come across this concept many times in everyday life: bronze, silver, and gold offerings. For example, the pro, business, and enterprise products offered by online file sharing website Dropbox are a G/B/B offering. Ideally, no more than a quarter of your customers should opt for the good option, while 70 percent should opt for the better or the best.

Why does a well-crafted G/B/B configuration/bundle work? Because you can steer customers to a choice based on whether they are price conscious (good), quality conscious (best), or somewhere in between (better). The core philosophy behind a G/B/B is that a significant portion of people avoid extremes when they are presented a choice; they choose the compromise option. Playing on this psychology, G/B/B configuration/bundling maximizes sales.

Think of a sales negotiation. If the salesperson only has one product to sell, the discussion with customers is black-and-white—a "take it or leave it" proposition. But with a G/B/B offering, the salesperson can switch between the good offer (if the customer focuses on price), the best offer (if the customer talks quality), or the better offer (if the customer wants both price and quality). In most cases, the better offer greatly increases the probability that a salesperson closes a deal. It also maximizes the new product's monetizing potential.

But a word of caution: While three is the classic number of product configurations/offerings, you could still use a G/B/B structure with a greater number of configurations—as long as you provide more value as you move from the good to best product configuration. Ideally, you should design each product to appeal to a substantial segment you have identified. In addition, the number of product configurations you decide on should be aligned with the number of distinct customer segments you have.

Insights, Tips, and Tricks

Before you rush headlong into figuring out your product configurations and bundles, here are 10 tips to guide you:

1. **Align with segments.** If you've followed the principles in this book, your offers should align with your customer segments. That is, they should reflect each segment's needs, value, and WTP. If you

don't design your offers with segmentation in mind, customers are unlikely to buy them.

2. **Don't make it too big.** Once you go beyond nine benefits or four products, your product configurations and bundles run the risk of exceeding psychological thresholds. Your product will start making customers' heads spin, and you will be heading toward producing a feature shock product!

3. **Make sure you and your customers both benefit.** The right product configuration and bundling provide benefits to both you and your customers (not just one or the other). The benefits to you should include more revenue (through increased acquisition and cross-selling), decreased price transparency, and higher customer loyalty (or increased switching costs). The benefits for customers include the added convenience of buying from a single provider, discounts, and an integrated experience from the bundle.

4. **Don't give too much away in your entry-level product.** In many industries, companies focus first on acquiring customers and then upselling. This strategy is often called *land and expand*. To increase customer acquisition, many companies pack too much into their entry-level product. But then they struggle to upsell customers since the functionality difference in the better or best product is marginal at best. Consequently, these companies land but don't expand. If more than 50 percent of your customers have bought your entry-level product, you most likely have this problem. If so, you should seriously consider removing features from your entry-level product. The ideal distribution of customers for a G/B/B product configuration strategy is 30 percent in good and 70 percent in better and best, with best being at least 10 percent.

5. **Hard bundling will not always work.** The standard approach is called a *mixed* bundle: The consumer has a choice of buying the bundle or buying the components in the bundle à la carte. But some companies are more rigid. They employ *hard bundling*, which means they do not give the customer the option to buy components of the bundle piecemeal. Some vacations, for example, are priced as all-inclusive—transport, hotel, meals, drinks, and activities; you cannot just book the hotel by itself. Hard bundling works when you have market power and are the dominant player. In almost all other cases, you should go with a mixed bundling approach.

6. **Individual prices need to be higher with mixed bundling.** If you create a mixed bundle and individual products are also sold separately, the à la carte price within the mixed bundle must be higher than the stand-alone optimal price in the unbundled situation. For example, if you hadn't offered a bundle in the pizza and breadsticks example (see Figure 6.3), you would have priced the individual product at $8. But if you offered a mixed bundle, you would price it higher—in this case, at $9.

7. **Don't forget bundle price communication.** Bundling offers you the unique opportunity to showcase your prices creatively and strategically. Suppose a customer really likes Product A and considers Product B a nice-to-have. Assume both were priced at $100 and you are prepared to give a 20 percent discount on the bundle. Saying "You get 20 percent discount on total price of the bundle" is totally different than saying "You get a 40 percent discount on Product A when you purchase it with Product B." Even though mathematically it amounts to the same price, customers are likely to find the latter option more appealing.

8. **Bundle with integration value so that 1 + 1 = 3.** Bundling is not always about discounting. In certain industries, such as software, you can sometimes charge a premium for bundling products together because customers are willing to pay for integrated product experiences (such as common user interface and seamless interoperability between products). In these situations, if you offer a discount on the bundle, you will hurt your bottom line two times over!

9. **Don't bundle for the sake of bundling.** You could lose a lot of money if you do. If customers would have purchased your individual products anyway, you are giving an unnecessary discount by bundling them.

10. **Exploit inverse correlations.** This is an advanced tip. If you find two customer segments with inverse preferences, you can bundle products together to serve both segments. For example, if one segment finds Product A a must-have and Product B a nice-to-have, and another segment finds Product B a must-have and Product A a nice-to-have, your best strategy may be to bundle A and B and sell one bundle to both segments.

YOUR BUNDLE CHECKLIST

We want to make sure you're fully prepared for product configuration and bundling. So along with our 10 tips, here are questions which will help you and your product team to develop the right product configuration and bundling strategy:

- **Goals:** How well does the product configuration/bundle advance your strategic and tactical goals?
- **Positioning:** Will the configuration/bundle enhance your company's differentiation as a solutions provider?
- **Cross-selling:** Will the configuration/bundle generate awareness for filler products that help you cross-sell?
- **Psychological thresholds:** Does the configuration/bundle exceed key psychological price thresholds? (It shouldn't.)
- **Killers:** Does the configuration/bundle avoid including features or products for which customers have a very low willingness to pay?
- **Synergies:** Do customers get more value when they use these features or products in combination instead of separately?
- **Convenience:** How convenient is our configuration/bundle for the customer?
- **Competitive reaction:** Can we structure our configuration/bundle in a way that avoids triggering an adverse competitive reaction?
- **Selling:** Does the configuration/bundle "speak" to customers?

WHEN *UNBUNDLING* IS THE RIGHT ANSWER

Sometimes the best bundling strategy is to *unbundle*. A number of companies have gone to market with a new product or service that broke apart the long-prevailing offering and item-priced features that had been all-inclusive. Ireland's Ryanair is perhaps the best example.

For much of airline industry history, carriers bundled most of the services they offered. The price the customer paid for a ticket included *everything*: baggage handling, food, drinks, pillows, and seat selection. The airlines saw it all as integral. How could any of those services be offered separately, unbundled?

Then along came Ryanair. Launched in Ireland in 1985, the airline struggled in its first few years of operation. In the early 1990s, with the goal of becoming Europe's first (and now largest) low-cost carrier, the company's leaders decided to take a page from U.S.-based Southwest Airlines' low-priced, short-haul strategy book.

But Ryanair took Southwest's strategy one giant step further: by rethinking product configuration and bundling. It decided to unbundle the airline offering. It charged one price for any seat on every one of its planes—no special business class. However, it sold everything else—baggage services, food, and so on—à la carte.[2]

In Europe, particularly in the United Kingdom, airline travel had been a luxury that many lower-income consumers couldn't even consider. Then, suddenly, this new airline was charging previously unthinkably low fares: £9.99 for a seat from Bristol, England, to Barcelona, for example. Travel habits (and customer segments) began to change. (The "crazy" £9.99 fare campaigns still occur as of this writing.)[3]

Ryanair made the bulk of its money through its unbundled product offerings. Customers paid a £6 administration fee (waived for those with a prepaid, £6 Ryanair Cash Passport); they paid £10 to reserve a seat (rather than grab the first available), and £15 to check a bag. By the time the average customer was done, that £9.99 fare was quadrupled.

The overwhelming reason Ryanair's unbundling strategy was successful is because customers paid far more attention to the base fare than to surcharges. In fact, most air travelers are about two times more price sensitive to the base fare than they are to the surcharges. Unbundling helped Ryanair achieve a much lower base fare, thereby making the offer look very attractive.

Since unbundling the plane ride, Ryanair's financial performance has been staggering. Its annual revenue has multiplied 50-fold over three decades to €5 billion. Net profits also climbed 35-fold, from €15 million in 1995 to €522 million in 2014.[4] Even more impressive, its market capitalization was €19 billion at the time of this writing, while Lufthansa's was €6.4 billion, even though the German airline's revenues were six times higher than the Irish carrier's.

More than two decades later, budget-conscious customers continue to *love* Ryanair's unbundling strategy. And so do the firm's shareholders.

Summary

Product configuration and bundling are your key building blocks for designing the right products for the right segments at the right price points. Product configuration is about putting the appropriate features and functionality—those customers need, value, and are willing to pay for—into the product; this process has to be done for each identified segment. Systematic product configuration prevents you from loading too many features into a product and producing a feature shock.

(*continued*)

(*Continued*)

Bundling means selling your products and/or services together. If done right, this will increase total profit because customers end up buying more than if the products were sold stand-alone. Also, customer satisfaction will go up because the buying decision is easier. Successful bundling benefits both you and your customer.

There are two key elements of the product configuration and bundling process: establishing which features are leaders (must-haves), fillers (nice-to-haves), and killers (features that will nix a deal if customers are forced to pay for them), and creating good/better/best options. While these might sound easy, they are two of the most difficult challenges.

Savvy product configuration and bundling decisions have propelled many new product launches, as firms like Microsoft and McDonald's can attest.

CEO Questions

1. What are the product configuration/bundles we plan to offer? Why did we pick these offers? Do they align with our key segments? If not, why not?
2. What are the leader, filler, and killer features for the new product or service our company is developing? How did we find out?
3. Have we explored a good/better/best approach to product configuration and bundling? What do we expect sales to be for each product configuration? Is the share of the basic product configuration lower than 50 percent? If not, why not?
4. Have we explored bundling our new product with existing products? What would be the benefits for us and the customers?
5. Have we considered unbundling as an opportunity? What would be the benefits to customers and our business (if any)?

CHAPTER 7

Go beyond the Price Point

Five Powerful Monetization Models

S o you've taken our advice in Chapter 6 and determined the right set of features to incorporate in your new product or service offering. You've also decided whether to combine it with other offerings. You know which of your features are leaders, fillers, and killers, as well as what product configurations or bundles to sell.

The next step is coming up with a monetization model. What is that? In a nutshell, it's how the customer pays for your new product or service.

This is no small matter. In fact, establishing a favorable monetization model can be as important as the new product itself and the price you charge for it. A highly innovative monetization model can make a new offering take off like a rocket.

A number of innovative—yet proven—monetization models are in use today: subscription, dynamic pricing, and freemium to name just a few. You need to choose one carefully; the right model can make or break your new product, your business, or even an entire industry. *How* you charge trumps *what* you charge.

That's a bold statement. Don't believe it? Read on.

How You Charge Trumps *What* You Charge

The first thing to realize is that most companies perpetuate the monetization model they've always used. They select a model without reflecting on it, thinking strategically about it, or testing it. That's a missed opportunity and a huge mistake.

Some of the world's most successful companies have made the biggest leaps by revolutionizing their monetization models. For example, take the "pay as you go" model. It's a model that has helped companies that provide hosting and cloud computing services, telecommunications, transportation services, construction machines, and aircraft engines (yes, you read that right!) achieve game-changing results.

Let's take a few examples. Xerox has been transforming its model through the years, charging some customers based on how much they use Xerox printing and copying equipment rather than selling or leasing those machines. Enercon, a German wind turbine manufacturer, charges based on the amount of electricity its customers generate. The more electricity the customer produces using Enercon turbines, the greater Enercon's revenue. Marketing software firm Adobe, after many successful years of selling software by the unit and charging a one-time fee, has moved most of its popular products to a cloud-based subscription model.

You might be tempted to think innovative monetization models are the preserve of newer companies—firms unconstrained by decades of conventional wisdom. But you'd be wrong. One of the most radical and successful monetization models was the brainchild of a 126-year-old company, one that virtually every driver knows: France's Michelin Group. Let's take a closer look.

Michelin: From Selling Tires to Monetizing Miles

Michelin has been known for decades for the quality of its tires, which have commanded a premium in the global marketplace. But in the early 2000s, Michelin's premium prices faced enormous pressure from a range of tire makers, including fast-rising Chinese and South Korean tire manufacturers.

Continuing to expect customers to pay a premium for Michelin tires—especially trucking firms, for which tires are a big cost of doing business—was the equivalent of driving on tires with nails embedded in them. It risked a blowout. And the executives at Michelin knew it. So Michelin, a company that has introduced numerous product innovations in its 126-year history (from the detachable bike tire in 1891 to the first radial tire in 1946 and the run-flat tire 50 years later), fell back on the strategy it knows best: product innovation.[1] It invented new tires that lasted longer—much longer, in fact. And it hoped it could retain its premium prices as a result, or perhaps even raise them. But competition in the tire market was relentless.

At the turn of the twenty-first century, the firm was ready to launch a new tire that would last about 20 percent longer. However, the head of sales predicted Michelin could only charge a few percentage points more for the new tires than it did for its standard tires. What's more, given that the new tires would last longer, they would reduce customer demand by 20 percent. Customers wouldn't have to buy Michelin's longer-lasting tires as frequently. To the company, a small increase in its premium pricing that would unleash a big drop in demand did not make sense at all.

With these hazards facing the firm, Michelin's executives realized they needed more—much more—than a superior tire. So they revisited Michelin's long-established monetization model—how the company charged for its tires. The new monetization model that Michelin's Fleet Solutions came up with in 2001 turned out to be as big a breakthrough as its longer-lasting tires: charging trucking fleets by the mileage they drove their Michelin tires, not by the number of tires they bought.

It was a bold move by Michelin, one that put its money where its mouth was. The company dubbed its monetization model "the TK"—short for ton-kilometer. Michelin started negotiating a per-kilometer rate with truckers, contract by contract.

Setting price by distance traveled delivered benefits to both Michelin and its trucking customers. The new approach allowed fleet managers to pay for performance rather than simply the privilege of owning Michelin rubber. What's more, it gave industrial vehicle owners the flexibility to manage costs appropriately in good times and bad times. If a recession set in, reducing demand for products shipped by truck and thus demand for trucking services, fleet owners would pay less for those tires since they were being charged by the kilometer, not by the tire.

Michelin took on the customer's cost of product problems; if a tire fails early, Michelin bears the risk. On the flip side, when tires exceed quality expectations—say, when they last 20 percent longer than before—Michelin generates 20 percent more revenue per tire.

Michelin's new monetization model allowed the firm to fully capitalize on its new invention—that is, to monetize a tire that lasted much longer than the previous generation did. And Michelin did this without having to spend more on sales and marketing to convince customers these new-fangled tires were worth the premium they were being asked to pay.

Michelin simply changed its monetization model. It was a brilliant move. Michelin soon boasted the biggest profits in the industry; by 2011, its earnings before interest and taxes were 25 percent higher than Bridgestone's and more than three times Goodyear's.[2]

Innovative Monetization Models: More the Rule Than the Exception

Since the turn of the century, innovative monetization models such as Michelin's have swept through other industries as well. One of them is the $369 billion global computer software industry,[3] where the "software as a service" monetization model has taken hold. In the construction industry, equipment such as backhoes and tractors now have sensors that transmit data when they're about to break down (so customers can fix them before they break). This demands a rethinking of the industry's monetization model. If you charge by the hour for an engineer to fix the equipment on site, your maintenance revenue may disappear. A better model might be to include proactive maintenance services into your machine's price and then increase that price.

With technological advancements such as these, increasingly the monetization model *is* the innovation. But those advancements have been in the making for a few years. For example, in 1999, a then two-year-old movie rental firm named Netflix began charging a flat monthly fee (a subscription model) for unlimited movie rentals by mail rather than the per-disk rental people paid at the neighborhood video store. Customers took to this model in droves, and Netflix later displaced Blockbuster.

Since 2000, the reigning monetization model for the online advertising market has been the auction. This is how Google has made most of its immense profits. While Google didn't invent the online ad auctioning monetization model, it undisputedly has been the best at perfecting and making money from it.

Uber has disrupted the taxi business with a dynamic pricing model based on supply and demand in a given location. Medtech and General Electric have begun charging hospitals and physician groups according to their use of medical equipment rather than selling or renting the equipment. Metromile, an auto insurance startup,[4] tracks customers' driving behaviors using telematics (onboard digital devices) and calculates their total premiums on a per-mile basis. These innovative monetization models have differentiated these companies and enabled dramatic success.

However, selecting the wrong monetization model can have just as significant an impact. A European trucking company found this out soon after signing a three-year contract to distribute a TV manufacturer's goods. The distributor charged the TV set maker a fixed price per TV delivered. Over time the size of the TVs increased exponentially, which meant the distributor couldn't fit as many TVs into each truck as it used to, and thus had to make more truck runs. Costs increased massively, but revenue did not because of the fixed price. Hence, the TV distributor ultimately lost money on the deal.

The TV set distributor learned a harsh lesson: *Monetarily, a bad monetization model can be worse than a bad price.*

Five Powerful Monetization Models

Sifting through dozens of pricing and revenue strategies, we have identified five monetization models that have been proven over time to help companies launch an innovative product or service, differentiate it, or dominate their marketplace. These five are not the only monetization models out there, but they are among the most valuable for new product launches.

Let's look at how each model works, its advantages, and the new technologies that make it possible, then how to decide which one best suits your business.

1. The Subscription Model

What Is It?   The customer provides periodic and automatic payment for continued delivery of (or access to) a company's offering. For example, customers may opt to subscribe to the *Wall Street Journal* rather than buying it on a newsstand. Netflix customers today choose among several subscription rate plans to receive video via digital streaming.

The number of companies embracing this model for products and services is exploding as the Internet has spawned a subscription economy (sometimes called "the membership economy"). Companies that offer subscription options for everything from clothing and shaving supplies (the Dollar Shave Club) to household goods are challenging established businesses.

The Advantages   The subscription model lifts lifetime revenue overall, and customer lifetime revenue specifically. A customer who buys the *Wall Street Journal* intermittently generally spends less money than a customer committed to a year of delivery. Obviously, this generates more revenue for the *WSJ*. A customer on subscription is also likely to stay for a longer time without churning (since you increase switching costs after getting the customer more familiar with your offering).

The *WSJ* loves subscription revenue models for their recurring revenue. For example, if the weather is bad or newsstand operators go on strike, a publication will lose sales. But with subscriptions, the money keeps coming, rain or shine.

While selling a long-term subscription is generally harder, it limits the number of buying decisions customers must make and locks them in. With a subscription, a newspaper buyer doesn't have to decide Monday whether to buy that day's edition. Add automatic renewal to the equation, and the company is in even better shape.

Subscriptions also open up cross-selling and upselling opportunities. Companies can use the data collected on subscribers to make other offers based on preferences and behaviors. Netflix has used its subscribers' movie-watching habits to create original TV series that have become huge hits, such as *House of Cards* and *Daredevil*. These shows have helped Netflix more than double its number of streaming service subscribers between 2012 and 2015, from 33 million to 69 million in 2015's third quarter.[5]

Last, the relationships between subscribers and brands also prove stronger and stickier than transactional ones. While the company gets to know the consumer, the consumer becomes more intimate with the brand and perhaps even emerges as an unofficial ambassador for the product or service, thereby increasing the brand's value.

Is It Right for You?   A subscription monetization model is an option for products and services sold both online and offline. Subscription models are also beneficial in industries where customers use the product continually. A great example is the music sector, where subscription plans for online music services from firms like Spotify and Pandora have taken a firm hold. In 2014, such streaming subscriptions accounted for nearly a quarter ($1.6 billion) of the global music industry's digital revenue, a six-fold increase since 2009.[6]

Subscription models also work in highly competitive industries in which market share is divided among many firms—a land-grab scenario. In these situations, subscriptions can help lock out competitors whose goods or services are only available on an individual transaction basis.

Last, subscriptions are becoming popular in industries such as software that formerly required customers to make big upfront investments to purchase the products. By letting customers buy the products in bite-size chunks, subscriptions make them more affordable and predictable for everyone.

2. Dynamic Pricing

What Is It?   A dynamic pricing monetization model is one in which a given product's or service's price fluctuates based on factors such as season, time of day, weather conditions, or other considerations that could impact willingness-to-pay, demand, and supply.

For decades, the airline industry pioneered dynamic pricing, changing ticket prices based on the time of booking, class of service, and other factors. As one of the pioneers of dynamic pricing, American Airlines' former CEO Robert Crandall, eloquently put it, "If I have 2,000 customers on a given route and 400 different prices, I am obviously short 1,600 prices."[7]

With rapid advancements in data collection and analytics technologies, companies in other industries can now use more complex algorithms to adjust prices more frequently. Uber is a prime example. The firm, launched in 2010, has disrupted the taxi business with a dynamic pricing monetization model that ties price to the real-time demand and supply of taxis. The benefits go both ways: to Uber's drivers and to the consumer. An increase in price during peak hours attracts more Uber drivers to meet the demand. Consequently, consumers don't have to fight for a taxi or wait in the rain trying to flag one down, and they're willing to pay more for that benefit. More on Uber in Chapter 13.

Dynamic ticket pricing is becoming more prevalent in professional and collegiate sports, with higher- and lower-profile games priced accordingly, even in the regular season.[8] Some supermarkets have applied dynamic pricing at the level of the individual consumer, offering personalized pricing based on repeat purchases.[9] Frequent buyers of a product will get a lower price to encourage the behavior; people who haven't bought the product before, or buy it infrequently, pay a higher price. French home improvement chain Castorama has installed electronic shelf pricing that adjusts prices in real time according to demand.[10]

But dynamic pricing can backfire. Coca-Cola began testing a vending machine in 1999 that automatically raised prices for its soft drinks in warmer weather.[11] The company abandoned the experiment; customers didn't like it one bit.

The Advantages   As the travel and hospitality industry has known for years, dynamic pricing boosts the monetization of fixed and constrained capacity. Companies don't want expensive, costly-to-maintain assets, like jumbo jets or five-star hotels, operating with empty seats or rooms. Dynamic pricing models let you adjust price (in this case lower) to monetize your unused capacity. Similarly, you can raise prices if your capacity is fully constrained. The more volatile the demand, the bigger the benefits from dynamic pricing. In addition, dynamic pricing can help a company that doesn't have capacity constraints, but whose demand and price elasticity is volatile. For example, UK grocery chain Tesco prices products higher in the evenings because high-income evening shoppers tend to be willing to pay more.

Is It Right for You?   First, dynamic pricing should be considered when demand and price elasticity in your market vary significantly. If they do, you then must ask what factors influence the volatility and whether you could set your price based on these factors. Second, you should consider dynamic pricing if your supply is constrained or fixed.

But dynamic pricing is a complex undertaking. Companies that wish to use it effectively must make significant investments in technology and business process changes.

As Coca-Cola and other companies have found, dynamic pricing can irritate customers who believe they're being taken advantage of. Dynamic pricing generally requires a customer base that is willing to pay a higher price for other benefits—like a taxi on a cold, rainy evening.

3. Market-Based Pricing: Auctions

What Is It? Auctions set prices based on competition for goods or services. They've been around for centuries. In fact, the first auctions date back as far as 500 BC.[12] Today, thanks to networking technology, it seems as if everything can be auctioned, from securities to artwork.

Auctioning is a primary way Google makes oodles of money. Google AdWords, which drives the advertising displayed alongside search results, is powered by an auction. Advertisers outbid one another for the most prominent placement based on keywords. During the first half of 2015, that auction-based ad business accounted for 70 percent of Google's $35 billion in revenue, according to company earnings reports.[13]

"Two-sided" marketplaces (those that connect sellers and buyers) have also embraced auctions. The most prominent is eBay, which has built an $18 billion-a-year business helping people sell household items through auction pricing. In a similar vein, Manheim, an automobile auction company (which we will explore in more detail in Chapter 9), is the world's largest auction provider for buying and selling used cars.

The Advantages With auction-based pricing, you can withdraw from the act of price setting and let the market figure out what it wants to pay. In other words, even though you are the seller, the market perceives you as the neutral party; customers outbid each other to buy and raise prices for you. In addition, when you use an auction model, you can influence the price without being too explicit about it. For example, you can set a minimum price for the auction and dictate how long the auction takes and the process of bidding.

Is It Right for You? Unlike the auctions of old, which required little more than a room, a podium, and a fast-talking auctioneer, today's high-tech auction-based pricing requires sophisticated systems and processes. If they are not executed properly, they can produce huge, costly mistakes.

The auction model might not work if the market has excess inventory and your customers have many options, or if you are in a competitive environment and don't have the pricing power required to make an auction model successful.

However, auctions are ideal for so-called seller markets, where inventory is constrained, the power is with the sellers (as owners of inventory), and demand is high. If you are one such seller or can become one, as Google did with AdWords, you should seriously consider this model.

4. Alternative Metric Pricing/Pay As You Go

What Is It?   Many companies have succeeded by pricing transactions on measures other than the industry per-unit standard. Often these alternative metrics are closer to product value and customer benefits.

Industrial giant GE has used such alternative metric pricing in recent years, embracing the power of analytics software, digital sensors, and data. In 2011, the company launched a big initiative to attach and embed digital sensors to its medical equipment, aircraft engines, power turbines, and other industrial equipment. The company generates $1 billion a year from the "outcomes-based" services it now provides—which, for example, help airlines identify problematic engines sooner and thus reduce downtime.[14]

Instead of selling or leasing a CAT scan machine or a jet engine, GE charges customers by the hours of usage for a medical practice or the miles flown for an airline. As such, customers pay when they use or benefit from the product. If GE reduces its customers' downtime, that goes into GE's pockets. It has monetized 100 percent of the value of its offering, exactly as Michelin has been doing with tires.

Software companies have also successfully employed alternative pricing metrics. A software company that produces lab reports increased revenue by 20 percent just by changing its pricing metric from fixed perpetual license to charging per lab report. It considered this alternate metric model to be much more aligned with the perceived value. The model also minimized customers' upfront investment commitments. Of course, this was also beneficial to the software firm since it could now charge a higher price for a lab report (compared with breaking even on the perpetual fee).

The Advantages   If your innovation enhances customers' performance in a way that is superior to the alternatives, the alternative pricing model might be for you. By aligning the metric to your customers' performance, you achieve full monetization potential. But you must be able to deliver on your promise, as Michelin did with its fleet operator customers.

An alternate pricing model can be very successful when you can align the metric directly to how customers perceive value. For example, let's assume you are a manufacturer of robotic surgery equipment that can be installed in hospitals. If a hospital is small to medium in size, they typically don't have the capital to invest in machinery you provide. The traditional way is to price by the upfront cost for the instrument. What if you price by surgery? This alternative is totally aligned with the value delivered to the hospital as compared to them paying a really high upfront cost. In other words, you are participating in the revenue your customers generate by using your product and services. Ultimately you can showcase your intentions as a win–win situation for you and your customers.

Finally, this monetization model could be effective if you are an adept predictor of future trends. For example, telecommunication providers have long anticipated the trends of increased usage of digital data and devices and have proactively changed their metric to "gigabyte-based pricing" or "device and gigabyte-based pricing."

Is It Right for You?   The alternative pricing model makes sense when your innovation creates significant value to end customers but you cannot capture a fair share of that value using traditional monetization models. Michelin is an excellent example of this.

This model makes more sense when you have total control over how customers use your product. For example, if Monsanto is paid via yield per acre, it must make sure that its herbicides are applied in farmers' fields as prescribed. Only then does Monsanto have full control over the impact of its products on customers. And this, in fact, is how Monsanto's monetization model works.

5. Freemium Pricing

What Is It?   With the freemium model, a company offers two or more tiers of pricing for its products and services, one of which is free. The goal of a freemium monetization model is to attract a huge customer base to the free version and later convert a significant percentage to paid subscriptions. This model is also called "land and expand." You try to land with a freemium offer and expand with paid offers.

Both LinkedIn and Dropbox are good examples of companies that have succeeded with freemium pricing. Customers with basic needs can access a limited version of LinkedIn's career networking and Dropbox's storage services for free. But customers with greater needs pay for more sophisticated features.

The Internet has greatly expanded freemium possibilities by reducing the cost of distributing many services to zero. In fact, freemium is now the dominant business model for many Internet start-ups, online service providers, software companies, and smartphone apps.[15]

The Advantages　Because freemium services lower the cost of customer entry to zero, they spur rapid adoption. The free offering becomes, in effect, a marketing tool for the premium offering. That helps companies reduce their cost of customer acquisition compared with more expensive traditional marketing and sales methods.

Is It Right for You?　The freemium model is definitely not right for everyone. It only works if you have a very low cost of production (preferably no production costs at all) and minimal fixed costs that can and will be offset by the generally smaller percentage of paying customers.

What's more, companies often struggle to turn the freemium model into long-term monetization. The land-and-expand approach fails for 90 percent of companies. (For an exception to the rule, see the LinkedIn case study in Chapter 13.) In fact, the number of free customers who convert to premium is typically below 10 percent in software companies. In video games, freemium games have an average life span of less than a year, losing 75 percent of free users after just one day and retaining just 2 percent after a month of play.[16]

If you decide to offer a freemium service, you must double down on your efforts to convert customers to the premium version. It is extraordinarily difficult to get consumers to buy something they previously received for free. One need only to look at the scores of Web-based businesses that failed to monetize free online offerings in the last two decades. For example, most newspapers (apart from ones like the *New York Times* and the *Wall Street Journal*) have failed to convert free readers en masse to paid online subscribers.

This is the same dilemma for Evernote, a mobile app that helps people take notes on the fly. The firm became one of the first "unicorn" start-ups, joining the exclusive club for private tech companies worth $1 billion or more. Despite reaching 150 million registered users this year, Evernote has been slow to generate revenue, according to *Business Insider.*[17]

To have a chance at converting free customers to paid customers, you need to test what benefits they will pay for and ensure a functional free experience. You also need to know exactly how many customers will actually be willing to pay. What's more, you must avoid giving the farm away for free because it will leave your premium offering with very little value.

Five Questions to Choose the Right Monetization Model

We have provided five monetization models and explained when they apply. These models are by no means the only ones you can use. You can also combine pieces of each one. For example, the $112 billion U.S. retailer Costco charges a membership (subscription) fee to use its warehouse stores on top of charging for products you purchase. OpenTable charges restaurants a monthly subscription fee and a transaction fee for every diner in a reservation.

Before implementing any of the models, you should have extensive conversations with customers and then test them. Whichever model you choose, it should not only play to your organization's strengths, but also benefit your customers. It should also take into account future trends for your product, company, and industry. Here are five questions to consider when assessing which monetization model is right for you.

1. How Likely Are Your Customers to Accept the Model?

Different customers like different pricing models. Is your model predictable, flexible, fair, and transparent enough for your particular customer base? Customers almost always have preferences for certain models. Make sure your model is in line with their preferences. Test out different models to discover your customers' favorites. One way to do this is to provide your customers with options, the prices of which always total the same amount (if you did the math), and ask them whether they have a preference or are indifferent. If your customers are rational they will always say they are indifferent, since the price is the same across options. However, we have done such testing hundreds of times and have yet to see the "indifferent" option win! People always have a preference.

2. How Will Future Developments Impact the Model?

Make sure you do scenario planning around the model. What are the key trends in your business? For example, if you're a mobile phone service provider, is the number of phone calls increasing or decreasing? How about the number of devices? What risks and opportunities do those trends present long term? How will the pricing metrics hold up? Michelin, for example, factored improvement in tire durability into its distance-based pricing model. Google anticipated an auction-based model would serve it well not only in the early days when prices would be low, but also later on as demand increased.

3. What Stage Is Your Company In and Does Your Model Choice Fit That?

A monetization approach has to suit your company's situation—its life cycle, competitive position, and relationship to customers. If you're a start-up, for instance, you may want to keep things simple and transparent, as payment processor Square did with its 2.5 percent no-hidden-fee model. A mature company may need to differentiate itself from rivals with a more complex approach. Also important is what you have in your innovation pipeline. When your new offerings come to market, will your model help you monetize them (as Michelin's model did with its new tires)?

4. What Are Your Competitors Doing?

The reason to ask this question is not to mimic your rivals' monetization approaches but to set yourself apart. Wherever possible, use your monetization model to create a competitive difference, as Netflix did to the point of transforming the video rental business and displacing video store competitors like Blockbuster. The question becomes especially relevant when competitors are not equipped to react to any model changes you can bring.

5. How Difficult Is the Monetization Model to Implement?

A monetization model is good only to the extent you can make it work. Assess factors like feasibility, difficulty of customer adoption, and scalability. Make sure you can measure the data necessary to enforce the pricing. In addition, you must be able to communicate the model easily to customers and partners. Don't exclude yourself from a particular monetization model based on existing infrastructure and system limitations, but be sure to factor in the additional investments needed to make the model work. Gauge the total cost of ownership and the ultimate return. Most of all, make sure your model is driving value to customers and your pricing is commensurate with the value you deliver.

The marketplace performance of companies such as Google, Netflix, Michelin, General Electric, and Uber irrefutably shows the power of choosing the right monetization model when bringing new products and services to market. These companies demonstrate that a winning monetization model can help a firm leapfrog the competition in ways even a winning product or service offering alone cannot.

The rapid evolution of the Internet and other technologies has created abundant opportunities to capitalize on monetization models that are new to your industry. You and your colleagues need to explore them, and quickly, to get out in front. Sometimes the best innovation is the innovation in the monetization model itself!

A FEW PRICE STRUCTURES THAT HAVE STOOD THE TEST OF TIME

We described in earlier sections how to choose one of the five monetization models. A *price structure* builds on such monetization models to account for different levels of usage. This is especially applicable when the monetization model is pay per unit, alternate metric, or subscription.

Here's an example: Say you are about to introduce a new payment processing service, and you've decided to charge 3 percent of each payment transaction. That's a simple monetization model—the alternate metric model. A more comprehensive—but also more complex—way to implement this would be to base that percentage on usage intensity. For example, the 3 percent charge per transaction is for customers that do between 100,000 and 500,000 payment transactions a month; a lower rate (2 percent) is charged to customers who do 500,000 to 1.5 million transactions a month, and so on. (See Figure 7.1.)

(continued)

(*Continued*)

With this structure, you are telling customers that the more they use your services, the better the rate they get. This could be more attractive to customers than a flat 3 percent rate no matter how many transactions they did.

That's a tier-based structure or, more specifically, a volume-based structure.

Now let's look at a matrix model. (See Figure 7.2.) Starting from the top left corner of the matrix, the rate gets progressively better for the customer as you work your way down to the bottom right. The key difference between the volume and matrix structures is that the matrix is a two-dimensional structure while the volume is one-dimensional. In Figure 7.2, the first dimension is volume and the second dimension is percent share of transactions (that is, the wallet share you receive). The logic is that the higher the volume of transactions *and* share of business you get, the better the rate for your customer. Note that the two dimensions could be any metric on which you decide to tier.

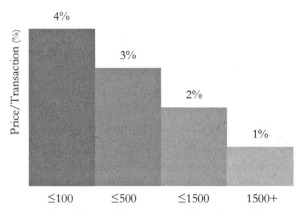

Figure 7.1   Tier-Based Pricing

	Price/Transaction (%)			
Below 30%	4%	3.5%	3%	2.5%
30% – 60%	3.5%	3%	2.5%	2%
60% – 75%	3%	2.5%	2%	1.5%
Over 95%	2.5%	2%	1.5%	1%
	≤100	≤500	≤1500	1500+

% Share of transactions

Transactions per month in thousands

Figure 7.2   Tier-Based Pricing in a Matrix Model

Summary

Monetization models can confer significant competitive advantage on a new product or service. How you charge trumps how much you charge. As the Michelin case showed, when done right, the best monetization models are a win–win for you and your customers.

Companies have countless monetization choices, but these five work well for most new product monetization: subscription, alternate metric, dynamic pricing, auction, and freemium.

You can also combine pieces of these five models for a mix-and-match model. Furthermore, by instituting two price structures (volume-based and matrix), you have the flexibility to adjust for different levels of usage.

Not all models are applicable in every situation, but the guidance in this chapter will help you winnow out your choices.

(continued)

(*Continued*)

CEO Questions

1. What monetization model do we envision for our new product? Why is it the right one, and how did we choose it?
2. Which models did we not pick, and why?
3. What are the most important trends in our industry? How do they affect our choice of a monetization model?
4. How do we plan to monetize our product if customer usage varies significantly? Which price structures have we considered and why?
5. Do we have the right capabilities and infrastructure to execute the chosen monetization model and price structure?

CHAPTER 8

Price Low for Market Share or High for Premium Branding?

Pick the Winning Pricing Strategy

At this moment in your product development process, you have had the "willingness to pay" (WTP) talk early. You understand how customer needs differ by segment, you've developed offerings for each one, and you have picked the right monetization models.

Are you ready to set a price and launch your product? Not yet. Not before you establish a pricing strategy.

What do we mean by pricing strategy? Simply put, it is your short- and long-term monetization plan. At the highest level, a sound pricing strategy must have clear intent, quantifiable goals, and a time frame for execution. Figure 8.1 is a simple example of a high-level pricing strategy.

Let's examine this strategy. The firm's objective is revenue growth by establishing a premium price in core segments and increasing the consumer base in growth segments. That's a clear objective. The time frame: over the next two years. Good; that's concrete. The third element is the firm's market position: It will follow most of the market leader's pricing moves. That makes perfect sense because the market leader sets consumers' price expectations.

Over the next two years, we plan to increase revenue by 40 percent. We will accomplish this by establishing a premium price versus the market leader in core consumer segments and discount the price in growth consumer segments. This is because we believe in the following opportunities/challenges in our market:

1. We can't make drastic price moves: The market leader sets pricing expectations for our consumers.

2. We won't lose many core consumers: These consumers are relatively price insensitive and brand-loyal, even if we charge a slight premium.

3. We can communicate our price advantage in growth segments: Consumers in our growth segments are more price sensitive and try to directly compare prices to those of our competitors.

Figure 8.1   A Sample High-Level Pricing Strategy

The next element is also important: how the firm will treat each customer segment. The firm will lure consumers in growth segments with a slight discount while charging loyal customers a slight premium. This is in line with the value the product delivers to each segment.

Finally, the word "because" is the most important word in this or any pricing strategy. It forces you to think through your pricing strategy thoroughly and also ensures that you are able to articulate this to your team to gain their buy-in.

The example is a simple one. Nonetheless, you should be able to state your pricing strategy as simply as this one because it will set your new product's pricing direction.

Yet your pricing strategy doesn't end there. You should then develop a more comprehensive strategy. In the next section, we'll explain the four building blocks you'll need to create a comprehensive and effective pricing strategy.

The companies who are the best at developing new products in the ways we've described in this book take the time to painstakingly document their pricing strategies. But they don't then put that document on a shelf to collect dust. Rather, they make it a living and breathing document—one they update continually. By doing so, they find their pricing strategy is handy. It enables them to get organizational leaders on board, avoid knee-jerk pricing reactions in the face of slack demand or competitors' pricing moves, and fully monetize their new products.

Now let's look at how you can develop such a pricing strategy.

Creating the Pricing Strategy Document: The Four Building Blocks

Like a recipe for a great meal, a solid pricing strategy document must have the right ingredients. It must also have a process for adding those ingredients in the right sequence. Let's review the ingredients, or building blocks.

Building Block #1: Set Clear Goals

Without a clear goal, you won't have an effective pricing strategy. It's that simple. A clear, overriding goal is a prerequisite because different goals can lead to contradictory strategies and actions. For example, if you want to maximize market share, you must choose strategies and price levels that will be different from the goal of maximizing total profit.

So which goals are most important for your new products? Revenue? Market share? Total profit? Profit margin? Customer lifetime value? Average revenue per unit? Something else? Whichever goals you choose, you cannot maximize all of them at the same time. In setting goals, you must make trade-offs.

Here's an example: Assume you could sell your product at either $10 or $15. Further assume when you sell your product at $10, you get 100 customers, and when you sell it at $15, you get 80 customers. So how should you price your product? Will you take 20 percent fewer customers in return for a 20 percent increase in revenue?

Now let's say the cost to make your product is $7. If you sell it at $10, you have a 30 percent margin. If you sell it at $15, you have a greater than 50 percent margin. So which goal do you want now? Is your answer different?

This is a simple example, but it proves our point that it is a difficult choice. Most new-product pricing strategy trade-offs are far more complicated than this. If you don't prioritize your goals and define your strategy, you will be in hot water when you take your product to market. You won't know how to act in the face of customer and competitive pressures.

Forcing trade-offs in goals is crucial. A workshop task we call *Goal Allocation Exercise* helps companies do that. Every workshop participant is ideally from a company's C-suite. We ask them to allocate 100 points to a series of goals. That puts each executive in a trade-off mindset. "Should I allocate 20 points to this goal, or should I allocate 60?" The more points an executive allocates to a given goal, the more important that goal is relative to the other goals.

Figure 8.2 shows the output from one of our recent client workshops. It's easy to see the massive differences in each goal's importance among the CEO, CMO, head of sales, CFO, and head of procurement. This executive team was shocked. Walking into the room, they thought they were aligned on the purpose of the new product. The problem was they never put themselves in a situation to make trade-offs across goals. After the workshop, they had deeper and more objective discussions. Eventually, they agreed on the product's priorities: Maximize market share but ensure an overall profit increase of at least 10 percent.

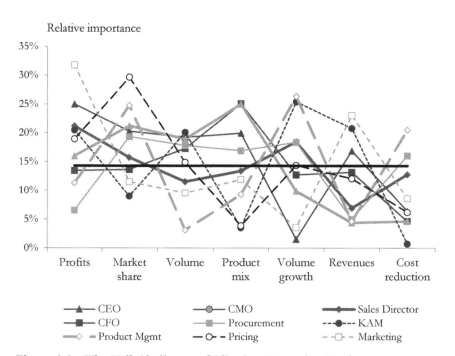

Figure 8.2   The Tall Challenge of Aligning Executive Goals

Building Block #2: Pick the Right Type of Pricing Strategy

Forcing trade-offs in goals is critical, but it won't be enough. Your goals must be in line with your pricing strategy. The good news is only three types of pricing strategies matter: maximization, penetration, and skimming. Let's look at each.

Maximization: This strategy maximizes your goal (such as profit or revenue) in the short term. Most companies choose this strategy for new offerings. You determine the optimal price—the point on the price elasticity curve at which the profit or revenue curve reaches its maximum. (We explain this in the sidebar later in this chapter.)

Companies typically choose a maximization strategy when their customer segments don't have early adopters with disproportionately more WTP. Or they choose this strategy because gaining a huge market share rapidly is not worth the expense of lower revenue or profit. In other words, these companies see little difference between the optimal short-term price and the optimal long-term price.

In choosing a maximization pricing strategy, you must have a number of options in mind. Senior executives often don't see the connections among price, volume, and profit. They believe these numbers are independent of one another; for example, they believe that if they raise price, volume will stay the same and profit will increase. If only that were the case! With a price response curve that shows the elasticity of your product, you can show these linkages. Later in this chapter we describe in detail the power of the price elasticity curve and how you can use it to arrive at the optimal price point.

Doing this kind of homework helps you avoid driving blind. Let's assume your team recommends a $100 starting price. Your CFO wants to raise it to $110. With the price elasticity curve you have proof in your hand. You would be able to say "We can certainly raise the price to $110, but then we lose X percent volume. Can we take that risk? Is that the better option?" By quantifying each price option's revenue, volume, and profit implications, you can be sure not to veer off the pricing strategy.

Penetration: With this pricing strategy, you intentionally price your product lower than in a maximization strategy to rapidly gain market share. This is also known as a *land-and-expand* strategy. When should you choose it? In some markets you must gain share quickly, especially in those dominated by network effects or where customers are highly loyal to the first brand they choose. If you gain customers early in such markets, you are better positioned to maximize customers' lifetime value from future sales and upsells. With a penetration pricing strategy, you make a grab for market share and then expand. This has been Samsung's pricing strategy in the smartphone market; cloud software companies have used this strategy after introducing freemium models. E-commerce market maker Ariba provides a great example. When the firm opened its online doors, it made all its money from buyers, not sellers. The service was free for sellers, and sellers typically brought buyers to the system. Over time, though, the company started monetizing its offerings to sellers. Today, Ariba generates as much revenue from sellers as it does from buyers.

Facebook is another great example of a hugely successful penetration pricing strategy. Most advertisers couldn't be bothered with the social network in its early days—until the free-to-users service had amassed hundreds of millions of eyeballs. But by 2014, with more than 1 billion Facebook members, advertisers were spending $12 billion annually on Facebook ads. That's huge revenue. Facebook has become immensely profitable as well, generating $7 billion in profits in aggregate from 2009 to the first half of 2015.

A penetration strategy might be right if you also plan to hike prices in the future. For example, Toyota's luxury car brand Lexus raised prices in the U.S. market more than 40 percent five years after it entered the market with a penetration strategy.[1]

A penetration strategy might also be the right strategy for you if you are in a position to rapidly gain share, bring down unit costs, and purposefully price low to create barriers to entry. In such a case, even if you operate at a laser-thin margin, you might still make up for it because of your very high volume of sales. Think Amazon. Think Uber. More on the Uber case study in Chapter 13.

But a word of caution: A penetration strategy is the riskiest from a profit and revenue standpoint. You must focus as much on expanding revenue from customers as you do on landing them in the first place. Or you need to gain huge market share rapidly. And you'd better be able to follow through on those future price increases if you had planned them while deciding on this strategy. We have seen many companies, especially in Silicon Valley, incessantly talk about future revenues as a justification for picking this strategy but hardly come close to achieving it, even years after they launched! One such firm is LivingSocial, which had raised more than $900 million in venture capital to create a business that sent e-mail coupons to consumers to shop local businesses (similar to Groupon, taking a cut of the transactions). But by 2015, LivingSocial was struggling. Four years of losses had piled up to more than $1 billion. Said a *New York Times* story: "No one paid much attention to how the company would ultimately make money."[2]

Skimming: Here you first cater to customers with a higher WTP—the early adopters. Then, you systematically decrease price in order to reach other customer segments with lower willingness to pay. Your initial price needs to be higher than the price you would have charged had you chosen a maximization strategy. A skimming strategy is especially appropriate if you have a significant number of customers who are willing to pay a higher price than others for your product. Put another way, your customers' WTP varies greatly between early adopters and late followers. Some prime examples are buyers of movies, music, online games, high-definition TVs, gaming consoles (such as Microsoft's Xbox video game console), smartphones (Apple iPhone, for example), and some automobiles. These customers won't wait for a product to become mainstream. It gives them bragging rights; they want to show it off to their peers.

Two other scenarios make skimming the right choice. One is when the product represents a breakthrough—an offering that delivers far superior value. The other scenario is when you have production capacity constraints in the initial launch periods but must mass produce in the future.

A classic way to implement skimming is by combining product and pricing actions. Here's how this works: You launch the higher-end product first, skim the market, and then launch lower-end products. A great example of this is when Porsche launched its four-door car, the Panamera. It first debuted the eight-cylinder model to skim the market, then released the lower-priced six-cylinder model a year later. (More on Porsche in Chapter 13.)

Building Block #3: Develop Price-Setting Principles

Now that you've chosen the right pricing strategy type, the next step is to create rules for the tactics you'll need to execute your strategy. By determining your price-setting principles early, you can keep your overall pricing strategy on track and avoid knee-jerk reactions after your product launch. (More on this in Chapter 12.) These are the top five operational parts to consider:

1. *Monetization models:* We showed you many monetization models in Chapter 7. Which one or ones will you use for your new product? Will your monetization model be the same across all customer segments? Will it change over the life cycle of the product? You must put the answers to these questions into your price strategy document.

2. *Price differentiation:* Will you differentiate your price? If so, what are the differentiating factors (for example, by channel, industry vertical, and region)? Will you maintain a maximum spread for your range of prices (say, all prices must be within 200 percent of the average price)?

3. *Price floors:* Will you have a price floor below which you will never price? Will you have a floor below which you will never discount (such as 50 percent maximum discount)?

4. *Price endings:* Literally speaking, how would you "end" all your prices? What will the numbers on the price tags and catalog look like? From our vast project experience, the most common price endings are 0, 0.50, 0.99, and 0.95 (that is, $30, $29.50, $29.99, or $29.95). These endings are more important in business-to-consumer (B2C) than business-to-business (B2B) markets. In B2B, whole numbers typically are better.

5. *Price increases:* Will you increase price over time? If so, how much and at what frequency?

Figure 8.3 is an example of what your price-setting principles might look like in practice.

1. We will adopt a profit maximization strategy.

2. We will price on a subscription basis.

3. We will differentiate pricing by industry vertical and region.

4. We will never discount beyond 50 percent; we will never price below $25 per month.

5. We will end our prices in x.99.

6. We will increase prices over time using annual escalators, and the size of yearly adjustments should be around 3 percent above inflation rate.

Figure 8.3   Examples of Price-Setting Principles

Building Block #4: Develop Principles for Reaction

You should plan not only what your launch price will be, but how you'll react once your product hits the market. Here again you will need a set of principles to guide your actions.

Price reaction principles come in two varieties: those based on how customers behave (such as promotional reactions due to lower-than-expected demand) and those based on how competitors behave with their prices. Planning your reactions is much like playing chess and thinking a few moves ahead. Companies that don't think ahead react spontaneously and make unintentional yet avoidable mistakes. We say more about this in Chapter 12.

Promotional Reactions   These principles should include whether and how to promote your product and who will receive those promotions and when. You should determine your promotion price and decide what types of promotion you *won't* resort to, such as cash-back offerings.

These promotions are tactical instruments, but decisions on how to use them are *strategic* decisions. Your pricing strategy document should clearly lay out your promotional principles. For example, you might want to gain a low-entry price image through price promotions (like the Every Day Low Price at Walmart). Or you could skimp on promotions because you've chosen a premium strategy (like Apple). Or you might do something in between. The most important aspect of promotional reactions is to decide early which principles you will base them on.

Competitive Reactions   These principles help you think through countermoves against your rivals. Before you react, you *must* anticipate competitors' moves, understand the reasons behind their moves, and prepare for possible counterreactions to your moves. To do so, you should conduct war-gaming sessions prior to launch. These sessions should include questions such as:

- How might the competitors react, and why?
- Are competitors likely to react only once?
- If we match a competitor's price, what will be the impact on our revenue and profit?
- What counterreactions do we expect to our reactions?

1. We will offer promotions only to new customers. The duration of promotional pricing will not exceed one month and will never be >25 percent.

2. We will add value to preserve the price (e.g. premium features, services) as long as the price cut from the competition is less than 20 percent. We will only start price reactions if the price difference gets to be more than 20 percent to the next best competitor in the market.

Figure 8.4   Examples of Principles for Promotion and Competitive Reactions

From the outcome of these war-gaming sessions, you should distill the key principles that defined your reactions to competitive moves. We say more about this in Chapter 12 on how to avoid knee-jerk reactions. Figure 8.4 is an example of a few promotional and competitive reaction principles.

We have shown you the four building blocks for developing an effective pricing strategy. Properly done, this strategy will become the tool that gives you pricing power. And pricing power is exactly what you want to have with your great new product. As Warren Buffett nicely summarized, "The single most important decision in evaluating a business is pricing power."[3] Companies that have a well-defined pricing strategy are 40 percent more likely to realize their monetizing potential than those that don't have one.[4]

It's hard to beat those odds.

PRICE OPTIMIZATION AND PRICE ELASTICITY

The most important input for optimizing your price is the price elasticity curve (also known as the *demand curve* and *price–demand relationship*). It shows how much the sales volume of your product decreases and increases if you move your price up or down:

Price Elasticity = Change in Sales (%)/Change in Price (%)

To calculate the price elasticity and profit curve for your new product, you need two sources of data: your analysis of what customers are willing to pay (discussed in Chapter 4) and your costs (both variable and fixed). Everything else is simple math.

Here's an example. Figure 8.5 describes a product launch. At a price of $100, you would sell 1 million units per period. If you charge less, sales go up (1.35 million at a $70 price point). If you charge more, sales go down (to 600,000 at a price of $130).

With that information, you can calculate revenue (price x volume). By factoring in the variable cost of $50 per unit and the $25 million fixed cost for your factory and staff, you can now calculate profit (revenue − cost). The table shows the profits for the seven price points.

To maximize profit, you would set a price of $110. While your volume would be 10 percent lower than if you charged $100, you would make up for it with a higher margin per unit. But if you wanted to maximize revenue, you would set a price of $100.

Note the patterns in the chart. At lower prices, revenue is relatively stable. But volume and total variable expenses increase, which massively reduces profit. At higher prices, you have lower total variable expenses, but your revenue falls faster and therefore reduces profits. The profit impact is significant: A $20

Price scenario

	1	2	3	4	5	6	7
Price ($)	70	80	90	100	110	120	130
Volume (mill. units)	1.35	1.22	1.1	1	0.9	0.75	0.6
Revenue ($m)	94.5	97.6	99	100	99	90	78
Var. cost ($m)	67.5	61	55	50	45	37.5	30
Fix cost ($m)	25	25	25	25	25	25	25
Profit ($m)	2	11.6	19	25	29	27.5	23
Profit change (%)	−93	−60	−34	−14	0	−5	−21

Figure 8.5   Price Scenarios for a New Product Launch

(*continued*)

(Continued)

pricing error can easily cost you 20 percent of your total profit. Rule of thumb: The smaller the margin per unit, the bigger the impact of suboptimal pricing.

Sometimes companies prefer to illustrate these relationships in a graph (see Figure 8.6) rather than a table. In either case, the most important input for calculating your optimal price is the shape of the price-elasticity curve—its steepness and level. The steeper the curve, the more sales volume you lose when you raise prices. For example, if you increase your price by 5 percent, volume falls 10 percent. Your price elasticity is then −2 (−10 percent/5 percent). That's a steep curve.

If your new product has high price elasticity (a steep demand curve), you will have a relatively low margin (in the optimum). The other way around is true as well: Low elasticity leads to a high optimal margin.

Many companies think price elasticity is a theoretical concept. It is anything but. Every product—from a Rolls Royce to a pack of chewing gum—has a price elasticity curve. If you don't determine the elasticity curve for your product and use it to price that product, you will not get to your optimal price. There's no escaping this fact.

Furthermore, because price elasticity varies greatly across products, when you set your curve you cannot use general assumptions or an industry average. (Figure 8.7 is a representative sample of price elasticities from our recent experience.) You must measure or estimate the price elasticity level for *your* new product—and no one else's.

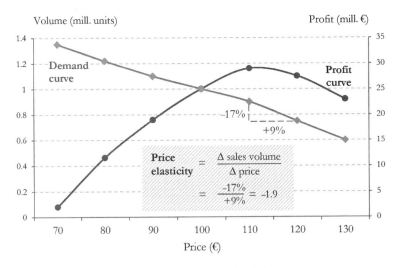

Figure 8.6   Another Look at the Price Elasticity Curve

Product examples	Elasticity range	
Price promotions	< -5	Very high
Real commodities	-5 to -50	(< -5)
Airlines	-1 to -5	High
Automotive (standard brands)	-2.5 to -5	$(-2.5$ to $-5)$
Tires	-1.5 to -4	
Consumer goods	-2 to -3	Medium
Luxury cars	-1.5 to -3	$(-1.5$ to $-2.5)$
Computer/ software services	-1.2 to -2	
Differenitiated industrial products	-0.5 to -2	Low
Mobile telephony (air time)	-0.5 to -1	$(-0.5$ to $-1.5)$
OTC drugs	-0.5 to -1.5	
Mail/ postage	-0.2 to -0.9	
Innovative pharmaceuticals	-0.2 to -0.7	Very low
Bank deposits	-0.1 to -0.5	$(0$ to $-0.5)$
Spare parts	0 to -0.8	

Figure 8.7   Price Elasticities for a Basket of Goods

Summary

A pricing strategy is your short- and long-term monetization plan. The best companies document their pricing strategies and make it a living and breathing document.

Documenting your pricing strategy will help get the executives in your company on the same page; more important, it will help keep you accountable. The price strategy document should have four building blocks.

First, set clear goals and prioritize among conflicting goals (for instance, price to maximize revenue but ensure a 10 percent profit increase). Second, pick one of the three types of pricing strategies: maximization, skimming, or penetration. Third, set price-setting principles that define the rules of your monetization models, price

(continued)

(Continued)

differentiation, price endings, price floors, and price increases. Finally, define your promotional and competitive reaction principles to avoid knee-jerk price reactions.

Companies that have well-defined pricing strategies are 40 percent more likely to realize their monetizing potential than firms that don't have them.

CEO Questions

1. Is there a pricing strategy document for our new product? If not, why?
2. What are our pricing strategy goals? What are the relative priorities across goals (revenue, profit, share, customer lifetime value, and so on)? Is the management team aligned on these goals? How do we know?
3. What pricing strategy type (maximization, penetration, or skimming) did we pick? Why did we choose it?
4. What is the price elasticity of the new product? What does the pricing response (price elasticity) curve look like? What is the revenue/profit maximizing price point? How do we know all this?
5. Did our team clarify the price-setting principles such as monetization models, price differentiation, and price endings? How do these principles compare with the ones we follow for existing products? Have such principles worked for us in the past?
6. Do we have plans to deal with customer and competitor reactions? Who developed the plans, and how? Are those plans frequently updated?

CHAPTER 9

From Hoping to Knowing

Build an Outside-In Business Case

A critical step in your new product development process will be making the business case for it inside your organization. Even though this will be for *internal* purposes, you must get *external* input—specifically, your target customers' willingness to pay (WTP) for your product (Chapter 4). That doesn't exist anywhere within the four walls of your company. You have to go out and get it.

Your very first version of the business case should be created right after you determine the high-level WTP for your product. You need to keep evolving it as you define your customer segments (discussed in Chapter 5), determine product configurations and bundles (Chapter 6), select a monetization model (Chapter 7), and set your pricing strategy (Chapter 8).

In this way, your business case document will be an up-to-the-moment reflection of your product's evolution and the most accurate representation of its monetization potential. It will be a living, breathing document—one that you continually update with your latest knowledge about the market opportunity at hand.

The business case that global car auctioneer Manheim put together for a new service is a great example.

How Auto Auctioneer Manheim Tested a New Offering

Since its launch in 1945 as an auctioneer of used automobiles between car dealers, Manheim has grown into a multibillion-dollar global enterprise.

Now based in Atlanta and a subsidiary of $17.5 billion Cox Enterprises, Manheim remarkets about 7 million used vehicles a year. The company provides not only the auction services, but also a host of ancillary services to help dealers buy and sell vehicles from each other: financing, title work, transportation, and repair.

In 2011, Manheim leaders considered launching a service that would give dealers the option to return the vehicles they purchased within a certain time period, no questions asked. The additional peace of mind for the dealers could accelerate conversion and sales—or so the thinking went.

The concept generated great excitement in the top management team at Manheim when they first met to discuss this idea. Some executives were convinced of the new service's appeal. They believed the new return policy offering was a surefire winner. Their gut feeling was that they didn't need a business case. They told themselves, "In the interest of time, we should get moving." There were some who wanted to take a more conservative approach to the new offering. They suggested testing it in a small way—say, a limited offering with a few dealers or region of dealers—before committing a lot of funds to it. A few others doubted the viability of the concept from a risk and returns standpoint. "What if dealers return too many cars?" they asked. "What if it costs us too much to provide such a guarantee? What if we need to pull back after launch?"

This situation would be familiar to most of you. A new idea always has proponents and people who question its efficacy. When met with such a situation, many companies end up in decision paralysis, and the new product idea sits on the shelf rotting. This was definitely not the case with Manheim, which has a great culture oriented toward taking action. The product strategy and leadership team agreed to test the idea in the market, conduct customer research, and develop a robust business case before embarking on a long journey of productizing.

Vishaal Jayaswal, Manheim's head of pricing and value management, was asked to help figure out whether customers would value the service in the first place and, if so, how much they would be willing to pay for it under various conditions.

Jayaswal began to assess what factors would impact WTP, such as a time limit on returns, the make and model of a car, or a car's mileage. What would the demand for such money-back guarantees look like at different prices?

To get that, Jayaswal commissioned a value research study in 2012 and began having early WTP talks with customers (talks of the type we discussed in Chapter 4). The company discovered dealers loved the idea and were willing to pay for it. More important, Jayaswal found WTP varied by dealer and situation. For example, dealers that were more price-sensitive and willing to assume more risk were only willing to pay for a short-term guarantee.

Other dealers were more risk-averse. They were willing to pay a higher price for a 21-day return option, which gave them more time to spot deal-ending defects. Their WTP also varied by the type of car (defect rates on used cars can vary substantially from brand to brand and model to model) and its condition.

Ultimately, Jayaswal's pricing strategy recommendations were based on several elements: a) the business risks Manheim was assuming; b) the value to customers of different guarantee services; c) customers' WTP for them; and d) how much demand changed at different price points (the price elasticity curve, explained in Chapter 8). In other words, the recommendation tied the four critical elements together—**price** (WTP), **value** (to customers), **volume** (the expected demand at those price points), and **costs** in delivering the service (including the risks based on probability of car failure within the warranty period). That helped the product strategy and leadership team develop an airtight business case. It was a business case built on a foundation of real customer feedback rather than on internal assumptions and opinions.

With statistically significant survey data, the product team could simulate how demand would vary across different price points. They could point to the type of inventory on which Manheim would offer guarantees, as well as the revenue potential those guarantees generated. They could simulate what would happen if Manheim lowered its price significantly, and how much more market share the company was likely to gain if it chose a penetration strategy.

And most important, the business case demonstrated what these and other scenarios would mean to Manheim's revenue and profits—its bottom line.

The executive management had the data they needed to make a concrete decision. Manheim had based its business case for this new service on undeniable facts, especially the two most important ones for any new offering: Will customers buy it, and if so, at what price?

Branded as the DealShield Purchase Guarantee,[1] the new service debuted in 2012. Today, it lets dealers who purchase a vehicle at a Manheim auction return it for any reason for up to 21 days and 500 miles from the time of purchase at any Manheim auction location. The price for the service depends on the risk of the transaction, including the condition of the vehicle, reconditioning expenses to get the auto ready for retail sale, and market conditions.[2] By 2015, DealShield had protected billions of dollars in vehicle purchases and generated significant revenue and profit for Manheim.

Why WTP Is Essential For Your Business Case

Think back to the last business case you or your colleagues were asked to write for a new product. How did you arrive at your prices? Did you compare your product to other products in the marketplace, or did you actually ask customers what they'd pay for it? Did you know in advance what would happen if you increased your price by, say, 20 percent—how it would affect demand and thus volume?

If you are like thousands of companies we've seen over the years, you probably didn't. These firms *did* have business cases. But only about 5 percent had the essential information, on customers' WTP.

When you think about it, that's amazing.

If you don't know how much customers might pay for your proposed product, how much they value it, how demand (that is, *volume*) will likely change based on its price, then how can you trust your business case? The answer is, you can't. Put another way, if there is minimal WTP, you would rather find that out as early as possible (before sinking in too many resources).

Much in the same (sane) way we helped Manheim create a solid business case for DealShield, we convinced the top executives at a software-as-a-service provider to dump plans for a new low-priced entry product. (It was a "freemium" model of the type we discussed in Chapter 8.) The price for the base service was to be zero so customers would sign up en masse. The hope was many or most would move to the premium service at some point. Several of the firm's top executives were emotionally attached to their freemium model. This company had enjoyed rapid revenue growth, and they had good reason to believe in their pricing instincts.

However, when we helped the company create a detailed business case, we became the bearer of bad news to this faction of the top team. Our model revealed a freemium service would greatly cannibalize the firm's low-priced products, which had gainfully served as the entry-level offerings. In no way would the additional number of freemium customers offset the sizable revenue lost from customers switching from the low-priced to the freemium version. After hearing that, the executive management walked away from the concept, thanking us heartily for bringing them the bad news. Better now than later.

Your business case must model the linkages among the four elements of price, value, volume, and cost. When you do that, your monetary forecast will be far more precise.

Building a robust business case with these linkages will help you avoid the monetizing innovation failure types. How so? Making this kind of business case will alert you to a product that will be dead on market arrival—the dreaded undead. In some cases, customers will be willing to pay much more than you anticipated. If you don't know this, you'll underprice your innovation and leave money on the table (i.e., produce a minivation). To prevent a feature shock, a business case that prioritizes features based on how much customers are willing to pay for them will show which features you should focus on and which you should discard. You will be able to discover whether a market *does* exist for some newfangled offering and is willing to pay a sizable price for it (thereby uncovering a hidden gem).

A business case should be a living document that keeps you grounded on the true monetization potential of your innovation. As time goes by, the problems of business cases lacking information on value, price, cost, and volume only get compounded. Companies make isolated adjustments to one of the four elements without taking into account their interdependencies. For instance, the R&D team increases its cost estimates, leading finance to raise prices to hit target profit margins, all without addressing volume or value. Finance raises the price, but the company has no idea whether customers will actually pay it and what demand will look like after the price adjustment.

That's why you need a strong business case with WTP information and the linkages intact. That's why you can't succeed without one. Without it, you're just guessing about your innovation's monetization potential.

You can get the customer WTP in many ways. We listed them in Chapter 4. The essential point here is to do it and include it in your business case.

Nine Steps to Build a Living Business Case

We hope we have convinced you of the need to craft what may be a much different business case than the type your company has required to date for new products. So how do you create such an airtight business case, one that will help you monetize your new offering?

Here are nine steps to build a business case that will maximize the value of your new products or services over time. The first is the most important:

1. **Forget the way you do business cases today.** Nearly every business case we've reviewed in our firm's 30-plus years of business is a static document whose purpose is securing funding for a new product. By static, we mean it's created once to get funding approval, and then it's put on a shelf where it collects dust. Instead, a business case must be a living document, one you update before and after launch with new data on pricing, costs, volume, and value. You can use it to test assumptions about these four elements and how they interact with one another throughout the product life cycle, not just at the funding stage. It will help you respond effectively to competitors' moves before and after your new offering hits the market.

2. **Assemble the basic ingredients.** Incorporate market size, volume, customer segments, offer structure (configurations and bundles), value, WTP, a monetization model, costs, and competing products and their pricing.

3. **Include price elasticity.** Most companies avoid exploring price elasticity at this point, but we find it to be *the* critical element in business cases. When the price of a product goes up, sales volume tends to go down. If you've included that dynamic in your business case, you can make more accurate and better decisions if you add features that affect pricing. For example, you'll know how much volume will go down if you raise your price. Now the tough discussions can begin: Do we really need a certain feature that's

costing us a lot and driving up our price? Do customers value it? What is the demand?

4. **Apply data-verified facts.** You need to use figures based on real facts. Without data, many are tempted to overstate the size of their target market, for example, or to create unrealistic adoption assumptions. Such guesses will come back to haunt you later, when you have to explain why sales are grossly under target. Topics that typically require data-validity checks include market size, ramp-up times, churn, and cannibalization assumptions.

5. **Add risk assumptions.** You need to attach risk assumptions to any input parameters that are inherently uncertain. For example, your manufacturing cost per unit will increase if a key supplier goes belly up and you must source from higher-priced suppliers. If that's possible, you must mention that in your business case. To pressure-test your business case, you should add these risks and calculate best- and worst-case outcomes of input parameters. A more sophisticated tactic would be using Monte Carlo simulations. They will enable you to gauge the probabilities of your projected outcomes and model uncertainty using probabilistic distributions. Software such as Oracle's Crystal Ball (a popular plug-in to Microsoft's Excel spreadsheet software) allows you to model such assumptions easily.[3]

6. **Be realistic about goal tradeoffs.** It's nearly impossible to maximize a new product's profit, revenue, volume, and margin all at once. You have to prioritize your goals. Raising prices almost always lowers volume and thus revenue. Lower prices typically increase volume. Understanding and making these trade-offs through "what if" scenarios is a key ingredient for a best-in-class business case.

7. **Consider competitive reactions.** Make sure your business case models your rivals' possible reactions. Will they reduce prices? Will they increase service levels? Then, plan for how you'll respond to those reactions. An effective business case is dead serious about these competitive scenarios, and it quantifies their impact. We'll discuss this in Chapter 12.

8. **Don't focus the business case on just the new product.** As much as your business case must financially justify your new product, make sure you assess its overall impact on your company. If the new product will cannibalize sales of existing products, you must factor

that in. And, of course, if it cannibalizes too much, you won't have a strong business case.

9. **Keep checking in.** A strong business case will help you make decisions throughout the product development process and beyond. At each decision point, make sure the four pillars remain integrated, consistent, and in line with your company's strategy. Your model for pricing, volume, cost, and value needs to hold up at each stage of the development process.

Shaping a business case that gathers reliable information on customer WTP, value, volume, and cost is not simple. It takes time, effort, and money. However, the return will far outweigh the investment.

Most of all, a strong business case will help you turn your hopes of launching a successful new product—defying the 72 percent new-product failure rate—into informed confidence that you actually will succeed. By helping you create the right ambition for your new offering, a strong business case will let you extract your new product's full market potential.

Summary

Products are almost never launched without some sort of business case. But 95 percent of the business cases we've seen are built from the inside out, not the outside in. Consequently, they fail to account for critical market information, particularly customer WTP and price elasticity.

If you don't know what your customers will pay for your new product and how demand changes when you change the price, you simply don't have a business case. Without this information, your business case will only tell you what you want to hear.

Moreover, most business cases are static documents, employed to gain budget approval. Once the money has been allocated, they are quickly forgotten. That's a very limited use of a powerful tool. A business case that's a living, breathing document will help you figure out how to react effectively once your product hits the market and theory becomes practice.

To create this kind of business plan, you need to gather data on the four pillars: value, price, cost, and volume. Then you must integrate them because they all affect one another. This starts with including the WTP data discussed in Chapter 4.

The nine steps in this chapter will help you create an airtight business case.

CEO Questions

1. Does our new product business case include customer WTP data? What price elasticity is assumed in the business case? How did we come up with it?
2. Are we modeling the four critical pillars in our new product business cases: price, value, volume, and cost? How are we making sure the linkages are preserved when we make changes to one of the elements?
3. Are our business cases living documents that we check and update at project milestones? When was the last change, and why did we make it?
4. Does the business case help us simulate different scenarios that may occur after product launch so we can make better decisions throughout the product's life? What is a good example?
5. Does the business case anticipate potential competitive responses to our launch and suggest how to react to them? How did we get to these competitive responses? What assumptions were made?

CHAPTER 10

The Innovation Won't Speak for Itself

You Must Communicate the Value

Y ou've designed a great product. It answers a market need. You did extensive work to determine the right monetization model, and you developed a winning pricing strategy. Now it's time to let your customers know about your product. For a successful launch, your marketing and sales teams must be strong in communicating and selling the value of your product to customers. As management guru Peter Drucker once said: "Customers don't buy products. They buy the benefits that these products and their suppliers offer to them."

It sounds easy, but consider this: You have thought about your innovation for months or even years. You know the product inside and out. However, a salesperson may only have 10 minutes with the customer. Your customer might stay on your website only for five minutes. An advertisement may only run for 15 seconds. That marketing message, that sales pitch, and that ad must clearly articulate the value to customers in a very short period of time. If they don't, the would-be customer tunes out.

How can you maximize your acquisition success? You need to start by articulating benefits—not features—and focus on the most important ones. You need to speak the customer's language, not your language. Finally, you need to get your marketing and sales teams involved early in the product development process.

We examine each of these practices in this chapter, and more. We also explain why most companies struggle with value communications when it comes to new products. We'll explore the most frequent root cause of the problem: People in functions charged with communication are typically detached from the innovation process and thus *come in too late.*

A Few Shining Examples of Value Communications

When marketing and salespeople use compelling value communications, great things happen, as the following two examples demonstrate.

The first is a SaaS (software-as-a-service) company whose products streamlined and optimized warehouse and other supply chain operations for its customers. The software forecasted the customer's demand and helped it stock the right amount of inventory in its warehouses (thereby reducing the cost of carrying excess inventory). That helped customers get the right products to the right places at the right times. The software also automated the picking and shipping workflows in the warehouse and eliminated manual errors that had been par for the course. Lastly, the software provided a real-time view to coordinate the workforce. It also eliminated the need to pass paper documents around the warehouse.

It was evident to the SaaS company that its new product would generate great value for customers, and it wanted the product's price to reflect that value. Many of the firms the company thought of as peers priced on a per-user basis (for instance, $50 per month per user).

But the SaaS company knew this would be suboptimal (that is, a minivation!). It wanted to position its product, and its price, on the value it delivered. So the firm started by creating a spreadsheet salespeople could use with customers to quantify the payback on the product after asking a few basic questions about their operations. (See Figure 10.1.) The salesperson could enter such data as the number of hours the customer spent having warehouse workers manually pick orders from shelves (a task the software automated), the amount of inventory carried (the software would reduce costs of carrying excess inventory due to better forecasting), the number of shipping errors that occurred (the software would eliminate those), and the savings from eliminating paper documentation (by ending the paper shuffling, real-time coordination in the warehouse would greatly increase efficiency).

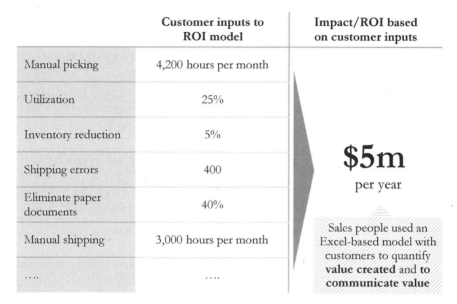

	Customer inputs to ROI model	Impact/ROI based on customer inputs
Manual picking	4,200 hours per month	
Utilization	25%	
Inventory reduction	5%	
Shipping errors	400	**$5m** per year
Eliminate paper documents	40%	
Manual shipping	3,000 hours per month	Sales people used an Excel-based model with customers to quantify **value created** and to **communicate value**
....	....	

Figure 10.1   Conceptual Example of a Value-Selling Spreadsheet

The spreadsheet then calculated the customer's total return on its software investment.

Voila! The value that the software brought to the table, in dollars and cents, became crystal clear to the software company's customers. The SaaS firm was able to easily justify the price the customer needed to pay for the software.

Along with communicating the dollars and cents, the salespeople also delivered a crystal clear benefit statement, one that captured the customer's attention because it was fully in line with the value they were looking for: a reduction in inventory carrying cost, greater warehouse efficiency due to automated workflows, and more. The result: Sales of its new product took off like a rocket.

The SaaS firm's approach was remarkably different from competitors, whose sales negotiations were still explaining features but not benefits. The SaaS firm's sales were many times higher than they would have been if it had opted for per-user pricing.

The second example is SmugMug, an Internet startup that lets people safely store, share, and sell photos online. SmugMug offered four customer plans. SmugMug loved the features of those plans, and so did its customers. But it offered simply too many features (100+) for the average customer to fully comprehend. (See Figure 10.2.)

Many customers simply chose not to purchase the product; they didn't know which way to go and which plan to select. As SmugMug continued to innovate and add more features to the plans, customers became even more confused. Sales were not picking up at the pace the firm expected. SmugMug cofounders Chris and Don MacAskill knew their innovation was a winner, and it was. The *Wall Street Journal* called SmugMug the "strikingly handsome photography site." *Forbes* called it "one of the top company brands in its field and one of the most-liked and most-respected personal brands." Nonetheless, the MacAskills had to solve their value communication and sales problems.

So the SmugMug founders revisited how they positioned their products. After scrutinizing their marketing messages, they realized they were spending a lot of time talking features and not benefits. SmugMug was trying too hard, and the value message was not reaching the average customer. The firm then revamped the messages for its packages (i.e. product configurations), using benefits—not features. They also moved the feature comparison to an optional section for those who still wanted to compare. They managed to condense the benefit statements from more than 100 to fewer than 10. (See Figure 10.3.)

The benefit statements, such as "beautiful design" and "unlimited storage," were music to many ears. The average customer could now quickly understand what they would get with each product offering. If you wanted only photo storage, you would choose basic. Want personalization? Choose power. Did you want to sell online? Choose portfolio. How about marketing what you sell online? Then you would choose business.

The messaging was simple with clear value statements. That was a big change from the way benefits had been articulated before.

With these changes, Chris and Don MacAskill nailed it. By excelling at value communications, SmugMug saw a double-digit percentage increase in revenue and conversion.

Sounds easy? It isn't. Most companies have great sales and marketing teams and spend oodles of time trying to craft the right value messages. Yet, we have seen far too many companies struggle to communicate the values their products deliver. The next section underscores the root cause for this.

COMPARE PLANS

Photo Website	Basic	Power	Portfolio	Business
Your own customizable website				
Responsive design—automatically adapts to mobile, tablets, and monitors	✓	✓	✓	✓
Fully hosted, unlimited traffic				
Ads and spam	Zip	Zero	Zilch	Nada
Unlimited photo and video uploads	✓	✓	✓	✓
Gorgeous, full-screen galleries				
Maximum photo file size	150 MB	150 MB	150 MB	150 MB
Maximum video file size	3 GB	3 GB	3 GB	3 GB
Video quality	1080p	1080p	1080p	1080p
Video clip length	20 min	20 min	20 min	20 min
Embed photos and videos on other websites	✓	✓	✓	✓
Add photos from Lightroom, Aperture, iPhoto, and more	✓	✓	✓	✓
Detailed statistics and analytics	✓	✓	✓	✓
Robust SEO tools, including meta tags and XML sitemaps	✓	✓	✓	✓

Community and Support	Basic	Power	Portfolio	Business
24/7/365 real-human support	✓	✓	✓	✓
In-depth help center guides you in making the most of your account	✓	✓	✓	✓
Video tutorials provide step-by-step learning opportunities	✓	✓	✓	✓
Live online SmugMug training events	✓	✓	✓	✓
Community forums for feedback, tips, and in-depth support	✓	✓	✓	✓

Customization	Basic	Power	Portfolio	Business
Create a completely personalized homepage		✓	✓	✓
Apply themes to add personal style to pages and galleries	✓	✓	✓	✓
Pick your own fonts and color combinations	✓	✓	✓	✓
Choose from 21+ premade site designs		✓	✓	✓
Create your own designs, no coding needed		✓	✓	✓
Create your own themes		✓	✓	✓
Personalize your site with easy-to-learn layout tools	✓	✓	✓	✓
Customize by simply dragging and dropping	✓	✓	✓	✓
Easily add slideshows, your logo, and more, anywhere on the page	✓	✓	✓	✓
Pick a favorite gallery style (six to choose from)	✓	✓	✓	✓
Put your logo or brand name on your site		✓	✓	✓
Use your own domain			✓	✓
Add optional customization via HTML and CSS		✓	✓	✓

Organization	Basic	Power	Portfolio	Business
Easily organize your photos and website	✓	✓	✓	✓
Quickly access any page, folder, or gallery on your site	✓	✓	✓	✓
Manage settings on images, galleries, and folders	✓	✓	✓	✓
Bulk manage images with drag-and-drop functionality	✓	✓	✓	✓
Bulk delete images and galleries	✓	✓	✓	✓
Drag images into galleries, galleries into folders, and folders into folders, up to seven levels deep	✓	✓	✓	✓
Sort photos by date, caption, and more	✓	✓	✓	✓
Add captions and keywords to photos	✓	✓	✓	✓

Safety and Security	Basic	Power	Portfolio	Business
Every image backed up with Amazon Web Services	✓	✓	✓	✓
Access cloud storage anytime, anywhere	✓	✓	✓	✓
Copyright is always yours	✓	✓	✓	✓
Retrieve your original photos and gallery backups at anytime	✓	✓	✓	✓
Password-protect folders, galleries, pages, and your whole site	✓	✓	✓	✓
Unlist folders, galleries, and pages	✓	✓	✓	✓
Create private galleries	✓	✓	✓	✓
Make any folder, gallery, or page completely private	✓	✓	✓	✓
Opt out of search engines	✓	✓	✓	✓
Limit display size to keep originals safe	✓	✓	✓	✓
Set a custom right-click message for your images		✓	✓	✓
Limit access to your folders, galleries, pages, and site to specific people you choose			✓	✓
Add custom watermarks to protect images			✓	✓
Provide a private client area for your customers				✓

Sharing	Basic	Power	Portfolio	Business
Share via Facebook, Twitter, Google+, WordPress, and more	✓	✓	✓	✓
Publish photos to albums on Facebook	✓	✓	✓	✓
Allow visitors to download an entire gallery of photos	✓	✓	✓	✓
Embed slideshows in forums and blogs	✓	✓	✓	✓
Give pages custom, easy-to-remember URLs	✓	✓	✓	✓
Send photos easily via email	✓	✓	✓	✓
Create virtual collections of photos you love	✓	✓	✓	✓
Create Smart Galleries for automated collections	✓	✓	✓	✓
Allow friends and family to upload to your galleries	✓	✓	✓	✓
Enable or disable comments	✓	✓	✓	✓
Moderate comments	✓	✓	✓	✓
Get email notifications for comments	✓	✓	✓	✓
Edit, archive, and share on-the-go with our free mobile apps	✓	✓	✓	✓
Display geotagged photos on interactive maps			✓	✓

Prints and Gifts	Basic	Power	Portfolio	Business
100% Print Satisfaction Guarantee	✓	✓	✓	✓
Order prints and products with EZPrints	✓	✓	✓	✓
Enable/disable product sales from any gallery	✓	✓	✓	✓
Fully hosted shopping cart and checkout	✓	✓	✓	✓
Order prints, canvas, and more right from your site	✓	✓	✓	✓
Order products like mousepads and more	✓	✓	✓	✓
Create custom greeting cards	✓	✓	✓	✓
Allow family and friends to order photo cards from your site	✓	✓	✓	✓
Credit card processing and customer service included	✓	✓	✓	✓
Buy photo books, framing, etc., from multiple vendors	✓	✓	✓	✓
Ship anywhere	✓	✓	✓	✓
Get special SmugMug discounts with other companies		✓	✓	✓

Figure 10.2   SmugMug's Pricing Plans before the Change (100+ Features for Consumers to Sort Out)

Source: Smugmug.com

Figure 10.3   SmugMug's Revamped Plans with Clear Benefit Statements

Source: Smugmug.com

So Why Is Value Messaging Difficult?

The problem usually begins with a disconnect between the frontline sales and marketing teams responsible for communicating the messages and the innovation team driving new product development. The sales and marketing teams often are far removed from the innovation teams and are brought in toward the very end to pinch hit, to market and sell a product. By the time they join the process, though, it is typically too late. They were not part of the value-to-customer story that drove the product design process and pricing. Nonetheless, they are told to craft the value story and sell it. Strange, but true.

Without real information, they sit around a table to brainstorm ideas and develop a value story, which might not match the discussions the innovation team had when it designed the product. Sometimes the marketing and sales groups don't seek input from the innovation teams and they try to run with what they have, since they feel they already know their customers. This gets complicated quickly.

But even if marketing, sales, and product development managers convene to hash out the sales and marketing messages, the right communications often don't emerge from their meetings. As the teams try to reconcile divergent views of the product's value, the loudest or most senior voices in the room win the message-framing battle. And in too many cases, the winning message is different from the value proposition defined during product development, the one that excited potential customers.

Most companies do not pay enough attention to this gap, believing the handoff from R&D to sales and marketing is a standard business process. But in practice, it's not. It requires special effort. Great new products, even when they are priced right, don't sell themselves. Marketing needs to promote them, and sales needs to sell them.

Telling a compelling value story is well within every company's ability and means. It's not about getting a top Madison Avenue ad agency. Instead, it requires adding key marketing and sales people to your innovation teams from the very start. This helps them fully comprehend the value messages that resonated most with customers from the get-go and lets them give valuable input to the new product design process. This also enables salespeople to focus their conversations on value, rather than price. More on this in Chapter 14.

Now that you have understood how value messages can get scrambled, let's shift gears and learn about how to fix it. In the next section we provide three steps to get this right from the start.

The Three Steps to Create Great Value Communications

Step 1: Develop Crystal-Clear Benefit Statements— Not Feature Descriptions

A company that excels at value communications articulates its products' benefits in meaningful terms to customers. This is not about describing product features. A feature belongs to the product; a benefit belongs to the customer. Value is a measure of the benefit to the customer. Communicate benefits, not features. Take each feature and ask yourself this: What does the customer achieve because of this feature? If you are still unsure about how to phrase your product's benefits, probe your customers about their pain points and how your product would solve them. Ideally, you should understand how customers measure their performance—and how your offering would affect those measures. Once you know that, you can tailor your messages to the customers' priorities. You should also quantify the relative value of your product: the value it would deliver compared to the value your customer gets today from other offerings.

To be more specific, when you create a value message, you should determine the customer purchasing criteria and how your product or service might perform on those criteria compared to existing alternatives. Such information can be captured in a 2×2 matrix that we call the *matrix of competitive advantages*, or MOCA for short. (See Figure 10.4 for an example.)

To create this matrix, you list the relative importance of your innovation's benefits to customers on the y-axis. On the x-axis, you rate your innovation's performance against the competition—not as you see it, but as your customers see it. The benefits your product delivers that are most important to customers and that competitors can't match (top right quadrant) are the ones to emphasize in your sales and marketing messages.

But those aren't the only benefits to communicate. For the ones in the lower right quadrant—benefits you are better at delivering than competitors but which are less important to customers—you are trying to convince customers these benefits are more important than they might realize. However, if you can't prove it, don't emphasize them in your value communication.

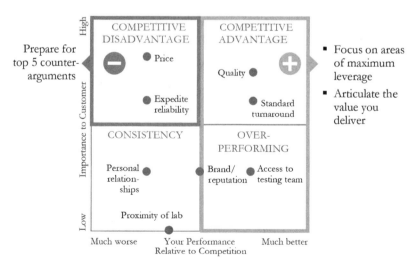

Figure 10.4   Matrix of Competitive Advantages (MOCA)

The factors in the top left quadrant represent your competitive disadvantages, and you should prepare arguments to defend them.

Using this matrix, creating value communications will become more structured. It will also become easier to get all the innovation team members (R&D, product, sales, and marketing) on the same page.

A few more tips when creating benefit statements:

- When communicating the benefit statements, it's easy to fall into the trap of thinking your features are the same thing as the benefits to your customers. They aren't. Take the case of Carbonite, the online data storage and backup company. The firm used to describe the storage amount for data backup services to consumers as "20 gigabytes." While an IT professional would understand how much storage that figure represents, the average consumer would not, and therefore they couldn't assess the benefit in a meaningful way. The offer of 20 giga-bytes was most likely much more than what a majority of consumers would ever need. But the words "20 gigabytes" certainly did not identify a problem or a solution. Carbonite changed its description to "unlimited storage," and the message truly resonated. Consumers could say, "With this service, I don't have to worry about running out of online storage space." In reality, most consumers might still use less than 20 gigabytes, but the positioning strongly helped increase customer conversion.

- Customers are hardly interested in how you created your innovation or how much you spent on it. What's fascinating for you is not necessarily fascinating to your customers. Americans didn't buy Thomas Edison's incandescent bulb upon learning that he tested over a thousand filaments before settling on tungsten. It was a heroic feat of innovation, but most Americans never knew about it, nor would they have cared. They bought Edison's bulb so they didn't trip over their kids' toys in the dark. And a message along the lines of "the product is good because it has seven patents" is pretty meaningless as well. Your customers couldn't care less.

- You should also communicate those benefits with extreme brevity. Come up with a handful of words for a headline or sales pitch—not a line the length of Lincoln's Gettysburg Address (which by public speaking standards was a very short speech indeed, at only 272 words). The top-level messages about the core benefits to customers matter greatly. They must be short but sweet. You should test the messages with customers before finalizing them. Take the example of LinkedIn. In reformulating its Talent Solutions offering, the company found customers were clearly willing to pay for the opportunity to recruit "passive" job candidates—people not actually looking for jobs because they already were employed. LinkedIn's communications centered on recruiters' newfound ability to approach millions of these passive job candidates. The company led its messages with the very simple but very successful value message: "Find and engage the best passive talent."

- Last, remember that passion can get in the way of communicating value. This happens when product and marketing professionals try to jam every feature and benefit statement into marketing and sales communications. Encourage the innovation cross-functional team to practice restraint and communicate only what matters most to customers.

Step 2: Make Your Benefit Statements Segment-Specific

As described in Chapter 5, homogeneity is one of the biggest wrong assumptions you can make in your new product design. Your customers are different. The same value messages are not likely to work for all of your customer segments. You should tailor your value messages to the needs of each segment. Marketing software maker Adobe, for example, does a great job of describing the right plan for the right segment using the right value message. (See Figure 10.5.)

Find the plan that's right for you.

There's a Creative Cloud plan to fit every individual and organization.

Individuals	Photographers	Students and teachers	Small and medium business
Tet the entire collection of creative apps and more – for just $49.99/mo.	Includes Photoshop CC plus Lightroom for desktop, mobile and web for US$9.99/mo.	Save 60% on the entire collection of Creative Cloud apps. Just $19.99/mo.	Get the entire collection of creative apps and business services – including easy setup and license management – for just $69.99/mo.
Choose a plan I Buy now >	Learn more I Buy now >	Learn more I Buy now >	Learn more I Buy now >

Enterprise	Schools and universities	Governments
Customized provisioning and deployment, plus enterprise-level	Flexible licensing and desktop deployment starting at US$14.99/mo.	Industry-standard technology. Enterprise support Secure deployments.
Learn more >	Learn more I Buy now >	Learn more >

Figure 10.5   **Adobe Creative Cloud's Messaging for Each Customer Segment**

Source: www.adobe.com/creativecloud.html

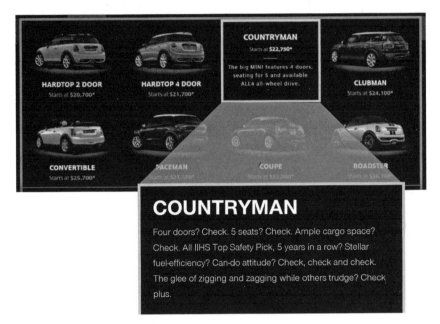

Figure 10.6   Value Message for the Mini Countryman

Source: miniusa.com

For Adobe's Individuals segment, the messaging includes "getting all the creative apps" and "being able to search 45 million stock images and videos." For the Enterprise segment, Adobe's messaging is "customized provisioning deployment," "enterprise level support," and "streamlined license management and deployment." The messages are quite distinct from segment to segment.[1]

Another company that creates great segment-specific message is Mini. While the car company has eight models (from the Hardtop two-door to the Roadster), each one has a very specific value message attached to it and a benefits statement that is exciting to read. For example, the value message for the Countryman is highlighted in Figure 10.6.[2]

Step 3: Measure the Impact and Refine Your Value Messages

Just as we urged you to craft a business case (described in Chapter 9) to be a continually updated document, you should check and recheck the viability of your marketing and sales messages. Specifically, you need to measure customer perceptions of the value you are communicating.

You should be prepared to refine your messaging if customers don't believe the value is clear and compelling.

A way to do this is to run a MOCA analysis as described in step 2 on a regular basis. If the messages you are communicating are too far afield from the messages that matter most to customers, you need a new strategy.

Summary

Mastering the art of value communications is just as important as mastering the process of designing products that customers will pay for. If you can't clearly communicate that value, how can you expect customers to understand why they need your new offering and why they should pay for it?

While it sounds simple in theory, we routinely see companies struggle with crafting their value communication when it comes to new products. The most frequent root cause of the problem: People in functions charged with value communication are typically detached from the innovation process and thus *come in too late.*

To fix this, integrate marketing and sales into the innovation team. Follow the three steps mentioned in this chapter to create compelling messages—those that communicate benefits (not features), are segment-specific, and are monitored and continually improved.

CEO Questions

1. What benefits do our customers derive from our new products? Have we quantified these benefits? How did we go about it?
2. Are the marketing and sales teams involved with the innovation team from the get-go, or are they plugged in toward the end of product development to create the value messages? If the latter, how do we fix the situation?
3. To what extent are our value communications in tune with the benefits customers perceive? Have we tested our messages? If so, how? If not, why not? How do the messages change by customer segment?

4. Did the entire innovation team (R&D, product, marketing, sales) check and approve the value communication materials we developed? How closely? Did anyone object? If so, why?

5. What processes do we have to measure the effectiveness of our value messages? Have we used the matrix of competitive advantages as a framework to create our value messaging? How regularly are we planning to measure the effectiveness of our value messages?

CHAPTER 11

Use Behavioral Pricing Tactics to Persuade and Sell

Sometimes Your Customers Will Behave Irrationally

People make decisions based on both rational and emotional factors. For example, imagine you are on a beach on a hot day and you crave a cold beer. A friend offers to bring you one from the only place nearby that sells beer—a fancy resort hotel.

How much will you pay for the beer?

Now imagine you are on a beach on a hot day, craving a cold beer, and a friend offers to bring you one from the only place nearby that sells beer—a small, run-down corner store.

How much would you be willing to pay for the same beer now?

Remember: The beer is the same, the weather is the same, and, best of all, you don't have to move. Your friend is willing to make the beer run.

When asked, people typically are willing to pay twice as much for the beer from the resort as from the run-down store. From an economic perspective, this makes no sense; it is, in a word, irrational. Behavioral economics springs from this recognition that buyers are not always rational actors. Their willingness to pay (WTP) for your product is not solely based on the value they get from it. Psychological factors also can play a big role. We refer to the pricing tactics that play to this irrational side of customers as *behavioral pricing*.

The topic of behavioral economics is of growing interest in academic and business circles. It was first popularized by researchers Daniel Kahneman, Amos Tversky, and Richard Thaler in the 1970s and '80s. Dan Ariely's amazing book, *Predictably Irrational*, expanded the field's followers. But while a number of books have explored behavioral economics, the literature on behavioral pricing is sparse, especially as it relates to monetizing new products. This chapter attempts to address that gap.

In discussing the concept of value pricing and its components (especially WTP and value messaging) in Chapters 4 and 10, we explained how to appeal to the customer's rational side. We explored how to match the price of your offering with the value customers perceive that offering gives them. That's the rational side of pricing.

Behavioral pricing is a separate matter. It calls for refining your product offers and the messages you create about them to make it easier for customers to compare, decide, and purchase. And making it easier doesn't necessarily mean providing information for logical, rational analysis. Sometimes, that data only makes deciding harder. *Behavioral pricing* is the magic that happens when *value pricing* meets irrational customer psychology.

All of us are subject to behavioral pricing every day. Consider what happens when you walk into a movie theater. When you belly up to the concession stand, do you wonder why the price of the large soda ($5.99 at a theater near one of us) is just a buck more than the $4.99 small soda? The reason is the price of the small serving makes the large one seem less expensive, and thus more attractive, even if you're not that thirsty and the small soda is all you really want. Such offers, promoted to make another product look better, are called *anchors*. The small soda makes the more expensive option look like a bargain, and who can resist a bargain? That's the only reason for a $4.99 small soda at all.

Price anchors are one of several pricing tactics that play to the irrational side of customers. How you communicate your pricing to customers, and how you frame a conversation to deal with customer irrationality, can substantially impact how well your new product sells and the price you get for it.

This is an important step you should take at the very same time you factor your product's value to customers into your pricing. Pricing that doesn't consider the irrational aspects of customers is likely to be suboptimal.

If you think behavioral pricing applies only to consumer products and services, think again. It does not. In fact, behavioral pricing is just as crucial in business-to-business (B2B) settings. In both cases, you are selling to people, and understanding their psychology and how they buy is important whether you are pricing candy bars or bulldozers.

The Behavioral Pricing Dilemma of an Internet Start-Up Company

Back in 2012, we worked with an Internet start-up that wanted to increase revenue from service providers. The company already had a "good, better, best" product lineup. But close to 60 percent of its customers selected the good or entry-level offering. The firm launched a large study to determine whether it was possible to steer more customers to the more profitable premium offerings.

The study uncovered a number of insights, two of which were the most consequential:

1. The firm's customers had key psychological price thresholds—limits to what most of them would spend, depending on the product configuration. Those price thresholds were $49, $99, and $199. Our client had three offerings priced at $49 (Basic), $79 (Standard), and $149 (Advanced). The fact that the firm's pricing was below customers' psychological thresholds suggested it could raise prices without hurting demand.
2. Our client was giving away too much value in its low-end offering. No wonder almost 60 percent of the service providers had chosen it! More important, by providing too much value in the entry-level offering, the firm had unintentionally made its higher-priced offering less attractive. Even though the Standard offering had more value than the Basic offering, customers failed to appreciate that additional value (for the additional price). The Basic offering was too good, and the Standard offering looked expensive given the incremental value it offered.

The findings pointed to two recommendations that could raise average revenue per subscriber: increase prices of the Standard and Advanced offering to customers' psychological price thresholds, and make those offerings more attractive. The company's CEO reduced the functionality of the Basic offering but kept the same price. The price of the Standard and Advanced offering were increased to $99 and $199 respectively. The CEO also redistributed the existing features among the Standard and the Advanced offerings to make each of them more compelling. Last but not least, a fourth offering, an ultrapremium offering with new functionality (aptly named Premium), was created and priced at $299.

The impact was immediate and substantial. The number of Standard and Advanced premium products sold rose significantly, even though their prices went up. The financial impact was substantial: an average revenue per user (ARPU) increase of 36 percent and a 29 percent increase in monthly recurring revenue (MRR) from new customers. The company's annual profit jumped many times because the new products came with little additional cost to the firm.

Of the 29 percent total increase in MRR, the firm attributed roughly 14 percentage points to behavioral pricing and 15 percentage points to changes in the core product configurations. This is behavioral pricing at its best.

If you work at a multibillion-dollar company, you aren't likely to get a 14 percent revenue increase using behavioral pricing; a 1 percent to 3 percent sales boost is more likely. But remember, the pricing tactics we're talking about here don't necessarily require rejiggering the functionality of your product offerings. You won't need to increase your costs very much to get that revenue increase. In other words, all of that extra revenue goes directly to your bottom line.

Why is that kind of revenue and profit boost possible? Why did the Internet start-up company's customers flock to its higher-priced options? Three reasons stand out.

One, reducing the functionality of the entry-level Basic offering made the offering immediately above it much more attractive to buyers who previously would have been misclassified as price-sensitive.

Two, the Premium offering came with a premium price: $299. That made the Standard and Advanced products look more attractive. The

Premium offering was the anchor, the Internet start-up company's version of the movie theater's small soda. The offering's sole purpose was to make the other products look like bargains. It drove a higher percentage of customers who wanted a high-quality solution—but still loved getting a deal—to choose the Standard and Advanced product.

Three, a few customers were willing to pay the premium price for the premium offering with the most functionality. We have seen this time and again: Certain customers will always go for the most expensive product in a lineup, the one they perceive to have the highest quality. They believe you get what you pay for and that they deserve the best. As pricing experts, we have come to accept this as a fact of life.

In the end, behavioral pricing helped turn a good vanilla cake into a four-tier torte with gourmet toppings (see Figure 11.1).

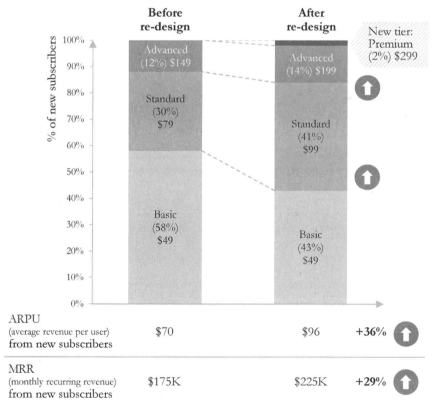

Figure 11.1   Redesigning an Internet Marketplace's Product Lineup

While such stories make behavioral pricing exciting, we need to temper expectations. You can't base your price-setting strategy only on behavioral techniques. Rational tactics, those that discern what customers value and what they are willing to pay, are prerequisites. Combining rational and behavioral pricing approaches is the most effective strategy.

With that caveat, let's explore six behavioral pricing tactics that work really well for new products. They work even better than you might imagine.

Six Behavioral Pricing Tactics That Make the Difference

These tactics can markedly increase the success of a new product launch. Based on behavioral economic theories we've tested in many different customer settings, these six tactics become more powerful when you combine them. Here they are, along with examples that illustrate them:

1. **Compromise effect:** Make decisions easier for people who can't choose.

   When given a set of choices, people will avoid extremes. For example, imagine you are in a wine store and want to buy a bottle. You find three options: a $10 bottle, a $25 bottle, and a $40 bottle. Which one would you pick? When asked this question, most people would pick the $25 bottle to avoid the extremes ($10 seems cheap; $40 is costly). Of course, some price-sensitive people will pick the $10 bottle, and some quality-conscious people will pick the $40 bottle. But by introducing the $25 wine, you just made the decision process much easier for everyone, including those who can't decide whether to go with price or quality. They'll choose the middle option. This strategy is very common in both B2B and business-to-consumer (B2C) companies. Imagine you work in sales at a B2B company and you're negotiating a deal with a potential customer. You can steer the conversation based on whether the customer is price- or quality-conscious and force a compromise. Recommendation: If you are launching a new product, plan on having a compromise option.

2. **Anchoring tactics:** Set the context for value.

   We illustrated two examples of anchoring—the movie theater concessions and the Internet start-up company. Anchors make the other options look attractive. Another illustration of anchoring is *The Economist* magazine's A/B pricing experiment, which Dan Ariely described in his book. The experiment divided people into two groups, A and B. The A group was given two choices: $59 for an online-only subscription and $125 for a print-and-online combination. The B group was offered three choices: $59 for online only, $125 for print only, and $125 for the print/online bundle. The $125 print-only option was an anchor. It made *The Economist*'s print/online bundle for group B look like a great deal; the online edition seemed like a freebie, a throw-in. Some 84 percent chose the print/online bundle in group B versus only 32 percent who chose that bundle in group A.

We have helped companies in a variety of industries—Internet, media, and financial services, to name just a few—institute such successful anchoring strategies.

Anchoring is a crucial behavioral pricing tactic in B2B sales negotiations. If you start with a high price, inevitably you will end up at a higher net price when the negotiation concludes. Anchoring lets you establish a reference point that will influence subsequent offers and shift the range in your favor.

An anchor works because it shapes the customer's perception of the possible price outcomes. It also creates room for price concessions. To prepare for such concessions, one of our clients always opens a negotiation with a statement such as: "This new proprietary part is priced at a 40 percent premium over standard versions because of significant development costs and superior technical advantages. But since you have been a great customer, we can bake in some price concessions."

This lets our client frame all subsequent conversations with customers who ask for discounts because it set the 40 percent premium as the starting point, the anchor. The firm always nets a higher price than if it had not used an anchor. Recommendation: Make sure you have an anchor product in your new product offering portfolio, and start every B2B sales negotiation for new products with a high anchor price.

3. **Using price to signal quality:** If it costs more, it reinforces the customer's perception of quality.

A product's price sends a powerful signal about its quality. Low price equals low quality; high price equals high quality. The premium pricing for the iPhone when it first launched in 2007 was essential to positioning it as a quality product. If Apple's Steve Jobs had debuted the iPhone at $49, it would have been a terrible mistake. The price would have won market share by undercutting competitors, but it also would have depressed prices for all future smartphones, and Apple would not have become the most profitable company in the world today. Instead, the $599 price for the most popular iPhone signaled that the Apple smartphone was a quality product and always would be.

Pricing also has a psychological effect on how consumers view a product's effectiveness. In a 2008 study, Ariely and his colleagues gave two sets of participants the same pill, telling them it was a painkiller. Informed that the price was $2.50 a pill, 85% of the participants in the first group said the pill reduced their pain. Told the painkiller's price was discounted to 10 cents, only 61% of the second group believed the pill reduced their pain. Interestingly, not only were both groups given the same pill, but the pill was a placebo. The price—not the pill—relieved the pain.[1]

Let's be clear: We're not advocating deception; we're not saying you should sell people something that isn't worth the price. Rather, we're highlighting how a price can powerfully signal quality. Recommendation: Pricing your product too low is worse than pricing it too high. If you start high you can still go down; if you start low you can hardly go up. Therefore, when launching your new product, beware of a too-low price. It can ruin the perception of product quality in the mind of the buyer.

4. Razor/razor blades: Get a foot in the door.

Customers are influenced by costs that are immediately in front of them. Even if they calculate their total cost of ownership of a product over time, they will be swayed by the initial costs. Let's say you are a manufacturer of a coffee machine, and you also make the specially formulated coffee that must be used with it. You plan to launch a new machine and new coffee bags. Let's also assume you are targeting a customer base that consumes an average of one pound of coffee a month per customer. You are considering two pricing schemes: Option A, which prices the machine at $480 and the coffee at $10 per pound per month, or Option B, which prices the machine at $120 and the coffee at $40 per pound per month. Even though a rational person would be indifferent to these options—over a 12-month period, the price for the machine and the coffee is the same—we have consistently found across industries that companies are better off with a scheme like Option B.

Why? The customer's upfront cost has a much bigger psychological impact than the total cost of ownership. Your pricing strategy should be to land a customer by showcasing the lower upfront costs and then expanding on a higher variable amount. Many companies now use this tactic. Computer hardware manufacturers sell cheaper and cheaper products but try to make more money on services. Consumer goods companies do as well—for example, a low upfront investment for a razor but, over time, investment in costlier razor blades; a low upfront investment in a computer printer but expensive ink cartridges.

To maximize your customers' lifetime value, you can use the same strategy to sell versions of your new product. First, sell a basic version of a product (land) and then upsell customers to an advanced version (expand) in due course. Software companies are famous for doing this. Retailers also offer certain categories of products at low prices (doorbusters) to pull more people into their shops and expand the number of products in each shopping cart.[2, 3]

Recommendation: Use this tactic only if you are 100 percent sure you can sell your downstream products to customers—your razor blades, printer ink, and so on.

5. **Pennies-a-day pricing:** Reduce sticker shock and build loyalty.

Amazon.com, the largest U.S. Internet retailer, now owns another title: the largest provider of cloud computing services, also known as infrastructure as a service (IaaS). The technologies involved—the servers and cloud environments—are well-known and widely available. Amazon's innovation centers on its business and pricing models for Amazon Web Services and Elastic Compute Cloud (EC2).

For small companies, investing in computing power and servers can be prohibitively expensive. And renting physical servers does not necessarily solve the problem because setting them up and staffing them pose financial and resource challenges. Amazon's EC2 solves this problem by allowing customers to rent computing capacity, not servers, and for finite amounts of time. In other words, customers use and pay for servers only when they need them, not all the time. That lowers the customer's total cost. But just as important, it lowers the customer's formerly high barrier to entry for tapping into a powerful computing infrastructure.

Amazon's EC2, a great technology innovation case, demonstrates the potential of behavioral pricing and the psychological impact of price levels. The company quotes low prices to reduce the chance of sticker shock and customer resistance. Instead of displaying prices in the hundreds or thousands of dollars per server, EC2 shows prices in dollars or even fractions of a penny for hourly prices.

Aside from fundamentally changing your business model to be like Amazon's, are there easier ways to use pennies-a-day pricing? Absolutely. And the simplest is breaking up time.

Companies often look to establishing annual contracts to ensure predictable revenue. But yearlong contract prices can look prohibitively expensive. Breaking that cost down into monthly installments makes the cost appear more reasonable. Instead of charging an annual price of $120, payments of $9.99 per month can have a very different effect on customer signups. Recommendation: Put the proper thought into framing your price to make it look attractive—not just in coming up with the price.

6. **Psychological price thresholds:** Avoid falling off the price cliffs.

You might wonder why you rarely see prices like $101 in retail; you almost always see $99 or $99.99. The reason is that customers typically have price thresholds in mind. The perceived difference between $99.99 and $101 is more than a dollar and a penny. More often than not, people will feel $101 is much more expensive than $99. From a study we did for an online subscription company, we demonstrate this phenomenon in Figure 11.2. You can see clear price thresholds at $40, $70, and $100. This company was much better off pricing its product at $69.99 than at $71. More than 20 percent of its customers wouldn't accept a $71 price. That was the price cliff. The $69.99 price helped the company avoid losing a sizable share of its audience.

Recommendation: Identify the price thresholds for your products and stay on the cliff.

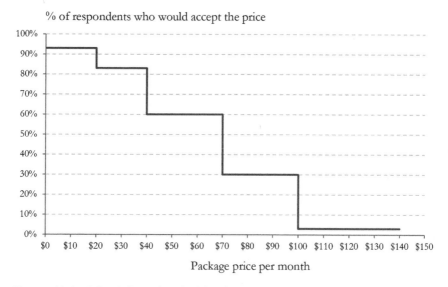

Figure 11.2   The Price Thresholds of an Online Subscription Firm

Don't Guess: Put Behavioral Tactics to the Test

As this chapter shows, there are very good reasons to use each tactic. Since the options are many, you need to do careful tests, track results, and choose the best tactics for your innovation. If you use too many tactics, you will confuse customers. If you use too few of them, you won't fully monetize your new product.

You have several ways to test behavioral pricing tactics. Here are three:

1. **Focus groups** provide customer feedback on potential behavioral tactics. They serve as small, controlled tests for understanding the thought processes driving product selection. You can watch how customers react as price anchors, deals, and other factors change.

   The results can steer you toward or away from some behavioral pricing tactics. In one focus group test we conducted, we gauged the impact of premium product anchors on a four-product lineup. Customers told us they would get very confused and leave a store display with the four products. This tactic just didn't work in the tests. The number of choices made the decision too complicated.

Had we blindly assumed the tactic would work as well as it did with the Internet start-up company mentioned earlier in this chapter, we would have led this company down the wrong path.

2. For online offers, **controlled A/B tests** let you assess click-through and conversion rates on different behavioral pricing tactics. They give you statistically significant data on the options with the best outcomes. But you must set up these tests correctly, which includes clearly defining your control and test cases. You must also divide the sample in each group so the customer populations are similar.

3. Run **large-scale experiments** when you need more information about customers than you can get from a controlled test. Studies can simulate a controlled test in survey mode; that saves you from having to launch a live test. This is particularly important in companies that must maintain price transparency at all times, and thus where launching a price test is not possible. An Internet company we worked with tested every behavioral tactic using off-line surveys before implementing them on its website. Such testing also allows you to try many ideas, even with the same people, because you can put them through many hypothetical situations.

As you can see, it's important to sweat these tests. They will help you set the right prices—and then stick to them.

Summary

Both rational and irrational factors drive customer purchases, and this applies to business customers and consumers alike. Behavioral factors influence whether customers purchase your product and which configuration they choose.

These six behavioral pricing tactics are among the most powerful for new product launches: the compromise effect, anchoring, price to signal quality, razor/razor blades, pennies-a-day pricing, and psychological price thresholds.

Before putting behavioral pricing tactics into play, you should try them out first through focus groups, controlled A/B tests, and large-scale experiments.

CEO Questions

1. Did we consider behavioral pricing tactics when developing the monetization strategy for our new product? If not, why not?
2. Of the six new-product behavioral pricing tactics (compromise effect, anchoring, price to signal quality, razor/razor blades, pennies-a-day pricing, and psychological price thresholds), which ones work for our new products? Why?
3. To be more specific: Do we have an anchor product for launch? Do we know the psychological price thresholds for our product? Have we spent time *framing* our pricing and not just coming up with a price point? How so?
4. How did we test the effectiveness of our behavioral pricing strategy? What were the results?

CHAPTER 12

Maintain Your Price Integrity

Avoid Knee-Jerk Repricing

S o now you know what it takes to maximize your new product's moneymaking potential before you bring it to market. But what if your product hits the market and the market is less than enthusiastic, and sales come in below expectation? After all, innovation does not come with a guarantee. What happens then?

What happens is that you will feel intense pressure from every corner of your organization to cut the price. That's almost always a bad idea.

In this chapter we will explain why this happens; how you can resist the pressure to lower the price you've so thoughtfully and carefully set (because you followed the steps outlined in the previous chapters); and what you can do instead.

When sales volumes don't meet projections in the first few weeks after launch, you've reached a moment of truth. And in that critical moment, far too many companies flinch, cutting their prices because they feel they must.

But reducing your price so soon sends an unintended message: that your new offering has less value than you initially communicated. In effect, you're telling potential buyers your company has made a mistake, in quality or otherwise. But even if you have a quality problem, a price cut won't fix it. In fact, it could make matters worse for you.

Here's a great example of a company that didn't flinch in the face of bad market news and resisted pressure to cut prices: Apple's April 2015 introduction of the much-hyped Apple Watch. At first, it was available only through Apple's website, and the cheapest version was priced at $349—not very cheap. With options including stainless steel and gold finishes, it could cost as much as $17,000—a true luxury purchase.

However, Apple's launch largely drew negative reactions. One stock analyst noted that a components supplier for the watch had produced fewer units than projected, hinting at underwhelming sales. His comment appeared in a July 31 *Wall Street Journal* headline that sniped, "Glimmers Emerge on Apple Watch Sales, and They're Not Pretty."[1]

Highly influential product reviewers gave the watch decidedly mixed reviews. Yahoo's David Pogue simply wrote, "You don't need one."[2] The *Wall Street Journal*'s Personal Technology Editor, Joanna Stern, gave it a positive review but told consumers they should wait for future releases, when the watch would be better.[3]

All of this was not what Apple wanted to hear. Yet despite the negative press, despite the warnings of purportedly in-the-know investment analysts and reviewers and the rumors of lagging sales, Apple did not drop its price. It held firm.

By October, after the summer of discontent, the lowest-price version of the Apple Watch was still $349.

Based on International Data Corporation and investment analyst estimates of Apple Watch sales from April through September 2015 (the second half of Apple's most recently completed fiscal year), Apple sold an estimated 8 million watches. Assuming most sold for the entry price of $349, that would make it a $2.8 billion product in its first six months of life.

Not too shabby for a new product.

By being resolute on prices, Apple avoided the typical response when new products meet mixed market reactions. Most companies quickly seek to placate customers, investors, and reviewers by cutting prices.

We call that losing price integrity. Products lose integrity when a company's knee-jerk response to a lukewarm early market reaction is to reduce their product's price in the first few months. You don't want to do that. Here's why.

The Importance of Patience in Maintaining Price Integrity

You don't want to lose price integrity because it creates two large hazards: *eroding profits* and *eroding customer lifetime value*. If you developed a price elasticity curve in your new-product plan, you did lots of hard work to arrive at your price. Don't be hasty and abandon all that work at the first sign of weak sales. You'll instantly give up the profit margin you targeted in your plan, and that profit will be gone forever.

Your business case should tell you how much profit you will sacrifice if you knock the price down 5, 10, or 20 percent. If you make such a price cut, it cannot be repaired easily. You'll wind up losing profits over the lifetime of your relationship with customers.

By making a knee-jerk price reduction, you may also do major damage to your brand. Cutting your price could permanently damage your brand by creating a negative perception of its quality. If your customers perceive your discount as signaling a lack of confidence in your product's value, they may not want to buy it at any price.

Holding onto your price is especially important in the first few months after a product arrives. Think of your pricing as the narrative you're creating about your product's value to customers. If you release a product and cut the price a short time later, what you're saying is, "Sorry, we made a mistake."

That said, sometimes it is not that black and white. Occasionally, you might have to cut your price to gain traction. If you do, make sure you are in the driver's seat to avoid rash moves. You need to plan this out and ensure you will get something in return if you give in on price. This would preserve your price integrity.

Why are knee-jerk price reductions so common for new products shortly after they hit the market? Well, when initial sales disappoint, that's a scary time for your team. It has invested a huge amount of time, energy, money, and career capital in the product launch. And now it's not going well. The temptation is to do something—right now!—to jump-start sales. The most obvious tactic is to cut the price.

One European company was not prepared for lower-than-expected sales of a new product. After its product hit the market, a competitor launched an aggressive effort to win back business in the Netherlands. Its sales manager for Holland (where the firm had a 70 percent market share) let his European head of sales know about that. The head of sales panicked, asking the CEO for his support to start discounting across Europe to keep sales high. The CEO, now worried about similar scenarios in markets around the world, told the global head of sales that he was free to make any pricing cuts he felt were necessary until the end of the year.

The firm's pricing strategy had wilted away *in a single day*—mainly because it was unprepared. (See Figure 12.1.)

But this is when successful innovators must remain cool, calm, and collected. If you haven't anticipated the possibility that sales might lag, and you haven't planned a response, this is no time to overreact. This is a time to stop and think. Either something has changed that you had not anticipated, or your original plan had a mistake. You will be much better off responding after you analyze what just happened rather than thrashing about with a new promotion or price cut.

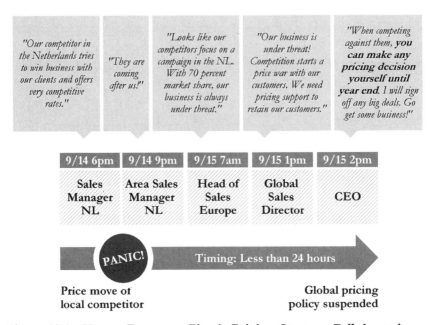

Figure 12.1   How a European Firm's Pricing Strategy Fell Apart in One Day

Showing patience about pricing is more important than fretting over sales numbers in the first months after a product launch.

Think price last.

How to Prepare for Post-Launch

The post-launch phase is typically hectic for the product team. Your product is finally in the market. Everybody is nervous. What are the initial customer reactions? Are they as good as we estimated? Are sales according to plan? What is the competition doing? And so on.

This is also a period in which many mistakes are made, because of the hectic pace and because actions are taken too spontaneously. Of course, you cannot plan everything in advance. But you can prepare for the most common reactions to avoid those spontaneous mistakes.

Here are some tips and tricks to keep in mind when preparing for post-launch.

1. Be patient addressing post-launch problems. They typically come in only four varieties, and you can prepare for them: (1) the market doesn't understand your product's value or you didn't explain it well; (2) your competition undercuts on price; (3) the competition launches a competing product; and (4) regardless of what the competition does, sales are below plan.

Being patient doesn't mean doing nothing. Rather, your firm must take all-hands-on-deck action to determine the cause and solution to your post-launch sales problem. Your task force should include all relevant business functions—sales, marketing, finance, product development, product management, and so on. The task force's first task is to pinpoint the reasons for the problem.

What if a competitor undercuts your price? This recently happened to an industrial products manufacturer. The firm asked us to determine the causes of disappointing sales of a new product. We examined everything. The culprit turned out to be a competitor's preemptive price cut. Anticipating our client's new product, the competitor offered huge temporary discounts that required high minimum purchase orders—all before our client had shipped one new product. By the time the product hit the market, customers had already stocked up on the competitor's discounted product and had no room for the new one, even though it had better quality.

Alternatively, your poor sales could be due to a feature problem, a distribution channel problem, a market awareness problem, or a quality problem. If you've done your pricing strategy work properly, you probably don't have a pricing problem. But you need to search far and wide for the source of the sales problem.

BMW did this in 2001. The company traced the reason behind the slow sales of its new 7 Series sedans. It found that European customers thought it was ugly. (Americans did not.) BMW decided to keep the car's price high. If people do not like the car, they will not buy it, even if it is 10 percent cheaper. Instead, BMW reduced its sales targets—not its price—and started working to design a face-lift right away.

2. Go beyond financial KPIs and track monthly outcomes. To measure the progress of new product launches, most companies track only financial key performance indicators (KPIs)—typically volume, revenue, and profit. These measures are grossly inadequate. You must also track sales, customer metrics, and operational metrics to keep a pulse on your new product after launch. Sales KPIs such as win-loss ratio, percent deviation of final price from target price, average sales quoting time, and price as a reason for win/loss will give you crucial insights on sales team performance.

If you are losing a high percentage of deals or your sales greatly and consistently deviate from your target plan, or if the sales force complains that price is the only reason they're losing deals, you could have a sales training problem. Or you may have to revisit your pricing guidance.

KPIs such as number of escalated deals (where someone higher in the organization approves a price), price changes upon deal escalation, and the number of rejected escalated requests will shed light on the health of your sales operations. If the approved prices are the same as requested prices, your sales operation has essentially instituted a rubber-stamping deal escalation process. A healthy escalation should always have reasonable amounts of pushbacks, changing prices on at least 30 to 40 percent of all deals.

By the way, be prepared to learn that your price might not be high enough. The number of escalated deals is an important KPI here. Having too few escalated deals could indicate the sales team is finding it too easy to sell. You need to ask yourself whether you priced your product high enough.

As a rule of thumb, at most 20 to 30 percent of your deals (depending on industry) should be escalated. Last, KPIs such as price difference achieved across segments and how often features are used indicate if your customer segmentation strategy is working and if your customers get value from your product.

3. Do deal "deconstructions" regularly. You need to dissect the reasons why you're winning and losing deals. You should bring together a cross-functional team (including sales, marketing, pricing, finance, and product) that was involved in the deal. The objective is to fully deconstruct the deal to understand whether product strategy, price strategy, and value communications were applied correctly. Through the deal deconstruction process, you can identify weaknesses and, more important, best practices to be applied to other deals. This step is important; it rallies the sales troops and gets them aligned on successful practices. But you must frame these deal deconstructions as a learning experience, with no repercussions for a particular function or group. You want an open and honest assessment of what happened and what else could have been done, not a finger-pointing session.

4. Advocate pricing patience: Make your team come up with three nonpricing actions before you approve a price decrease. Spontaneous price reactions—usually price decreases—are a typical problem in the post-launch phase. This is an understandable but wrong response. If sales are below plan or, say, competitors slash their prices, companies look for a quick fix. Lowering prices seems ideal: You can do it right away, without any investments, and see quick results. But, as we have stated in this and other chapters, this is extremely shortsighted. You run the risk of a significant downside.

Pricing patience is an important capability of every organization. But as simple as it sounds, it is the most difficult thing to get across to executive leadership. To maintain and institutionalize price patience, here's an approach that typically works: Before getting approval for a pricing reduction, make your team come up with three nonpricing alternatives. If the action must be a price cut, the team must explain why it is superior to the nonpricing alternatives.

Nonprice actions can include increasing advertising or adding to the value of the product. You could give customers a higher-end product at the same price. That will help you preserve your price. Even if you lower your price, you should ask customers for something in return. That something could be a longer-term commitment, greater volume, introductions to departments you have not sold to, endorsements and references, or joint press releases. Or it could be something else—as long as you're getting value for giving value.

A telecommunications firm in Latin America instituted the rule of forcing managers to come up with three nonprice actions before making price cuts. A board member of the company stated afterward: "This simple rule had the highest impact we have ever seen and instilled the right discipline we were seeking. It was simple and everybody understood it."

5. Before reacting on price, war-game your competition's counterreactions. This is another simple way of avoiding a knee-jerk price reduction. Write down how you expect your major competitors to react. Then simulate your position after that reaction: projected sales volumes, market share, profit, and so on. If you built your business case on the principles we presented in Chapter 9, you will be able to anticipate your competitors' reactions.

If your war-gaming shows you will be worse off if you reduce your price after the competition attacks, then don't. Look for other strategies. Why make things worse for yourself? This may sound like simple common sense, but you'd be surprised how many companies just don't budget for competitive reactions. If you took this approach to playing chess, you'd lose in a few moves.

6. Unusually high sales could be a high-class problem. This is the hardest problem to acknowledge, and it requires the same disciplined solutions as unexpectedly low sales.

You launch your new product and a wonderful thing happens: Sales volumes are way beyond expectations. Time to celebrate? Not so fast. You actually might have a problem—pricing lower than you needed to and leaving money on the table. That, of course, means you have a minivation. Did you simply misjudge your market size, as PlayMobil did when demand outstripped its supply? Or does your main competitor have manufacturing problems?

Of course, higher-than-expected sales is a good problem to have. That's why most companies do not view it as a problem or, if they do, they do not examine it. But too-high sales should be examined as rigorously as disappointing sales. So, once again, use a cross-functional team to find out the key reasons for the bigger-than-expected success. Then develop a plan that solves this "problem." If your product delivered more value than you thought customers were expecting, raise your price. But do it carefully, and in several steps.

We've seen this happen many times. In the 1970s, Mercedes introduced a new SL car. The model sold out in a few months, and would-be customers were put on a waiting list of two years! Mercedes learned its mistake quickly: Its price for the new SL automobile was about 20 percent too low. However, it could raise the price only 3 to 5 percent a year. So the automaker had to wait a few years until it reached the optimal price level. In doing so, Mercedes left hundreds of millions of dollars in revenue on the table.

The Mercedes example shows the importance of getting the right price at the beginning. When you don't—when you severely and needlessly underprice your new product—you should accompany price increases with small product improvements that justify the price hike.

You can also try to convince customers to accept longer delivery terms. But you'll need to manage that process with, for instance, frequent updates on the status of their orders. The idea is to lock in your customers as strongly as possible to avoid giving your competitors the sales just because you're having trouble keeping up with demand. Alternatively, you could make greater supplies of the premium versions of your product and reduce supplies of the entry-level version.

But in general, be careful about overly increasing the price if you find yourself in similar situations. Customers will despise you, and competitors will see an opportunity to undercut you. Alternatively you could accelerate the development of the next generation of products and offset prices in the future releases.

Price Wars: The Only Winning Move Is Not to Play

Price wars are about seeing who can lower prices the most. You don't want to start one, and you don't want to be the first one to move. Ultimately, a price war has only one winner: the supplier with the lowest cost. Most likely, that's not you.

Price wars have deadly consequences for new products, yet as our research shows, managers are not only strongly tempted to use them, but also in denial about how they start. In our firm's 2014 Global Pricing

Study, 83 percent of companies had felt increasing price pressures over the past two years. The biggest reason: low-price competition, either from new attackers or from incumbents. That pressure fuels price wars.

Everyone hates price wars, but no one wants to admit starting one. Fifty-eight percent of the survey participants said they were currently in a price war. (About 19 percent observed a price war in their industry but said it hadn't affected them.) An overwhelming 90 percent of those fighting a price war said that the competitors started it. A mere 5 percent said they started the price war intentionally, and 5 percent said they started it accidentally.

It's logically impossible that almost 90 percent of the time the price war is the other person's fault. That's denial. The truth is it takes two to tango.

With that in mind, CEOs and other business leaders can coach teams to treat price wars with extreme caution and not act on fear. At the root of such fear is misunderstanding: Competitor A wants to hit back at Competitor B because B stole a customer. Competitor C perceives that as a frontal attack, which provokes A and B to counterattack.

You need clear communications to avoid such misunderstandings. You must understand the reasons behind competitors' pricing moves. Leaders must ensure their teams know the unfavorable outcomes of price wars.

To avoid surprises that encourage price reduction thinking, put in place processes for updating models and forecasts regularly with new market information, then make people accountable for delivering on those forecasts. Make sure your models and forecasts include price elasticity assumptions.

Summary

Losing price integrity with a new product means you're cutting prices unnecessarily or too soon when sales are slower than expected. That erodes profit, customer lifetime value, and your brand.

To maintain price integrity, you need to take a cross-functional approach to diagnosing the problem. It may turn out you don't have a pricing problem at all. It may be the inability to communicate the substantial value of your product, a quality problem, a sales-force training problem, or another problem. Don't assume first that you put the wrong price on your product.

That requires patience. Successful innovators teach their teams how to avoid confusing pricing problems with the quality and communications problems that can beset a new product. They do not approve price cuts before their team has suggested at least three nonprice actions that could be taken.

If demand for the product far exceeds expectations, examine this "problem" rigorously as well. If the analysis suggests a large price increase, implement this in several small steps. Raising prices too fast can generate a customer revolt.

Perhaps most seriously, innovation leaders avoid price wars at nearly all costs. They realize it's a slippery slope to counter competitors' price reductions with more price reductions. Only the lowest-cost competitors can win that war.

CEO Questions

1. If sales are below target, what are the real reasons? How did we find out?
2. How would the suggested measures solve the problems we identified?
3. Does the way our product is perceived in the marketplace (by customers, channel partners, and so on) match the way we perceived it in our planning/business case? If not, what are we doing to correct that?
4. If competitors decreased their prices, why did they do so? What could be their goals?
5. What is the best possible reaction strategy? If the decision was to change our price, what nonprice measures were discussed? What competitive counterreaction do we expect? What situation will we be in after competitors react?
6. How was our sales force prepared for the launch? (You should ask for the messaging strategies they were given to respond to competitors' responses.)

Part Three

Success Stories and Implementation

CHAPTER 13

Learning from the Best

Successful Innovations Designed around the Price

Throughout the last nine chapters, we've used anecdotes from real companies to illustrate our nine steps for designing new products around a price. They have shown what happens when companies monetize innovation this way—the new revenue they can generate, the higher profits they can earn, the more on-target innovations they can invent, and the customer devotion they can create.

In this chapter, we go beyond anecdotes and present case studies of seven companies that have profited handsomely from the "design the product around the price" approach to monetizing innovation.

The cases are a strong mix, in multiple ways. They represent a mix of Business-to-Business (B2B) vs. Business-to-Consumer (B2C) examples, traditional innovations vs. disruptive innovations, and they span a wide variety of industry verticals including automotive, software, and pharma.

We begin with Porsche, an example you might remember from the beginning of the book. The Porsche case here is a deep dive into two highly successful products that enabled the firm to break out of its sports car niche: the Cayenne sport-utility vehicle and the Panamera sedan.

Following Porsche is the story of LinkedIn. The case study shows how LinkedIn has grown its business social network, including the recruiting-tools side of the marketplace. And grow it did: a 36-fold revenue spurt in that part of the business in just five years.

The third case study is Dräger Safety. It makes products that detect hazardous gas in underground places like mines and sewer systems. You'll read how Dräger Safety used the rules outlined in this book to launch a hit new gas detector.

Following Dräger, we get under the hood of Uber, a company that needs no introduction. If you are one of the millions who've hailed a cab by using Uber's wildly popular mobile app, you're already familiar with how it works. But we go beyond the app and show you that the pricing model of Uber is an innovation by itself.

Our fifth case study is on a company much older than Uber: Swarovski, the Austrian maker of luxury crystals. We will show how the firm revamped its product development process, which has reshaped the products it makes and how it capitalizes on them.

We follow Swarovski with the story of Optimizely. Its founders can lay claim to helping President Obama get elected to his second term. Optimizely is a software-as-a-service (SaaS) firm that helps companies improve their ability to test and personalize their online presence. The Optimizely case is worthwhile reading for start-up companies who want better ways to assess the market potential of a new product or service concept, what it must do for customers, and how to price it for success.

Our last case study is an innovative pharma company. We explain how this firm radically revised the way it assessed the commercial viability of the new drugs it develops. Due to confidentiality, we disguise the name of this firm.

The Porsche Story—Veering Off the Sports Car Track to Create Two Winning Vehicles

Porsche's approach to product development fully embodies the principles of this book. The German automaker's story demonstrates how executives can make innovations outside their core business pay off.

Porsche has followed the innovation paradigm of "design the product around the price" so rigorously during the two decades we've worked with them that it has become an integral part of the organization's culture. Not coincidentally, over that time, the company has generated impressive growth and innovated continuously, with consistently high profitability. In fact, in terms of profit per car sold (before tax and interest), Porsche tops the automotive industry.[1]

In 2013 and 2014, the Stuttgart-based company's operating margin was far above those of the three far bigger German luxury automakers Audi, BMW, and Mercedes.[2] And while Porsche may seem to be a small company, in fact its 2014 revenue ($19 billion) would rank it in the top half of America's Fortune 500 companies.

Since its founding in 1948, Porsche had been known in the twentieth century for only one kind of vehicle: high-performance sports cars. Consequently, its 2002 launch of the Cayenne, a sport-utility vehicle (SUV), seemed a huge gamble. However, few auto industry watchers were privy to the pricing and development research Porsche had done on the Cayenne long before the launch. The watchers couldn't know the Cayenne was less of a gamble than a rational line extension of the Porsche brand.

Porsche planted the seeds for the stunning success of its Cayenne—and later the Panamera, a family-minded, four-door luxury sedan launched in 2009—in its upfront product development. The mandate that Porsche's top executives handed down to the developers of both products was to rigorously determine what features, improvements, and other aspects of the cars customers truly valued, and how much they'd pay for them. This monetization principle was instrumental to the Cayenne's and later the Panamera's overwhelming market success.

So exactly what kind of success are we talking about? The Cayenne became Porsche's bestselling vehicle. In 2015, the company sold more than twice as many Cayennes as it sold 911s (about 73,000 versus 32,000).[3]

The Panamera has been a big hit as well over the last five years. Porsche sold about 22,000 Panameras in 2014, around 1,000 more than the Boxster roadsters it delivered that year.

Here's how Porsche pulled off these two new-product successes.

Atypically Early Customer Research

About four years before introducing the Cayenne and Panamera, Porsche conducted initial research, including high-level telephone surveys with potential customers in its most important markets.

Porsche's surveys confirmed what the company hoped they would: Customers would view a Porsche SUV and family sedan to be in keeping with the brand's image, and they wouldn't detract from its reputation for building leading sports cars. Just as important, the customer surveys provided detailed input that Porsche used to fine-tune each concept. For example, the Panamera's potential customers wanted a full-size sedan with plenty of trunk space, but with 100 percent Porsche (sportiness) DNA.

The customer surveys also helped Porsche find the proper price positioning for the two cars—that is, the price range, not the exact price point. For the Cayenne, the survey told Porsche it could charge a significant premium over other SUVs. For the Panamera, Porsche learned it could position the car at the upper luxury segment level (e.g. Mercedes S-Class) and thus significantly above the Mercedes CLS level (a four-door Mercedes coupe about the size of the Panamera, but with a 15 percent lower price than the S-Class). This was welcome news.

Finally, each survey gave Porsche important initial insights into both cars' market potentials and key segments. For example, many people liked the Porsche brand and would love owning a 911 sports car, but they couldn't afford it as an additional, just-for-fun car. But with the Cayenne or Panamera, a Porsche fan's everyday family car could be a Porsche. Moreover, Porsche 911 owners would not have to drive another brand's cars for family errands; they could make every vehicle in their garage a Porsche.

But Porsche is also a brand that polarizes consumers. From its surveys, Porsche found it had a customer segment that would never buy an SUV or sedan from Porsche, no matter how great the vehicle. With this information, Porsche had an initial quantitative sense of the market potential for Cayenne and Panamera. The survey data became crucial inputs to each vehicle's first business case.

Deciding Which Features Should Be In or Out

With initial research showing Porsche had real opportunities with an SUV and a four-door family sedan, the next step was to determine exactly what had to be in those vehicles. The company knows designing a viable vehicle means giving customers the features *they* want, not what Porsche wants. For Cayenne and Panamera, it conducted extensive value analysis (as discussed in Chapter 4) to determine the features for each car.

Porsche did its value analysis in so-called "car clinics" in exhibition halls, where it rented competitors' cars and presented them alongside the new Porsche models. It then invited potential customers to evaluate the vehicles.

Of course, part of what Porsche asked these potential customers about was their willingness to pay (WTP) for the cars. This, too, went above and beyond the industry's typical customer research. Most automakers only gather customer perceptions, asking such questions as, "Do you like the car overall, the front, the interior?" or "How do you like this feature?" and "Would you be interested to buy?" But they typically don't take the next crucial step and ask the WTP questions (as we explored in Chapter 4).

This information was indispensable to Porsche. It gave the firm specific price ranges for the Cayenne and Panamera. And by gauging customers' reactions to each proposed feature, the company had the data to make sure each car's design and product configuration were on target.

No feature is sacrosanct at Porsche; even the smallest features are carefully considered. For example, Porsche initially thought small hidden cup holders in the Panamera dashboard would be sufficient. But the research showed customers wanted much more. Managers decided to not only include the dashboard cup holders, but also to invest in an expensive redesign of the middle console to do full justice to what customers said they valued, wanted, and were willing to pay for.

A crucial design and product configuration decision for Porsche was to determine which features should *not* go into the Cayenne and Panamera. Here again, Porsche breaks from the pack. At many other automakers, arguments abound over why certain features *shouldn't* be added to a car. At Porsche, the burden of proof is always on why a feature *should* be included. Porsche puts every feature on trial. The argument that "everybody else does it in this segment" does not fly.

A key step in this process is deciding which features will be standard equipment and which will be options. What matters most is customers' value and WTP for each and every feature. If nearly all customers have a relatively high WTP for a certain feature, Porsche makes it standard in the vehicle. If only some customers will pay, Porsche makes it an option.

Porsche conducts this rigorous analysis on every one of its new car models. Consequently, its cars have some of the longest option lists of any automaker. But Porsche also makes more money from those options than most rivals do. And by turning so many features into options, the company avoids building an overloaded, overpriced base product.

At Porsche, the process of deciding which features are in or out is long and sometimes cumbersome. However, it enables the company to avoid costly feature mistakes that rivals make.

Creating a "Living" Business Case with True Price Optimization

For the Cayenne and Panamera, Porsche's business case included a market simulation model of the entire relevant market for the vehicles. Each business case showcased Porsche's customer WTP data, value analysis of features, and price elasticity. All of this was based on detailed research in the United States, Europe, Asia-Pacific, and all available market data (market size, sales volume of competitors, and so on).

Using its market simulation model, Porsche had a firm idea of consumer demand for the cars at each price point. (That should sound familiar; it's the price elasticity/demand curve we explored in Chapter 8.)

In this exercise, Porsche did not consider the Cayenne's impact in isolation. It also looked at the product's effect on the company as a whole: additional revenue, profit, and related factors. Porsche carefully analyzed whether new products would cannibalize sales of other Porsche cars. It only approved new products if they increased Porsche's *total* revenue. In the cases of the Cayenne and the Panamera, the company found cannibalization would be relatively low.

That holistic approach is rare in the auto industry, a business in which the number of car models has exploded since the 1990s—even though every market but China has shown little growth. The lineups of the major automakers are extensive. As such, Porsche's competitors are weighted down with car models that cannibalize sales of their other models. But for Porsche, adding new products that don't boost overall revenue is, as they say in Germany, *verboten*.

Porsche's business cases for the Cayenne and Panamera are living, continually updated documents. The company even revisits a business case after a vehicle's launch to check the accuracy of the sales forecast and capture lessons for the next new-product development process.

Appealing to the Early Adopters: Porsche's Skimming Strategy

From its customer research, Porsche knew its new SUV and family sedan would stir high interest. Potential customers had told Porsche they had a high WTP for both the new cars; they saw real value in them. Therefore, for the Cayenne and later the Panamera, Porsche initially came to market with only the premium eight-cylinder engine models. The company waited a year before rolling out less expensive six-cylinder models.

That allowed Porsche to skim the cream of its market segment— the customers who wanted to be the first on their block to own a sporty SUV or family sedan from Porsche. Those customers had to buy the higher-priced (and higher-margin) models, even if they didn't value an eight-cylinder engine.

Porsche's C-Suite Task: Planting New-Product Monetization into the Company's DNA

Porsche's top managers, right up to the CEO and the board, drove the "design the product around the price" innovation approach. Through their conversations and their actions, Porsche's C-suite has infused the principle into the company's DNA.

The company has long referred to its DNA as "The Porsche Principle." This broader guiding philosophy is to "always get the most out of everything . . . to translate performance into speed—and success—in the most intelligent way possible." But to make monetizing innovation part of that philosophy, Porsche's top executives knew they constantly had to lead by example.

How did they do that? When the firm's product developers started the Cayenne project, the C-suite rented and test drove rivals' cars to gain firsthand knowledge about their road performance.

In its car clinics, focus groups, and other research activities, Porsche's top executives eagerly spoke to participants to gather feedback. They also intensively watched focus group videos and returned to the product development teams with specific questions. These actions sent an inarguable message to the teams: *This exercise is important.*

That kind of top-level interest and support, for customer research on a new car's value and customers' WTP for it, is rare among the world's automakers—and we know most of them. Top management also made sure that all relevant functions—sales, marketing, product, strategy, after sales, market intelligence, finance, controlling etc.—were represented in the new product team. With that approach, all monetization aspects were evaluated holistically, if possible in a quantitative way. Decisions which would only support sub-goals of specific functions but contradict the overall Porsche goal were avoided.

Finally, the teams had to present the monetization strategies for the new Cayenne and Panamera to the full board. That, too, created a very clear message to Porsche's product development teams—the board recognized the importance of the new Cayenne and Panamera *and* their monetization strategies. Needless to say, it also helped the teams get the time and money necessary to design and price those products right.

And *right* they were: By 2014, Porsche was selling more than twice as many nonsports cars (about 135,000 Cayennes, Panameras, and a newer SUV called the Macan) as the sports cars and roadsters it's been identified with for nearly 70 years.

Porsche is a study in how a company can transform itself through disciplined innovation. It succeeded by making bigger, bolder new product decisions based on painstaking upfront work on exactly what customers needed, valued, and were willing to pay for.

LinkedIn—Monetizing the World's Largest Professional Network

LinkedIn was launched in 2003 out of the Silicon Valley living room of entrepreneur Reid Hoffman. By "connecting talent with opportunity at massive scale," the site has grown to more than 400 million members worldwide. A driving factor of LinkedIn's success has been the values and principles driving day-to-day decisions. CEO Jeff Weiner explains, "There are six values . . . and by far the most important one is members first. We as a company are only as valuable as the value we create for our members."[4]

The Mountain View, California, firm started with a concrete goal to create economic opportunity for every member of the workforce. LinkedIn has done so by giving its members a platform through which they connect with others, find job opportunities, and share knowledge.

While the service started off as free, LinkedIn had clear monetization goals. From the start, the team was highly focused on the members-first philosophy, adding value to members and monetizing that value. The strategy has paid off handsomely: LinkedIn is now a $3 billion business and operates in more than 200 countries.

Designing Products Based on the "Members First Principle"

From day one, LinkedIn held an unwavering focus on delivering value to members. The benefits of this focus are evident in the company's success. Here are but a few examples of products that have fueled LinkedIn's fortunes, starting with a product that allows members to send private e-mails through the LinkedIn platform.

Designing and Pricing a LinkedIn E-mail System Right Building the largest professional network provides LinkedIn with a flurry of competitive advantages. One of these is the ability to let you contact professionals you don't personally know, but want to network with. This ability was productized as the LinkedIn InMail.

Since its inception, InMail has been a premium feature. The price, first set at $10 per InMail, seemed expensive. However, LinkedIn strongly believed that messaging someone you didn't know was a privilege. After confirming with customers that they valued the feature (and were willing to pay for it), LinkedIn was ready to go to market with the InMail product.

Incidentally, the higher price also generated positive externalities for members. Setting the price at a premium preserved the quality of the marketplace and gave the service additional legitimacy. Had InMail been free, spam messages may have flooded members' inboxes and devalued the network. In this case, a higher price actually *increased* value for customers.

Before going to market, the "members-first" philosophy drove the LinkedIn team one step further—recognizing the uncertainty members faced whenever they sent an InMail to a stranger, the team created a response guarantee. Members would only be charged for an InMail if they received a response. With powerful value messaging to communicate the credibility and guarantee of the InMail, member adoption of InMail rose significantly. In the many years since its inception, it has become a "leader" feature for members with paid subscriptions.

But that's not the end of the story. Fast forward to January 2015. LinkedIn tweaked its InMail policy, again in a way that put members' needs first. The adoption of InMail had grown significantly, and LinkedIn needed to reevaluate the overall health of the marketplace. The new policy flipped the original on its head: If a member received a response to an InMail within 90 days after they sent it, it would be credited back to them (and they wouldn't pay for it). If there was no response, you would pay for the InMail. The policy discouraged recruiters from sending generic InMails that generated few responses and thus created a poor member experience.

We must point out that LinkedIn changed its InMail policy 12 years after the site opened for business. Had the company launched its InMail program with this policy, few members would have used the service; the site didn't have enough members at the time. It made sense only when LinkedIn had become highly popular, with hundreds of millions of members.

Creating Products for Recruiters and Members   From the beginning, LinkedIn was keen on monetizing both sides of the two-sided marketplace it served. On one side would be members, who created résumé-type profiles and built their professional connections through the platform. On the other side would be recruiters. LinkedIn is one of those rare two-sided marketplaces that monetizes both sides. Most two-sided marketplaces monetize only one side—a missed opportunity!

LinkedIn gave the recruiters something they had dreamt about for years: ready access to professionals who were *not* looking for work. Nothing like it existed in the market. Like with InMail, LinkedIn set about designing a suite of recruiter products while keeping a focus on monetization by proactively identifying recruiter needs, values, and WTP. The results are stunning—the growth of Talent Solutions has been explosive and has continued unabated. By 2014, it had become a $1.3 billion business. And in 2015, revenue was 41 percent higher than the year before.

Meanwhile, on the member side, a growing percentage of users are signing up for premium subscriptions: 18 percent of LinkedIn's total revenue came from these subscriptions in 2015. These users pay extra for e-mail and search tools that help them find jobs and generate business leads.

Instituting a Rigorous Monetization Process

So how has LinkedIn gone from zero to $3 billion in revenue in a dozen years? The answer is nicely summed up by Andrew Freed, the head of Talent Solutions Marketing: "LinkedIn has put in place a rigorous process for monetizing innovation and has embedded that into the core philosophy and approach to bringing products to market."

Josh Gold, LinkedIn's global head of pricing strategy, describes how the company's new process works for monetizing innovations this way:

> *At LinkedIn we typically use a multi-step, iterative process to test new concepts with customers. As our confidence in the product's potential increases, we invest more time and energy into optimizing our go-to-market monetization strategy.*

More specifically the typical process steps are as follows:

- **Hypothesis development:** Innovation teams start with identifying the white space. They ask questions like "Where can we create and deliver differentiated value?" and "Which markets are underserved?"
- **Internal refinement:** A cross-functional group of internal experts comes together to refine and pressure test the hypotheses. These discussions bring together teams like marketing, sales, pricing, and product design.
- **Initial customer validation:** The team then starts validating product-market fit, perceived value, and WTP with target markets. Methods used include value trade-offs, ideal package (i.e. product configuration) creation, unaided WTP, and purchase probability (as outlined in Chapter 4). This typically occurs prior to writing any code.
- **The gut-check:** The concept must then pass an internal "smell test." The team typically pitches the product concept to LinkedIn sales reps—the people at the firm who are closest to customers. If both customers and the LinkedIn's sales team give the concept a thumbs-up, the product team has the green light to start developing it.
- **Building a precise model:** After this stage, typically a larger scale quantitative study is commissioned to get more precise inputs (on product configuration, price models, and of course the WTP), in order to build a robust business case (as outlined in Chapter 9). Such findings

are constantly fed to the product teams so that things are moving lock, stock, and barrel.

- **Paid pilots:** Instead of giving the product to beta-testers for free, LinkedIn typically goes to market and *sells* the beta version of the product. Why? It provides another layer of validation for the monetizing potential of the new service based on the value delivered. In the words of Josh Gold, "Our beta users have skin in the game by actually paying for the pilot tests." And there is a clear impact of having skin in the game: It generates better concept-testing feedback from the testers. It also allows LinkedIn to fine-tune the price levels prior to a full go-to-market launch.

In summary, what LinkedIn has is an extremely collaborative, parallelized approach with an extraordinary amount of rigor to monetization and commercialization. This robust process speaks volumes to LinkedIn's unwavering focus on providing value and identifying the monetization potential of that value long *before* that product comes to market. This is typically how LinkedIn designs the product around the value and the price.

Looking Ahead

Over the recent years, the firm has brought several new promising products to market. One such product is Elevate, launched in 2015. Products such as Elevate are crucial to LinkedIn's further evolution as an invaluable online tool to help employees progress in their careers, and employers find the people they need. Like Andrew Freed said, embedding the monetization process into the core philosophy and approach to bringing products to market at LinkedIn is the key to its continued success.

Dräger—Collecting the Specs for Successful Industrial Products before Engineering

Porsche vehicles and LinkedIn recruiting tools have an appeal that any consumer can understand. But Dräger Safety, Inc. makes products that most people will never see. A $1 billion unit of a $3 billion German company, Dräger Safety manufactures gas detection equipment. Its customers are mining, sewer cleanup, and other industrial companies that must keep worker environments free of toxic fumes.

Yet the rules of "design the product around the price" innovation apply just as much to B2B products like Dräger Safety's industrial tools as they do to consumer offerings. Dräger Safety has reaped the rewards of developing new products this way. Its experience illustrates the importance of talking to customers early about their needs and their WTP for products that meet those needs. Dräger Safety also shows the value of creating sales and marketing messages that articulate a product's value to customers and make it a must-have. Finally, the firm demonstrates why altering the strategy and culture of product development is just as important as changing the process—and more difficult.[5]

Dräger Safety began learning the power of this approach in the early 2000s, when Ralf Drews started running its global R&D. Drews, who joined the firm in 1991 as a mechanical engineer, had climbed the ranks to become global R&D vice president. In 2008, he was promoted to president and CEO.

The company had a long history of manufacturing gas detection equipment, air quality monitors, masks, and other safety tools. Its engineers had spent decades developing devices to help make tough jobs safer. By 1937, the firm created the Dräger Tube, a portable gas detector that measured the levels of carbon monoxide, methane, and other harmful gases in a mine.

Decades later, after a complete rethinking of its innovation process, Dräger Safety brought to market another industry-leading product, the X-zone 5000 gas detector. Let's examine the before-and-after picture of Dräger Safety's innovation process.

The Limitations of the Old Innovation Process

At the time Drews took over the firm's R&D, its longstanding product development process typically began with a bunch of engineers brainstorming in a whiteboard-filled conference room. As Drews says, it was emblematic of the so-called "fuzzy front end" of innovation—when a new product is often a nebulous concept.

The primary input for product development came from Dräger Safety salespeople. From their rounds with customers, they came back to R&D with customer suggestions and complaints. However, used as customer research for product development purposes, such feedback had severe limitations. First, it was anecdotal and thus might not broadly represent the customer base. Second, it reflected needs the customers could articulate and thus left out their unarticulated desires. Third, it was gathered in an unstructured way, which made it hard to know the relative importance of any customer suggestion. Finally, it was filtered through the eyes of the sales force and thus wasn't direct from the horse's mouth.

For those reasons, while it was valuable, the sales force's input couldn't drive product development, Drews believed.

There was one other not-so-tiny flaw in using the sales force as the firm's market research team: The sales team would come to R&D and say the price of a proposed new product had to go down and the performance had to go up at the same time. Not a big surprise. No salesperson wants price to be a customer objection. However, if the price had to go down, that meant the firm's production cost had to drop as well, otherwise the price reduction would pinch margins.

Competitors' products were another input to new product designs. When competitors added features to their own products, Dräger Safety salespeople lobbied hard to match the features.

The scene at Dräger Safety provided the perfect recipe for a feature shock. Nobody rigorously examined the value each feature delivered to customers. The firm's entire product definition process was unstructured—in part because customers were treated as one segment and because Dräger had no systematic way to prioritize their needs.

As a result, Dräger Safety created too many products overloaded with features and overengineered to deliver those features. That led to lots of overpromising on customer delivery dates because the company's feature-laden products were a bear to manufacture.

The messy product development process created internal havoc as well. Frequent changes to product specifications delayed schedules, which deeply frustrated the R&D team. On top of that, the sales force applied constant pressure to reduce prices, which in turn forced Dräger Safety engineers to change their designs in order to trim manufacturing costs.

In short, the fuzzy front end of innovation led to overengineered, one-size-fits-all product specifications, scope creep (in which the list of features kept growing), an unclear selling story, and mediocre product margins.

Bringing Innovation to the Innovation Process

When Drews became global head of R&D in 2000, he said "enough" to the old product development process. He forced R&D to flip it: Start with the true voice of the customer, not the internal view.

"Thinking about how to monetize a product during the front end of innovation gives a firm a very good chance that it can come up with something great," Drews says. Without it, he believes, firms are likely to create an average or losing product that tries to do too many things. "A powerful innovation approach is to find out both the articulated and unarticulated needs of the customer," he says. The unarticulated needs can lead to the biggest innovations, Drews says. "The key is to understand how much value your innovation provides customers in solving *their* problem."

At Drews's insistence, Dräger Safety reversed its innovation process. It began with engineers and others from the new product team going out in the field and observing customers. The X-zone 5000 gas detector started this way, with Drews himself observing customers who drilled for oil and gas and firms that deal with sewage. "You really want to understand how people are dealing with your equipment," he says.

For example, Drews and other Dräger Safety employees went to such dark places as pipelines and parts of Hamburg's sewage canals to talk to the workers who spend 80 to 90 percent of their job time underground. The Dräger Safety crew asked them for pointed advice on how to improve the firm's products. They spoke with workers who monitored manholes and operated underground in sewage canal pipes. These workers, called testers, must continually sample the air from canals to detect toxic or combustible gases.

The interviews found the testers had two main problems. First, pedestrians often accidently kicked the gas detectors into a canal because they didn't see them. Second, when it rained, a tester had to stay out in the rain rather than work from a truck, because the detector's visual alarm wasn't bright enough and the audio alarm wasn't loud enough.

Dräger Safety's new X-zone 5000 portable gas detector addressed both issues. Resembling a mini R2-D2 from the *Star Wars* movies, the small, three-legged device stands 20 inches high and 12 inches wide and weighs in at 15 to 22 pounds, depending on the size of the battery. The $4,300 product provided big process cost savings for customers, despite commanding a price premium of 35 percent above its next-best competitor.

The X-zone 5000 became a huge hit. Product sales were 250 percent higher than expected, margins proved far above average, and the company won a German safety award for the product.

So what led to the X-zone 5000's roaring success? Dräger Safety had shown the concept of X-zone 5000 to customers before engineers even started to develop it. Customers loved how the X-zone 5000 addressed their biggest pain points, with its distinct visual appearance and improved alarms.

The new innovation process produced another benefit, one that went beyond creating an on-target product: pre-selling the new product long before it was available. "By doing such voice-of-the-customer research, you can 'test-sell' your product even though you haven't even started the product development process yet," Drews says. "Then, when the customer asks when he can have it, you know you created a very powerful product idea."

A company will have far more confidence that its product development investment will pay off. "With this kind of upfront customer feedback, it is much easier for top management to approve significant funding for a new product," Drews says.

Institutionalizing the Innovation Monetization Process

After it saw the big financial return on the X-zone 5000 and several other successful pilot cases, Dräger Safety decided it had to institutionalize this new product development approach for every new product idea. The new process (called CPM, for Customer Process Monitoring) begins before a new product is designed. The research and value analysis part of CPM has five phases:

1. **Defining where to focus the target market in terms of geographic region, application, and industries.** Dräger Safety concentrates on its most important industries and chooses product features largely on the basis of what those markets require.
2. **Identifying key decision makers and influencers.** In Dräger Safety's case, it's almost always a customer's buying center—a group consisting of a safety engineer, procurement professional, and a

technical or plant manager. Each person has different requirements and degrees of influence on the buying decision.

3. **Launching qualitative research to observe and interview customers in their environments.** In this phase, the company gathers invaluable data on how customers will use the product. The firm also identifies unarticulated and articulated needs (as we discussed in Chapter 4), especially those that lead to "wow" features.

4. **Conducting a quantitative survey.** While the qualitative research provides a wellspring of feedback on relevant features, the quantitative survey assesses customers' WTP in absolute terms, and relative to competitors' offerings. The company uses conjoint analysis and other techniques. From this research, Dräger Safety identifies needs-based segments, customer groups with homogeneous requirements, values, and WTP. For example, for the X-zone 5000 research, sewage customers said a watertight housing was very important and they were willing to pay for it. In contrast, petrochemicals customers showed less interest and almost no WTP for that feature.

5. **Assessing competitive products.** Before it establishes the value proposition and selling story of a new product, the firm spends considerable time to understand the strengths and weaknesses of competing products. "Your product cannot and does not have to be better than competitors' products in every function," says Drews. "You must pick your battles so that your product is stronger than competitors' products in key functions for your target segments."

As a result of its CPM process, Dräger Safety's new-product plans are no longer ruled by anecdotal evidence from salespeople about the importance of certain features. The company has learned that many proposed product features are of little interest to customers, and thus they have little willingness to pay for them. This was a revelation to Dräger Safety's R&D team. Knowing which features customers don't care about and won't pay for has helped the team to significantly reduce the cost of new products.

With all this information, Dräger Safety then created a full-fledged product concept. Features that differentiate a product and generate value for customers (especially those "wow" features) pass the test; they're baked into the product concept. Costly and unimportant features fail the test, and they are omitted.

Because Dräger Safety is vitally interested in meeting the often varying needs of different segments, it creates variations of each product. This was the case with the X-zone 5000 gas detector. For example, the sewage market version of the product came in a more expensive, watertight case.

Creating Winning Sales and Marketing Messages

After Dräger Safety creates a robust product concept, its next monetization task is to create the all-important messages for marketing and sales campaigns. The first job here is creating *selling stories*—narratives that articulate the product's value to each influencer and decision maker in the purchasing process. But before it starts printing marketing and sales collateral—indeed, even before it starts developing the product itself—Dräger Safety gauges customer reactions to its selling stories.

You may be thinking, how can you ask customers about a new product that you haven't yet developed? How can customers react to something they can't see? Dräger Safety creates simple presentations that show key product benefits—exactly what customers get if they purchase the device. These presentations vary by customer role. For example, the purchasing function gets a presentation on the benefits it cares about. The safety engineers get a presentation on what matters to them, and so on.

These selling stories generate important conversations with customers—conversations that give Dräger Safety a much finer sense of how much customers want the product and what they'd shell out for it. All these conversations happen before a single product is put through the manufacturing process. In fact, they take place even before Dräger Safety's product design professionals start the engineering process. These conversations are critical because it is far better to "fail early"—to learn what customers do and don't value—before kicking off product development.

Only when Dräger Safety gets an overall positive market reaction to a new product concept will it launch into its product development process. That gives the R&D team a clear mandate and much higher confidence in the product specs.

Since it added CPM to the beginning of its product development process, Dräger Safety hasn't had to change product specifications in the product development phase—and if they had to change, it was tweaks rather than drastic modifications Drews says. This is the design the product around the price paradigm at its best.

Embedding Monetization into Dräger's Innovation DNA

Dräger Safety's version of monetizing innovation—of creating products around a price—has taken firm hold. The CPM work that started with the X-zone 5000 product remains an integral part of the firm's innovation process.

So how exactly did Drews bring CPM into the organization and make it stick? Launching successful pilot tests was a key element. While he headed R&D, Drews collaborated with his counterpart in marketing to develop the CPM process and institute it in a few pilot projects. The X-zone 5000 was one of them. Another pilot test, for a new "alcotest" product—shorthand for an alcohol breath-detecting device—became a major success as well. Sales of an entirely new generation of alcotest product were 10 times higher than the version it replaced. And the new product's profit margins were significantly greater than prior ones.

These pilots proved to be very successful. They convinced Dräger Safety of the power of its CPM innovation process. Before long, the company couldn't imagine doing R&D any other way. Now all relevant Dräger Safety innovations must move through the CPM process. Each new idea is presented to the firm's product portfolio board (which includes C-level managers), and the board makes the ultimate project decision: a yes or a no. Major projects that have not gone through the CPM process are not approved.

To make the CPM process stick in the organization, Drews and his peers from the marketing department hired people to run the new CPM group. The CPM managers were made part of the marketing/ product management function. In doing so, Drews and his marketing colleagues made a bold move to bridge the gap between R&D and marketing and demonstrate that the entire product development process had to shift from inside-out to outside-in thinking, rooted in customer desires.

As a result, Dräger Safety's product development projects are now spearheaded by CPM managers from marketing/product management. For Dräger Safety, outside-in thinking has become part of its innovation DNA.

But while such organizational and process changes are important to making a CPM process stick, they aren't the most critical ones, Drews believes. Changing culture and strategy are more important—and more difficult. In culture, a corporate DNA of "product first, customer second" is, in Drews words, a "huge animal" to address. In such companies, a CPM-like process is hard to accept at first because executives fondly remember times in the 1970s and 1980s when product development delivered big wins. When asked to institute a process like CPM today, executives will say, "Our old approach to product development worked before; why would it be different now?"

Companies can be equally resistant to the strategic changes that a CPM approach forces on management: a crystal-clear focus on key market segments. In developing a new product, the CPM approach requires management to decide which customer segments to emphasize over other segments. Sales-driven companies can perceive this as heresy; focus and priorities will limit sales opportunities, so goes the impression. That, of course, is a wrong perception. (See Chapter 5.)

These mindset, cultural, and strategic changes can only be driven from the top of an organization. That's the way Drews did it when he ran R&D at Dräger Safety, and later when he became CEO. But, he adds, the changes must also be driven by executives in R&D, product management, and marketing—the business functions critical to product innovation.

"Creating a CPM type of process is relatively simple," Drews sums up. "But deploying it and making sure it stays in place for every new product can be like climbing the Mount Everest."

Uber—Monetizing a Disruptive Innovation through Innovative Price Models

You want supply to always be full, and you use price to basically either bring more supply on or get more supply off, or get more demand in the system or get some demand out. It's classic Econ 101.

—Travis Kalanick, CEO and co-founder of Uber[6]

Uber is redefining the American success story. It is remaking an entire industry, changing the way we think about how people get from point A to point B. Although it is still privately traded as of this writing, Uber has one of the highest valuations of any U.S. company. It only took Uber five and a half years to surpass the valuation of 107-year-old General Motors.[7]

It has reached this pinnacle seemingly by magic. As others have noted, Uber, the biggest new player in the transportation sector, owns no cars. Wikipedia describes them simply as "makers of a mobile application providing access to vehicles for hire." Whereas Walmart stocks goods and Apple builds computers, Uber doesn't own or make or even store what it sells.

Think, for a moment, of the scope of that accomplishment! Imagine taking on a major sector of the U.S. economy, dominated by a set of well-capitalized players, without significant working capital and without inventory.

Those who know Uber best, the insiders, have an opinion on the company's amazing rise. They say Uber's success was powered by its revolutionary approach to monetization.

Uber Designed Its Innovation around the Price

There are two levers to Uber's pricing strategy—the dynamic piece and penetration pricing. Let's look at both of these closely.

Part One: The Dynamic Piece   What accounts for Uber's success? Fans of the service will point to the app, which allows you to know exactly when you'll be picked up, track your driver's progress, estimate your fare, and pay automatically with a pre-loaded credit card. All of these are great features, but no matter how amazing Uber's app may be, no matter how clean the vehicles or magical the customer experience, none of that counts when a would-be rider sees the dreaded words, *no cars available.*

According to Bill Gurley, an early investor and current Uber board member, that was one of the company's biggest challenges.

Even among the all-star team of Uber insiders, Gurley stands apart. On *Forbes'* Midas List, dubbed "The World's Smartest Tech Investors," Gurley has also served on the boards of GrubHub, Zillow, NextDoor, and OpenTable among several others. His blog, *Above the Crowd*, is a must-read for the growth capital community. And before he became famous, he was the lead analyst for the IPO of a little-known company at that time, Amazon.

Early on, according to Gurley, Uber had discovered that they were dealing with a highly price-sensitive crowd. "It became very obvious very early in the company that the elasticity was off the charts," Gurley says in a conversation he had with us.[8]

The key insight was that this did not just apply to the riders. It applied to the drivers as well.

Faced with a shortage of drivers to pick up weekend bar patrons just after last call, Uber "messed around with incentives," says Gurley. The results were surprisingly strong. By offering additional money, they were able to "move supply off the edge" and get more drivers picking up Bostonians at 2 a.m.

The company could have attacked the car availability problem by forcing drivers to sign up for quotas, as some firms do. They could have insisted on regular hours, graveyard shifts, and forced scheduling. Instead, they solved it in the most elegant way possible: with a monetization model.

This is what Gurley refers to as the "dynamic piece," also known as Uber's *surge pricing*. Today, in times of peak demand, the company charges customers more for a ride than during non-peak times. In Chapter 7, we discussed this approach under the name "dynamic pricing," one of the key monetization models powering many successful businesses.

In effect, Uber's platform has a customer pay the driver more during high-demand periods, so that the driver is willing to brave the elements—or skip their own New Year's Eve party—to give the customer a ride. If Uber had not implemented the dynamic pricing model, the alternative would have been to leave numerous customers in the lurch, complaining about availability and reliability. Such customer dissatisfaction would have severely hurt adoption. Instead, the dynamic model intentionally reduces demand and at the same time increases supply in order to maximize availability and reliability.

This model creates a platform where supply is controlled not by the company but by the independent contractors. And it works brilliantly. "I still find it *the* most fascinating piece of Uber, because we do no scheduling whatsoever," says Gurley. "We do millions of drives a day and we never tell a driver when to go to work."

Getting the Language Right   In Chapter 10, we described how value communication can sometimes be the most difficult task of all. This was one area where even Uber stumbled, discovering just how hard it was to communicate that dynamic pricing was actually good for the customer.

Many companies use dynamic pricing to charge more during peak periods. Think of a resort in the summer months or a stadium-adjacent parking lot on game day.

This is usually done to boost profits. But as discussed previously, Uber's goal was ensuring 24/7 availability of cars, come rain, sleet, or snow. Rather than pocketing the surcharge, Uber passes most of it on to their drivers.

Unfortunately, the term surge pricing does not communicate the value Uber brings to the rider, who otherwise might have been stranded: As Gurley points out, Uber's peak pricing typically occurs when every form of transportation is under stress.

"I would have called it availability pricing in hindsight," Gurley smiles. "Funny thing," Gurley adds, "Travis wanted to be extremely transparent with the customer and felt the name helped achieve that goal."

Part Two: Penetration Pricing   If Uber's drivers are price sensitive, its riders are doubly so. This meant that despite early positioning that framed Uber as a luxury brand—the company's original slogan was "Everyone's Private Driver"—Uber could not charge luxury prices.

In some ways, their customers' low willingness to pay forced the company's hand. "I would argue that it is tautological that you need to be the low cost provider when you have such high price elasticity," Gurley said. "Otherwise another person can come under you and take massive share because the consumer is telling you that price matters."

In order to get prices as low as possible, Uber knew it would have to cut down on its drivers' idle time. "Surge pricing plays a huge factor there," says Gurley. "It tells people when to be where."

As they get accustomed to the system, a driver's utilization rate, which is the percentage of time they actually have a customer in the car, picks up. Drivers and riders naturally find their fit in the company's highly-efficient marketplace.

As utilization rates increase, Uber can drive the cost down even more, generating what Gurley calls the "Uber virtuous cycle."

The company's key insight was that this pricing strategy—"pricing low on purpose," in Gurley's words—was critical to gain large market share with customers. "It is a longer-term game, because with lower margins you've got to get much bigger. But it was the right play," says Gurley. As discussed in Chapter 8, penetration pricing is a bigger (and riskier) commitment since with pricing low you operate at razor thin margins and you need to get much bigger fast. Few companies get it right; Uber was one of them.

More importantly, the price low strategy opened the door to a much larger consumer base. Having made it "a company mission" to push the price ever lower, Gurley says, "suddenly you can reach a market that is 20 times larger than what you would have had had you not messed with price."

In a famous blog post, Gurley wrote that Uber's skeptics did not fully "consider the impact of price on demand." He asked, "What if someone could run a more convenient, safer service at a much lower price and with much higher availability? You would end up with dramatically more rides—and that is exactly what is happening." He then pointed to the multiple markets critics had not considered, from public transportation to rental cars.

Even walking is not immune: If you open up Google Maps for certain destinations, you will be shown an Uber price as an alternative to taking a stroll—a brilliant way to pose the question, "How much is your time worth?" Gurley told us that this is all part of the overall corporate approach to pricing. "The lower I can get the price point, the more types of scenarios I can get the customer to think of this as an alternative to whatever the substitute was—public transport, renting a car, borrowing a car, owning a car, etc."

My Other Car Is an Uber   That last part is one of Uber's big upcoming moves: The ride service as an alternative to car ownership itself. Uber's big goal is to be a substitute for the automobile in your garage. Gurley points out that your car sits idle "95 percent of the time." If Uber can get the price per ride low enough, and ensure high enough availability, it just may make sense to sell your car and use the proceeds to pay your Uber bill, or avoid buying a car altogether. From a financial point of view, Uber simply substitutes for ownership.

To reach that level of affordability, Uber's leadership dreams of someday reaching "the Perpetual Ride," where a driver has a rider at all times in his or her car. That would mean 100 percent utilization. But could the company do even better?

UberPool may be the answer. By harnessing Uber's mighty math department, the company has created a system to bring together like-minded riders in big cities such as San Francisco and New York. Some customers actually prefer the experience, citing the potential to meet new people in a stress-free environment. Tourists and other visitors find it an easy way to get tips about the city they are visiting.

But the best thing about it may be the price. Since one driver is now carrying multiple riders, UberPool allows the company to exceed prior utilization, making the service proportionally more affordable. This not only makes Uber an increasingly-reasonable substitute to car ownership, but it makes it a remarkable challenger to existing forms of public transportation.

The "Everyone" Segmentation Plan Of course, some people will not take UberPool, no matter how reasonably priced it may become. As we discussed in Chapter 6, that is how you define a segment: a set of people who are willing to pay more for given features than other people, because they value them more.

For example, some people may be willing to pay a premium to arrive in convenience. These riders are a natural fit to the SUVs and limousines that make up UberBlack. Other riders simply want the no-frills privacy of UberX. Uber has been reaching new segments organically by creating customer experiences around different values and the segment's willingness to pay.

Not All Dollars Are Created Equal In addition to understanding what each of its customer segments wants and values, Uber understands what they want to avoid. That's why one of the best parts of Uber is that you do not have to tip. In fact, there's no way to do so. As with most of Uber's pricing model, this is by design.

"Travis could have very easily built a tip tool," Gurley notes. "One of the most keen insights in the history of the company is that the tipping moment causes anxiety. He wanted people to think it was their car and just get in and get out."

In Chapter 11, we discussed behavioral pricing tactics. You might think a dollar spent on a fare is the same as a dollar spent on a tip. Uber saw that from a behavioral standpoint, this was simply not true.

"I think a lot of these pricing and product decisions are about taking the consumer out of the uncomfortable or anxious place they might be at," says Gurley. "You need to remove the burden of decision making as to whether you need to give 5 percent or 10 percent when you are in a hurry; in exchange your customers would love you for it."

Summary: New Roads

Uber plans to eventually reach everyone. This means creating products to appeal to the elderly and differently abled (UberASSIST) with high-access vehicles manned by drivers capable of performing CPR. It even means UberChopper for those who can afford to pay to arrive ASAP. It also means UberEATS for people who want their food delivered on time. Uber has and plans to continue to leverage clever segmentation to stretch its net as broadly as possible. Ultimately Uber wants to—and is set on a trajectory to—be an alternative to car ownership itself. As Travis Kalanick puts it, "If something is moving from one place to another in a city—that's our jam."[9]

Swarovski—The Payoff from Crystal-Clear Ideas on What Consumers Will Pay

Divining what customers want from a new product—and how much they'll pay for it—long before the product is developed has been a winning formula for innovation success in companies new and old. Even companies that have done R&D for decades (like Porsche) can adopt radical new approaches. Of course, newer companies have the advantage of adopting newer approaches, as our case studies on LinkedIn, Uber, and Optimizely (later in this chapter) illustrate.

Yet companies much older than Porsche have also adopted the lessons of this book. One of them is Swarovski, which was founded in 1895 in the town of Wattens in the Austrian Alps. As the manufacturer of small crystals, product developers have learned in the last decade the importance of establishing what both business customers and consumers value in a new offering way before the engineering work begins.

The company was launched on the back of a process innovation. Jeweler Daniel Swarovski's business began after he patented a machine that ground crystals faster and more precisely than could be done by hand. The firm soon became known for its sparklers, which famously were worn by Hollywood stars like Marlene Dietrich and Marilyn Monroe. (In fact, two Monroe dresses glittering with Swarovski crystals became famous: the one she wore when she sang "Diamonds Are a Girl's Best Friend" in 1953's *Gentlemen Prefer Blondes* [10] and the one she wore to sing "Happy Birthday" to President John F. Kennedy at New York's Madison Square Garden in 1962.[11])

Today, 60 years after he died, Daniel Swarovski might not recognize the company he founded, which continues to be run successfully by his family. The Swarovski group is a $3.4 billion company with 30,000 employees and diverse businesses in 170 countries. By far the largest part of the group is the crystal business, with three-quarters of its revenue coming from jewelry, watches, fashion accessories, and other consumer products sold in 2,480 Swarovski stores around the world.[12]

Another big part of Swarovski's crystal business is the professional business unit, a B2B2C business. One important offering is loose crystals, sold mainly to wholesale, fashion, and jewelry makers. Another part is custom offerings that appear on such products as cellphones and furniture.

Because its products ultimately end up with consumers, Swarovski must keep its eye on consumers even as it develops and prices new products for its business customers. Knowing what consumers are willing to pay for clothes, jewelry, and other items adorned with Swarovski crystals has been crucial to fully monetizing its innovations with manufacturers, explains Christoph Kargruber, executive vice president of innovation and product management.

Let's see how they've done this for each of those offerings.

Loose Crystals for the Fashion and Jewelry Sectors

Swarovski's loose crystals business customers largely are fashion and jewelry companies, ranging from midpriced brands like Victoria's Secret to luxury brands like Jean-Paul Gaultier. With more than 100,000 products in its active catalog, Swarovski can provide crystals of pretty much any type, color, size, cut, and form imaginable.

Swarovski launches new collections of stones twice a year. With 100,000 products and new ones added every year, it is impossible for Swarovski to research exhaustively what customers would pay for the new offerings on its drawing boards. So what can Swarovski do to know whether its products will appeal to consumers, its ultimate customers, in the fickle world of fashion?

The company needed an effective and systematic way to get customer feedback on the value of its products early in its product development process. But rather than doing customer research product by product, in 2013 it began conducting extensive research and analysis to identify the product criteria or features that increased customer WTP. In other words, the company was hunting for the drivers of customer value. Swarovski's goal was to come up with a systematic monetization and price-setting process, one that would capture both business customer and consumer WTP, taking into account the complexity of the company's huge product portfolio.

Swarovski surveyed customers in more than 20 countries around the world. According to Kargruber, the company's product managers retrieved two huge insights after analyzing the data. One was that certain customer segments were willing to pay five to six times more for crystal products with sophisticated cuts rather than traditional ones. Stated our way, *cut complexity* was a major driver of customer WTP. The second revelation was that WTP increased with a crystal's brilliance. And as a crystal's brilliance increases with cut complexity, making a crystal brilliant through a sophisticated cut was potentially a very profitable endeavor.

To put its WTP data and drivers of customer interest into a pricing system that product developers could use, the company came up with five price tiers. Each one varied by the degree to which a crystal delivered the core customer benefits of brilliance and sophistication achieved by a complex cut. Products in each tier had the same prices, even though they were different in such aspects as form and color, as consumer WTP did not vary very much for those factors. To make the price-tier approach more comprehensible to customers, each category was given an appropriate name (from lower to higher price positioning): Essential, Classic, Advanced, Sophisticated, and Outstanding Crystals. The price span from the lowest to the highest tier was 650 percent.

With a price-tier system based on customer value, Swarovski could now make crucial design and pricing decisions early in a new product's development. And because it followed the philosophy of "design the product around the price," designers could start their work knowing the price range they were dealing with and what would drive customer value.

This was highly beneficial to Swarovski, Kargruber explains, because designers could now create new products to appeal to each price layer. The company must have products for all of them. Behind each category are one or more target segments; Swarovski wants to address all of them. The price-tier system also helps steer the firm's product development process according to market size. For larger segments, Swarovski needs more new products.

Another big benefit of the price-tier system is that the sales force now can easily explain the rationale of Swarovski's pricing to its jewelry and apparel manufacturing customers. There are only five price tiers—not dozens, as in the past—and the most expensive products are the most innovative and complex. Customers now understand why one product's price is so much more than another's, and that reduces price resistance.

Before it instituted the new process, Swarovski based its prices on "internal gut feeling," Kargruber explains, not customer value. The result was that many of the company's prices were wrong, and salespeople had to correct for that in their negotiations with their B2B customers, which sometimes led to steep discounts for some products. Today, that no longer happens. The sales force can now focus on its core task: selling.

Kargruber says the new process helps product managers make new-product pricing decisions more quickly, easily, and accurately. "And more important, the redesigned new product monetization process helped to bring up our margins significantly, which was the key goal of that initiative," he states.

Boosting New Product Success for Customized Solutions

The Customized Solutions unit that develops custom crystals for businesses also has adopted the "design the product around the price" approach to product development. Custom Solutions is a growing revenue source for the firm. Mobile phone makers like Samsung want cases festooned with Swarovski crystals to stand out from the plastic-cover crowd; furniture manufacturers are spiffing up their lamps, chairs, and other items with fancy crystals to catch the eyes of consumers in cavernous furniture stores.

Each of these products is customized for each manufacturer. The cases that Samsung's mobile phones will get are not what another mobile phone maker gets.

But the Swarovski crystals that create an attractive phone case or lamp are only part of what's necessary to entice consumers to buy them. Swarovski not only sells a customized product, it also sells the customized packaging, marketing and branding, promotion, and sales consulting that are crucial for these companies to create consumer demand. Swarovski is selling a differentiating *solution*.

Here, too, Swarovski has learned it must discern consumer trends and spot drivers to make its products more attractive. Understanding consumer needs, and what they'll pay for products that meet those needs, is still critical. Without this information, Swarovski would have no idea what Samsung's customers would be willing to pay for a Swarovski-embellished smartphone case, and therefore what Samsung will be willing to pay Swarovski for its customized crystals. But the Custom Solutions group knows the answer to this question because (in contrast to the loose-crystal unit) it conducts more detailed end-consumer research. Consequently, the firm knows the crystal designs that consumers covet and what they'll pay for them.

To optimize profits, it knows which consumer segments to pursue over others. For example, with mobile phone cases, Swarovski has found consumers across different markets will pay an unbelievable 120 percent more for a crystal-embellished case. That helps Swarovski convince mobile phone companies that the value of its case goes far beyond its manufacturing costs, and that having the Swarovski logo, designs, and crystals on their cases will command a significant premium in the marketplace.

That knowledge enables Swarovski to move off the cost-plus discussions on pricing that manufacturers try to pursue. Swarovski can show manufacturers how much additional profit they can make with Swarovski crystals attached to their products, even if Swarovski takes a greater share of that profit than it would have on a cost-plus margin basis.

The 120 percent premium consumers will pay for Swarovski smartphone cases varies greatly for other products, from as little as 30 percent to several hundred percent. Swarovski's data has focused the Custom Solutions group's strategy on products whose customer segments have a higher WTP for them.

What's more, knowing consumers are willing to spend much more for products embellished with crystals from Swarovski, the firm even manages to monetize their brand and logo. Because Swarovski has such a strong brand, firms with weaker brands have been seeking Swarovski out.

They are willing to pay for the spillover effect from having a Swarovski logo on their products.

Having nurtured and buffed a brand known for innovation and excellence for more than a century, Swarovski is now in a position to help companies without strong brands increase their own cachet. But this requires Swarovski to remain a top-of-mind crystal brand in the eyes of consumers and the businesses that resell its products. And that, in turn, means Swarovski must continue doing the research that shows why and how much consumers are willing to pay for its crystals and the products they brighten.

The Next Steps in Swarovski's Monetization Journey

It's been two years since Swarovski began adopting these approaches to monetizing innovation. Kargruber believes it will take the firm another one to two years to complete the journey. "You can't underestimate how long it takes to change a firm's product development approaches, especially to change the mindsets people bring to the innovation process," he explains. "It is not just a process change; it's a very different way of thinking."

Making these difficult changes cannot be ad hoc; the effort must be structured. Swarovski installed a pricing board of three people to guide and push the change process, including the heads of marketing, sales, and the controller. The board's mandate is to give clear direction, resolve conflicts, monitor the monetization progress, and make necessary corrections to the process. It meets six times a year and has proven to be effective in moving Swarovski from a "price the product" to a "design the product around the price" approach.

For the more operational monetization support, Kargruber has created a pricing office with two full-time employees based in the marketing organization. They report to him and help innovation teams apply the new monetization approaches.

With a "design the product around the price" innovation monetization process, executives on a pricing board to steer it, and support from Kargruber's group, Swarovski crystals are glittering even more brightly in the marketplace. "In hindsight, we should have done this even earlier," Kargruber says. Nonetheless, the company is quickly making up for lost time.

Optimizely—How to Price Breakthrough Innovation

Rapidly advancing technologies make all kinds of newfangled products and services possible, but innovators face a great monetization challenge: determining whether a brand new product can sell, and at what price, before investors pony up their money. Seventy-five percent of venture capital–based start-ups fail in the United States, according to a 2012 Harvard Business School study.[13]

But the story of Optimizely shows why this doesn't have to be. The San Francisco–based firm used the principles in this book to assess the market potential for its breakthrough offering long before launching it in the market—and knew that it would succeed at monetizing. Launched in 2010, Optimizely has become a Bay Area star, achieving triple-digit annual revenue growth since its start. Thousands of companies have used its products, including Dell, Netflix, and Disney.[14] Optimizely is now the world's most popular software for optimizing websites, creating and delivering more than 30 billion optimized visitor experiences.[15]

Founded by two former Google product managers, Dan Siroker and Pete Koomen, the idea for Optimizely emerged during Siroker's stint as director of analytics for the 2008 Obama presidential campaign. Siroker's team compared the effectiveness of web pages, e-mail messages, and other communications in order to boost donations, e-mail signups, and volunteers.

For example, they compared how website visitors react to different versions of a web page (to see which one would perform better). They were also able to measure the impact of changing specific web page elements, such as a picture or a headline. They found, for example, that a button reading "learn more"—rather than "sign up" or "join us now"—was more likely to get a visitor to give his e-mail address. A black and white picture of Obama with his family also boosted engagement with the site. When the image and the "learn more" button were combined, 40 percent more people entered their e-mail addresses.[16]

Optimizely's techniques helped the Obama campaign raise more than $100 million in additional donations.

From this experience, Siroker saw an opportunity to commercialize A/B and multivariate testing and launch it as a full-fledged software product. The software could help companies improve their website experiences for customers, which is especially important to e-commerce companies. Siroker's results from the Obama campaign gave him credibility.

First Up: Determining Whether Customers Would Pay

Siroker sought out his former Google colleague, Koomen, to investigate the commercial viability of the product. But instead of diving headlong into development, as many Silicon Valley companies would, they started having the WTP talk with potential customers.

"We had a strong belief many companies would find our technology valuable," said Siroker in a conversation he had with us.[17] "But we didn't really know just how many and whether they would pay for it. We also needed to find out exactly what benefits drove customer value and how much each customer segment would be willing to pay for different levels of value."

At the time, A/B testing was in its infancy, and Optimizely had no products to sell. But when Siroker presented his idea to e-commerce companies, they instantly recognized its value. They also expressed a high WTP, which was no surprise. If more customers engaged with their website, they were more likely to spend more time on the site, and therefore they would make more purchases more often. In other words, Optimizely's customers could generate incremental revenue by using the Optimizely software product.

Siroker and Koomen set out to create a world-class but easy-to-use online service on which businesses could run experiments about their websites and make informed decisions about how to change them. They worked with Stanford statisticians to develop a new, powerful, accurate statistical framework for A/B testing that would remove the guesswork from declaring a test successful and statistically significant. Siroker and Koomen set up shop in downtown San Francisco, near a swarm of other web companies.

Still, with no commercial competitors, how would Optimizely price its platform? To buy the Optimizely testing product, what capabilities would customers need? To answer these questions, Siroker and Koomen created a monetization task force, a team with members from product, marketing, sales, and finance. Their job was to determine which features were and were not important (the product configuration considerations) and the best monetization model. Should it be fee per transaction? A subscription service? Freemium? They also looked at pricing strategies and how much they could charge.

From their conversations with potential customers, the monetization team identified clusters, or segments, of the market according to the value they desired from different feature sets. With that information, they created packages (i.e. product configurations) that varied by value (features offered) and price. These packages, they believed, would satisfy companies across all sizes. They also defined the minimum set of features for the "freemium" product, and they outlined a clear and compelling land-and-expand strategy that would convert free users to paid users over time.

But the Optimizely monetization team was still missing a core ingredient: a revenue model that would be a win for both the firm and its customers. In other words, they needed a winning monetization model. So they set out to create one.

Understanding How to Charge

To the Optimizely monetization team, the question of *how* to charge was, in many ways, more important than how much to charge. The more a customer uses the product, the more benefits the customer derives. Consequently, the team wanted to base the monetization model on usage. Use it more, pay more for it.

But that model would be a bit unusual in the software industry (at least back in 2010). When the team looked at the software market, it found most SaaS companies priced their offerings on a per-user basis. Per-user pricing made sense, they believed, *if* customers got more value as more of their employees used the software—a network effect. However, the Optimizely monetization team felt per-user pricing had no relation-ship to their software's value. Of course, they were right. The number of employees in a company using Optimizely's service had no bearing on whether that company generated business value from the software. If Optimizely had charged on a SaaS per-user model, and only the few employees who worked on it were monetized, Optimizely would have left a lot of money on the table. They would have produced a classic minivation.

In addition, the monetization team also worried that customers would not be able to predict how many people would use the software. This would likely slow down the purchase decision.

After weighing these factors, the monetization team decided to charge according to the number of monthly unique visitors (MUVs) bucketed into an experiment. This metric was more in line with the value of Optimizely's product. It also enabled smaller companies with lower site traffic to afford Optimizely. As their use of the software grew, they would get more value from it and thus be in a better position to pay more as their website traffic grew. That's a win-win. Larger companies tended to have larger MUVs and already were in a good position to pay Optimizely a price commensurate with the value they gained from the product.

The MUVs model also enabled Optimizely to increase revenue from customers over time. The more tests a customer conducted, the more value it received from Optimizely, and the more it would pay in return for getting greater value. In addition, as a customer's web traffic grew, it had to spend more to maintain the same level of testing.

The MUVs pricing model also simplified Optimizely's sales process, since customers only needed to know their monthly site traffic (not how many users might use the software)—a measure they invariably knew. (If they didn't, it was doubtful Optimizely could help them. After all, it was software, not a magic wand.) The MUVs pricing model is exactly analogous to the Michelin monetization model described in Chapter 7: charging by the miles truckers drove the tires, not per tire.

Expanding the Product Portfolio

In 2014, Optimizely began gauging customer interest in a new product, Personalization, to help companies tailor their web experiences for customers in real time. The product lets customers tailor their website based on demographic and behavioral data on each web visitor. For example, a customer who purchased a backyard barbecue on the last site visit could be shown grill covers, sauces, and grilling tools. This kind of personalization creates customer loyalty, increases engagement, and can greatly increase the chances that a visitor will buy more on the site.

To validate whether customers valued their product and how much they would pay for it, Optimizely talked to a representative set of customers and prospects around the world. The answer to the first question was a loud and clear "yes!"

Optimizely then used the techniques mentioned in Figure 4.3 in Chapter 4 (including most–least and build-your-own) to break down a list of 15 product benefits/features into leaders, fillers, and killers. With this information, the Personalization product team created a good/ better/best package that tied the products to the right segments. But from a product portfolio standpoint, the team was left with two fundamental questions:

1. Should they bundle the Personalization offering with the Testing offering?
2. How should they charge for the Personalization product? Should its pricing be different than Testing's pricing?

To Bundle or Not to Bundle

To answer the first question, Optimizely took a closer look at each core market segment, breaking each into three groups:

1. Current Testing customers who might also value Personalization
2. Prospects who might want to purchase Testing and Personalization in a bundle
3. Prospects who only would want Personalization

Selling Personalization to existing Testing customers was a no-brainer, since it would be a natural extension to the software they already owned. For example, a retailer who is an existing customer and has tested several campaigns might want to personalize its home page for shoppers based on the test results (e.g., customize the web page based on current weather conditions in their region, or the consumer's purchasing history). But since Optimizely's current customers already subscribed to the Testing product, bundling the two offerings didn't help Optimizely answer the question of whether they should do it.

When the Optimizely team talked to prospects who hadn't purchased Testing, or Personalization, it learned their needs could be substantially different for the two products. One reason was that each product was not necessarily needed by the prospect organization at the same time. Most companies preferred to sequence the purchase of the products.

To further complicate matters, there was no clear consensus among the prospects on whether a prospect should buy Testing before Personalization or vice versa. A small segment clearly needed both products, but not so many to warrant bundling the two.

Everything pointed to keeping Personalization a stand-alone product, but under the same optimization experience platform that Optimizely was building. When customers used the products together, they needed to be seamlessly integrated, but one should be able to work without the other.

Optimizely chose this route: Customers who wanted both products could choose from the good/better/best options of Personalization and Testing (that is, mix and match between the products). This also allowed advanced users of the Testing product to purchase a basic package of Personalization to get started. As the customer advanced on the learning curve, retrieving increasing benefits (from advanced packages) would be possible.

Had Optimizely not validated the go-to-market approach (including value and price) with customers before it developed the offerings, it might have bundled them, trying to sell the two products together since this was the easiest thing to do from a product standpoint. At best, that would have created a minivation. We have seen many SaaS companies go down this path and then try to take a step back after the bundle's sales fall short of expectations. Optimizely's laser focus on having the customer conversations early in the product development process steered it to the (shall we say it?) optimal outcome.

Deciding How to Charge for the Personalization Product

With its Personalization product strategy in hand, the next step for Optimizely was deciding how to charge for it. Should it use the same metric it used for the Testing product, MUV? Using the same metric would keep things simple for both Optimizely and its customers because both products would have the same monetization model. However, Optimizely learned from its validation with customers and prospects that the usage of Personalization is likely very different than Testing. While Testing would be used periodically and for a specific experiment, Personalization would be used at all times for all site visitors; it was always on. Personalization only works when it's constant and universal.

Jill would not like it if the site were personalized on one visit and not on another, and why personalize for Jane and not Jack? Given that dynamic, customers would resist tying the price of Personalization to how much they used it.

After hearing this feedback, Optimizely chose a different pricing metric for Personalization: total site traffic. This metric was in line with how customers planned to use Personalization and get value from it. By measuring the value of each product differently, Optimizely could better defend the value of each. This, again, was a win–win for Optimizely and its customers.

The moral of the Optimizely story is that there is no one right answer for monetizing a suite of products. Had Optimizely kept its monetization model the same for the two products, it might have created a suboptimal outcome. By designing each product separately around the value and the price, Optimizely and its products have been a huge market success.

With 400 employees, the firm has continued to grow rapidly. It expanded its headquarters in San Francisco and opened five others in the United States, Europe, and Asia-Pacific.

Looking ahead, Optimizely has positioned its products as a website customer experience optimization platform, on which the company will add future Optimizely products. But before it launches those new products, the firm won't have to guess how many customers will want them and how much they'll pay. You can bet it will know.

Innovative Pharma—How a Customer Value Driven R&D Approach Boosts Success

The world's biggest pharmaceutical companies spend much more on new products than automobile companies and Silicon Valley firms do. In fact, large drug companies today spend on average of $2.6 billion to get a single new prescription drug off the ground.[18] It leads to severe pressure on their R&D, marketing, and market access organizations to avoid spending huge sums on new drugs that fall flat in the marketplace, even if they meet regulatory approval.

This was what drove a long-successful pharmaceutical company (whose name is being withheld at the company's request) to adopt the approach to monetizing innovation mentioned in this book. Despite its industry standing, the company faces strong competition, in part due to the biotech revolution of the past 20 years that has brought whole new approaches to finding cures to the world's illnesses. Top management of the company's life sciences division had the intent of improving its product development process to both reduce the risk that a new drug fails late in the development pipeline and to increase chances that the new treatment realizes its full clinical and market potential. That's a benchmark for success in this $4 trillion global industry.

Mastering the approaches laid down in this book has had two big and beneficial impacts on the company. First, the company can now determine very early in the development process which products to weed out of the pipeline for commercial reasons. It has a clear idea of which therapy their paying customers will value and which they will not. The benefit has been huge: freeing up money and people to work on the products with the best chances of clinical and commercial success. That kind of confidence is crucial to executives, shareholders, and scientists in an industry relying so much on new products.

The second big benefit is getting the market to embrace its new drugs faster. With better insights on what customers needed most and how to demonstrate that value, the company's product messages have been much more effective. This is critically important when thinking about the diverse groups of customers—including patients, prescribers, hospitals and integrated healthcare networks, and governments and insurance companies paying for the drugs. Each of them has different needs that often also vary by country.

This illuminating upfront market analysis was a clear departure from the industry's longstanding approach to drug development. Traditionally, life sciences companies had focused R&D on making sure their products were winners in the clinical sense. Developing a drug that alleviated symptoms or improved the quality of life without severe side effects was the path to regulatory approval, and that was most often the gateway to market access and commercial success. This company was no exception.

But that changed substantially for this and many other pharmaceutical companies over the past decade. Top management decided that in order to gain funding for a new drug in development, the pharma division had to prove that the new drug would be worth its costs in order to become a big winner with all their customers (especially payers) and not only with regulatory authorities.

Adopting a New Approach to Sizing up Opportunities

Top management at the firm realized they had to get better at picking winners, so they welcomed the "customer value–driven new product" approach. In this industry, customers include the physicians who prescribe drugs, the entities that typically pay for them (government and healthcare insurers), and, of course, patients themselves. All those influencers and decision makers on the drug-purchasing decision had to be considered in advance of the firm committing big dollars to developing a therapy. Shifting to this approach would require cultural and organizational changes that would ultimately take company management more than five years to complete.

First the executives had to sell the approach internally. One of the earliest internal presentations on the journey laid out three critical changes for the company to make.

Change #1: Listen to the Country Teams to Get the Insights on Market Access and Price Potential

The drug development division at headquarters started listening to its teams in the country markets and engaged them in the product development process. No one at a pharmaceutical company is closer to patients, physicians, and payers than the local teams consisting of medical, marketing, and market access specialists. Drug developers needed their input to assess a new compound's viability.

In the best case, the local teams serve as surrogates for customer input when primary research is prohibitively expensive. This has another benefit: It enables the country teams to assess early in product development which unmet customer needs a new product may be able to address—pending confirmation by clinical trials—rather than hearing about it from headquarters close to product launch.

When local teams provide customer insights, they feel committed to embracing the candidate product and prepare future customers wherever they are allowed to (note: Talking with customers about forthcoming new treatments is strictly regulated). In effect, the company created a tight and transparent information loop between its local market teams and the central decision makers. The final step was the creation of an internal information system for tracking and repeat utilization of earlier gathered information.

Change #2: Determine a Product's Clinical and Economic Value Much Earlier in the Process

The testing of a medical compound goes through several phases before it gains regulatory approval and listing on the reimbursement schemes of insurance companies or governments. The most critical and costly clinical trials take place in Phase III. The supporters of the company's new value optimization process argued that if they better understood a drug's clinical, humanistic, and economic value to patients, payers, and physicians by the end of Phase II, they could send fewer compounds into Phase III and provide them with more resources.

For this reason, the company focused most of its process changes on the early stages of product development. Its task forces created new process steps that gathered input from customer surveys.

But the task forces were realistic about the magnitude of short-term process changes that could be adopted. They decided not to try to foist major all-or-nothing change on the drug development process. That risked spawning heated arguments and alienating key team members.

Instead, the task forces urged noticeable changes in drug development but with minimal friction. Rather than trying to get product developers to strictly adhere to a new process, it was more important to communicate the ideas behind the process. What if few teams followed every new step? Not a problem. The way the task forces explained the new process conveyed what the teams needed to do differently, and why: Broader market insights gathered by the end of Phase II greatly increased the chances that the products with the highest customer value potential made it to Phase III trials.

Change #3: Increase Cooperation between Clinical Development, Marketing, and Market Access to Encourage Constructive Challenges

The company's clinical development and marketing groups once operated separately, while market access barely existed. Clinical development tested and shaped a product, and then marketing launched it. The new organizational alignment still called for several groups, but their tasks had to be closely intertwined. Marketing focused on the prescriber customer, medical on the patient and physician specialists, and market access on the payer customer needs. In that context, health-outcomes could develop the evidence for the economic value of the product, while the clinical research teams developed the clinical value of the product.

Cooperation between clinical development and market access professionals became much more extensive under the new model, each group keeping of course their own tasks and responsibilities. Clinical researchers had to improve their understanding of payer data requirements—the proof payers require to evaluate the drug and decide on price, reimbursement coverage, and market access. The market access staff had to get better at articulating, in a way that researchers could understand, what payers were looking for to optimize the likelihood of successful negotiations in the countries between the company and payers. Such enhanced mutual understanding would allow the researchers to adjust their clinical trials and other product development activities in a focused and timely manner.

The new process linked the teams looking at the economic value of new drugs with the teams looking at their clinical value versus competing therapies (in other words, value differentiation). This is essential to shifting product development to the model we are embracing.

Senior management approval and ongoing support helped the pharma giant reap the benefits of its new innovation monetization process. They gave the green light to the first change: moving value analyses to the front end of the product development process. That gave the task forces the license to prepare a global rollout, which the top management then approved.

Impact: Lower Risk, Higher Upside

What was the result of these changes? The pharmaceutical company actually lowered its risks by placing bigger bets. It did so by killing more products in early development than it previously had the courage—or evidence—to stop. Over time, the pharma company placed fewer but much larger bets rather than continuing to support all compounds appearing to have some clinical benefit. This goes against conventional wisdom, which says that a company mitigates its risk by launching more products and counting on the gains from a few winners to overcompensate for the larger number of less successful products.

The company's "customer value–driven new product" approach supports the opposing argument: Concentrating more dollars in fewer products is actually less of a commercial risk than spreading the risk across a large number of products or compounds. Why is this the case? Having a much more incisive understanding of the market and a drug's commercial prospects reduces risk significantly. With better tailored data about the clinical and economic value of a new drug, the company was able to develop a better view of whom to target with the treatment, how much to charge, and how to quickly get to market. This allowed the company to make much better decisions about how much money to allocate for Product A versus Products B and C. Having a deeper understanding of a few high-potential products is far better than a superficial understanding of many products.

The broader lesson is that in innovation, less is more. Having a deeper and more specific knowledge about fewer products is superior to knowing only general information about a multitude of new offerings.

The trials the pharma company needed to conduct to gather additional information can indeed be more expensive, risky, and time consuming. This is contrary to how R&D people are normally measured. When a pharmaceutical R&D team fights internally for R&D dollars, it doesn't want longer and more expensive trials. R&D people prefer their standard key performance indicators (KPIs), which are based on how fast they complete a trial and the number of positive outcomes (that is, the number of products that hit the minimum bar to get regulatory approval).

In the company's new system, new products must meet financial minimums, not just clinical or regulatory ones. By changing incentives for its research teams, the company encouraged them to embrace the process and to understand that the payer-rationalized trial design would make the entire company more successful in view of the increased likelihood of clinical and commercial success at and after launch.

Impact: Less Promising Candidates Killed Earlier

Since shifting its product development process, the company has stopped several products not because of clinical issues but because of poor market prospects: not enough differentiation against the standard treatment, lack of added value in the eyes of key payers, and so on. Today, senior managers are much more critical before they give the green light to taking a candidate drug into Phase III of clinical development. It has become clear that weaker candidates need to be dropped even earlier in order to clear the path for the better candidates that deserve the resources.

At first, all this was a culture shock for the pharma company because it used to define new product success as approval from the U.S. Food and Drug Administration, the European Medicines Agency, or their counterparts in other geographies. In the new system, it is okay if a candidate drug does not reach the approval stage—if the team identified this risk early enough and had the courage to pull the plug with convincing arguments.

This experience shows that long-established companies whose pipeline products require scientific breakthroughs can make the shift from an internally focused R&D approach toward an outside-in customer value–driven approach that strengthens the collaboration between the multiple areas of expertise.

In fact, for all companies with major R&D investments, the outside-in customer value–driven approach will help identify the losers earlier, allowing the company to commit and invest in the winning candidate drugs while boosting the business in the longer run.

This is, however, easier said than done. It requires full commitment from the top and will take several years to implement.

CHAPTER 14

Implementing the "Designing the Product around the Price" Innovation Process

Time to come up for air.

You've been immersed for many pages in our theory and practice of how to design a product around the price. By now, you know the nine rules for monetizing innovation laid out in Chapters 4 through 12. The case studies in Chapter 13 have shown you how companies can make money— a lot of money—by following the rules.

Some of the preceding chapters may have challenged your most deeply held beliefs about monetizing innovation and innovation processes, and some may even have made you uncomfortable. If you've gotten this far, though, you're probably convinced that you should give it a try. We're eager to have you start.

If you're like any good executive whose company needs to innovate successfully to keep growing, you understand that knowing something is quite different from making something work. You should be (and probably are) thinking about the mechanics of implementing this proven approach. You're asking, "What should we start doing tomorrow?" If you've been through other transformations (because that is what this is), you'll be wondering, "What barriers should we expect to face? How can we overcome them?"

That's what this chapter is about: implementing the nine rules of monetizing innovation in your organization. We explain what you need to do, whether you're a billion-dollar company or a start-up and whether you sell products or services to consumers or to other businesses. We provide the steps; you'll need to customize them to fit the realities of your organization. (As we've shown, in this world there is no such thing as one size fits all.)

The implementation has two phases: "Jump-Start and Pilot" and "Scale and Stick." Jump-Start and Pilot will help answer the question "What can we start doing tomorrow?" In Scale and Stick, we explain the processes, governance, tools, change management measures, and training you'll need to implement the new process to monetize innovation, and how to make it stick.

After that, we answer the question "What barriers should we expect to face?" We describe the pitfalls you must avoid because, again, this is a transformation. You're going to have to change some long-standing business processes and many aspects of your organizational culture.

Jump-Start and Pilot
Part 1: The Jump-Start

To jump-start, choose a few new products or services your firm recently brought to market. These offerings need to have been in the market long enough to judge their financial performance. The idea is to compare their performance with what was predicted in the business plan. Were they successful? How do you know? Do you believe it? Did you launch a feature shock, minivation, hidden gem, undead, or a big success?

We have created an online diagnostic tool to help you diagnose the strengths and weaknesses of your overall innovation process (http://www.monetizinginnovation.com). Ask your innovation team to go through each task in the tool and report back with the results. The results should give you a high-level gauge for the status quo. One caveat: Make sure their inputs aren't biased. The key to improving innovation is to begin by being brutally honest. If you find strong practices in certain areas, document them. If you didn't find any pockets of excellence, don't despair. That means you have a big opportunity to improve the way you monetize innovation.

Once you finish the diagnostic, it is time to go one level deeper. To do this, discuss the nine rules of monetizing innovation and the checklists of CEO questions (at the end of Chapters 4 through 12) with your team, specifically for the chosen products. What steps were missing in your current process?

Now it's time for you to start participating in early-stage research and development meetings and jump-start the process. Of course you don't want to drop in on your new product team unannounced. That will only make them anxious: What are you doing there? Is something wrong? Are you about to reprimand them? Is there a new order?

Well, there is, but begin tactfully. Let the new product team know in advance you want to attend these meetings and you'll be listening to their ideas and, most important, challenging them. That will prepare them and keep them focused on the guiding principles of monetizing innovation.

In these meetings, you'll need to begin by explaining your vision and goals for monetizing innovation. You'll have to educate (a polite word for "sell") new product team members on how an innovation process for designing a product around a price will make their work far more reliable and successful, not to mention profitable for everyone. Go through each of the nine rules and the steps each involves.

By now, you will have completed the diagnosis of your firm's current innovation monetization process. You should have a crystalline picture of its strengths and weaknesses. At this point, we predict you will be itching to try out some of the recommendations you've found in this book.

Part 2: The Pilot

For the pilot, select a candidate—a real, new product idea that is in your pipeline. If you are a multiproduct company, keep it simple. Choose one product that's representative of your business.

If you don't already have a cross-functional innovation team, this is the time to form one. It should consist of managers from R&D, product, pricing, marketing, sales, and finance. Choose a person to fill the crucial role of *monetization hero*. What's that again? That's the individual who will be accountable for the success of the initiative. Therefore, this must be the person in charge.

Remember the Optimizely case study in the last chapter? A key factor in the company's monetization success was appointing a monetization hero to the team and putting that person in charge. The monetization hero should have solid product experience and be familiar with your firm's existing innovation processes. This person should also have a broad perspective on the organization—especially the strengths, weaknesses, failures, and successes of the current innovation process. The monetization hero should listen for best practices that emerge in the cross-functional innovation meetings during the pilot phase.

Two rules of engagement for team members are critical for success in these innovation meetings:

1. Each member should hold the others accountable for the ideas they generate. That creates a culture of constructive conflict.
2. Empower people to say no. They must have the license to challenge features that will result in a feature shock or an undead. As we noted in earlier chapters, "less is more" goes sharply against the grain of product developers who believe more is better (and most of them do). But if people are afraid to say no, you'll be stuck in your old model, and the new monetization process will never get off the ground.

Jump-Start and Pilot also includes allocating budget to survey what target customers value about your product concept and, of course, their WTP for that value. You have to get a quantitative understanding of the size of your target market and the value customers place on your new offering. This data will give your R&D teams the directions they need for segmenting the product, product configuration, and bundling strategy: which features to include, which to exclude, and why.

Now you're ready to kick off the pilot and use the nine rules to monetize it. Since this is a pilot, you should be documenting what is and isn't working. But you should be intently taking your first product through all the nine rules and designing it accordingly. This is an iterative process, and you will not excel at every part of it on the first try. Your mindset needs to be "test and learn."

Scale and Stick
Part One: Scale

Scale involves identifying other kinds of products (in different business units, short versus long life cycle, and so on) to put through your program.

The idea is to select one product from each of your firm's primary product groups. This is critical in a large, multiproduct company because by piloting one from each group, you avoid the "big-bang" approach of having all product development initiatives cut over to a new process at the same time. You need to crawl before you walk, and you need to walk before you run.

The six elements of scaling are summarized below. They are largely applicable to multiproduct firms. If you are a single-product company or a small start-up, some actions may not fully apply to you, but we will still encourage you to read on and absorb the nuggets!

1. Consult the process and playbooks you created in the pilot phase. Put the steps of that process into a workflow diagram that people can understand. Decide whether any of these steps must be customized to the needs of a specific product or product group.
2. Dedicate a monetization team that will work across products. Based on the pilot's results, decide whether you need to recruit internally or externally for this team. The monetization team works on monetization every working business hour; usually this is a full-time mission. Depending on the complexity of the organization, the team could become its own department. A member of this team must work hand-in-hand with the cross-functional product development team as well as be part of all new product meetings. This structure has been instrumental to Dräger's and Swarovski's success. Their monetization teams work closely with the product teams every day, all the time. In a start-up company, the monetization team and the cross-functional innovation team can be one and the same. In bigger companies, it's better to form a team whose sole responsibility is developing and applying the new monetization process.
3. Assign clear roles and responsibilities to the cross-functional innovation team. Again, a monetization team member must attend all innovation team meetings. That person is accountable for making sure the

Rule	Product	Marketing	Sales	Finance	Monetization Team
1. Have the willingness-to-pay-talk early.	R	C	C	I	A
2. Define segments based on needs, value, and WTP.	R	R	C	I	A
3. Ensure bundling and packaging are not afterthoughts.	R	C	C	I	A
4. Choose your pricing and revenue model wisely.	R	C	C	R	A
5. Pick the winning price strategy.	R	C	C	C	A
6. Build the business case using WTP information.	C	C	C	R	A
7. Develop the right value message.	C	R	R	I	A
8. Employ behavioral pricing principles.	C	R	R	I	A
9. Maintain your price integrity.	I	C	R	R	A

Figure 14.1 Roles and Responsibilities for the Nine Rules of Monetizing Innovation. R: Responsible; A: Accountable; C: Consulted; I: Informed

innovation team implements all nine rules. Other functional team members should be responsible, consulted, or informed. (See Figure 14.1 for typical team roles and responsibilities.)

4. Make sure the cross-functional teams meet regularly and ask the right questions. Ask the CEO questions found at the ends of Chapters 4 through 12. Be prepared to seriously challenge each team to make sure they have the market segmentation, customer value, and WTP evidence in hand.

5. Track new-product performance using all the KPIs you've identified. Remember to use the sales, operations, and customer KPIs, not just the financial KPIs (which we explained in Chapter 12).

6. Implement a review schedule to measure the performance of products you've put through the monetization process. You need to determine what worked, what didn't, and what you'll do differently.

The Scale stage ends after you've finalized all your process documents and playbooks and put several new products through the monetization process. If everything has worked the way we believe it will, you should have a handful of roaring success stories that will help you in the next stage: making the new process stick so you don't backslide to the old ways of developing new products.

Part Two: Stick

Creating a culture that embraces the nine rules of monetizing begins with designing a training plan and a change-management plan. You will need to get all your teams fully competent at executing the nine rules. You must find the skills gaps (especially in product, marketing, and sales) and develop training programs to fill them.

Instituting a new product development process, especially in companies that have invented and commercialized products in a defined way for years, won't be easy. Your change management plan shouldn't underestimate how much resistance you'll face. You shouldn't let individual agendas delay or derail the cutover to the new processes. For every business function, your plan for managing organizational resistance should document a) why the change is necessary, b) what needs to be done, and c) how to do it.

In the end, if you want your company to fully adopt the nine rules of this book, everyone who plays a role in new-product success must buy into the need to make substantial changes.

But the change starts with you. You must lead by example. You need to start showing up at new-product meetings and asking tough questions. You must continue communicating the importance of developing and commercializing new products in this manner.

Telling success stories is the best way to convey the importance of monetizing innovation in the ways we've prescribed. Fortunately, you have them because you've conducted your successful pilots.

You will also need to be able to say "no." Nearly every product development pipeline we've encountered has undead products lying around, diverting resources, energy, and attention from more deserving ones. It's time for your organization to pull the plug on them.

Killing unworthy new-product ideas not only takes courage, it also takes practice. One of the best ways to do this is to create a list of the costliest undead products in your firm's portfolio. (You know which ones they are; you've read Chapter 2.) By getting your organization to kill these offerings, you will, in effect, be creating the right culture for successful innovation to flourish. Of course, this is a culture in which a "yes" to every new product idea (or feature) no longer rules. You could say it's a culture in which the old approval process shifts from "yes/ maybe/no" to "no/maybe/yes." It's a mindset in which every product has to earn its way into the market before it is launched. That's the Porsche way, as we discussed in the previous chapter.

Cultures built on yes/maybe/no may seem more exciting. But if every idea starts with a yes and you go all the way, by the time you can say no, it is far too late and the train has left the station—and so has your product.

Last, you need to reward the people who develop products customers love because they enlisted customers' input to design the product features and determine how the product is priced. Nurturing that kind of ambition requires providing *disincentives* for those who lowball the goals for a new product—its market potential, how much the market is willing to pay for it, and so on. Too many managers set low goals for new products—lower revenue targets, lower-than-necessary prices—with the hope that more customers will buy them. But by lowballing, managers are returning profits that belong in your company's coffers to customers in the form of ill-conceived discounts.

Does that sound right to you? We don't think so. Discourage lowballing and other incentives that encourage people to over- or underinflate a new product's potential.

The Nine Pitfalls to Implementing a New-Product Monetization Process (and How to Avoid Them)

The changes we recommended in this chapter will not be embraced joyfully by everyone in your company who participates in creating and commercializing new products. Bank on it. Time and again over the last 30 years, we have seen these nine pitfalls emerge. Forewarned is forearmed.

1. Putting All Your Eggs in One Basket

The process and playbooks you build cannot be dependent on just one person or one group. What happens when that person leaves? People do, you know. Teams change. Further, if the monetization team is held solely accountable for keeping the process going, and it alone knows the ins and outs of the new process and what needs to change, your company is vulnerable, especially if other teams (such as product, marketing, and sales) are disengaged and are just going along with it.

The process is important, and you have to implant it into the DNA of your organization. To do this, you must get every group equally excited, invested in, and motivated through incentives to embrace the change.

2. Not Forming a Cross-Functional Team

The cross-functional team is essential to creating a culture that designs new products around the price. In most organizations, R&D and product teams are tasked with innovation; marketing and sales are charged with positioning and selling the innovation. Without marketing and sales managers' early involvement in the new process, they are likely to fumble the ball when it comes time to market and sell your new product. They won't know how to communicate the value of your innovation. Months later, the customer value you ascribed to it early in the product development process will be lost in translation. Your disappointing revenue and profit numbers will reflect this failure.

3. Banking on the Big Bang

For a change as fundamental as the one recommended in this book, implementing it all at once is not possible. This is especially true in large, multiproduct companies. Sweeping, successful change requires incremental steps. Once you've piloted your first products and then tested, refined, and measured your first successes, only then can you scale.

Simply put, if you bet too much too early, you put your whole stake at risk. That's not wise.

4. Imagining One Size Fits All

Monetizing innovation is not a cookie-cutter process—not in this book, at least. One size never fits all. You must tailor all the steps we've outlined to your company's capabilities, skills, tools, existing processes, and culture.

5. Having Too Many Opt Outs

You get the new process into the DNA of your company only through repetition (especially if you are a big company or a multiproduct company). For achieving repetition, your team needs to adhere to the process and follow it through to the best extent possible. If there are too many opt outs, people will tend to revert back to status quo. Best-in-class companies institute automated workflows with stage gates, ensuring that a product passes one stage gate (with the right approvals) before it moves to the next.

6. Getting Blinded by Science

In the early stages of designing your product around a price, when you are having the WTP conversations, remember you're only trying to get to a ballpark idea of an acceptable price. As you keep designing the product, you must keep refining this estimate. Trying to optimize your price before you start designing produces a false sense of precision. You may get an A on your process but an F on your innovation. Applying the philosophy and principles you find in this book is far more important than applying its math.

7. Avoiding Messy Information

Be prepared: The information you collect won't be perfect. In this life, nothing is. Some of it will be confusing. Don't let that throw you off. Step back and draw pragmatic conclusions from the data you have, and don't follow the arrival of data that fails to align with it with a witch hunt.

If you accept that you will encounter messy information, you will be better prepared to take a step back and see the majesty and magnitude of the forest instead of all those twisty, confusing trees.

8. Cheaping Out

Everything has a cost. Make sure to allocate sufficient budgets to the steps outlined in Chapters 4 through 12. You must assign adequate people and budget. It will be more than you like; it will take time; and you'll have to fight for it. Failing to do so will sabotage everything you hope for, but when you get what you need, you'll find your investment will pay off in relatively short order.

9. Letting the C-Suite Delegate Everything

This last pitfall can do the most damage of all. In the Simon-Kucher & Partners Global Pricing Study we mentioned in Chapter 1, we found that companies in which senior executives led the change to extract full value from new products averaged 33 percent more profit than companies where executives delegated that responsibility. When C-level leadership is not committed in body and soul, if monetizing innovation is not one of your top two organizational priorities, and if that is not reflected in C-level involvement, we would advise you not to embark on the journey.

But If You Are Ready for the Journey. . . .

This book was written to illuminate the path that some of the world's most successful product innovators have traveled and to show you how you can do the same. You can, of course, choose to accept or reject our advice.

Given that our prescriptions for making this journey involve so many and varied radical changes for executives involved in product development, marketing, sales, and the C-suite, we expect many readers will wonder whether it's possible to implement these changes in their organizations.

In the 1999 science fiction movie *The Matrix*, the hero, Neo, is presented with a blue pill and a red pill and asked to choose. Taking the blue pill will allow him to continue to exist within the comfortable but fabricated reality of the Matrix. The red pill will push him into the real world to confront the difficult truth of his existence.

If your company's innovation process is built on hope—a gut instinct *before* you bring your products to market that they will pay off—your organization has chosen the blue pill. If some (or even most) of your innovations have paid off, you still have been building them on a tenuous foundation, one that could give way at any moment.

In a world in which innovation success has become more important *and* more difficult, we believe no company can afford to build its future on wishes, hopes, and dreams.

This book has attempted to show you the red pill. It may have made you uncomfortable; reality is often hard to face. It is always easier to take the blue pill and keep building products and slapping on a price that you hope will deliver a profit. But, if you want to transition from hoping to knowing, you must take the red pill.

That is the one that will set you on a fast trajectory to fully monetize your innovation.

NOTES

Chapter 1

1. Latest data from IHS Automotive (a research firm) says the global auto business is $5 trillion, https://www.ihs.com/pdf/MegaPlatforms_231671110915583632.pdf and Aftermarket2.pdf.
2. Chris Reiter and Christian Wuestner, "Porsche Has an Identity Crisis Amid Its SUV Success," *Bloomberg Business*, July 5, 2012, www.bloomberg.com/bw/articles/2012-07-05/porsche-has-an-identity-crisis-amid-its-suv-success.
3. Craig Trudell and Mark Clothier, "How Chrysler's Dodge Dart Missed the Mark," *Bloomberg Business*, January 31, 2013, www.bloomberg.com/bw/articles/2013-01-31/how-chryslers-dodge-dart-missed-the-mark.
4. Wieden + Kennedy, "How to Change Cars Forever," www.wk.com/campaign/how_to_change_cars_forever/from/dodge.
5. Richard Read, "Why Isn't the Dodge Dart Selling?" The Car Connection, January 22, 2013, www.thecarconnection.com/news/1081847_why-isnt-the-dodge-dart-selling.
6. Timothy Cain, "September 2015 YTD U.S. Passenger Car Sales Rankings—Top 158 Best-Selling Cars In America—Every Car Ranked," Good Car Bad Car, October 3, 2015, www.goodcarbadcar.net/2015/10/usa-september-2015-car-sales-stats-by-model.html. The Dart's sales in the first nine months of 2015 were 68,319 versus 278,742 for the Corolla and 249,749 for the Civic.
7. Sarah Green Carmichael, "The Silent Killer of New Products: Lazy Pricing," *Harvard Business Review*, September 9, 2014, https://hbr.org/2014/09/the-silent-killer-of-new-products-lazy-pricing/.
8. Dr. Rob Adams, "Market Validation," Texas Executive Education, University of Texas McCombs School of Business, www.mccombs.utexas.edu/execed/take-a-class/marketing/market-validation. Accessed January 28, 2016.
9. http://www.wsj.com/articles/SB10000872396390443720204578004980476429190
10. Martin Grueber and Tim Studt, "2014 Global R&D Funding Forecast," *R&D Magazine*, December 2013, https://www.battelle.org/docs/tpp/2014_global_rd_funding_forecast.pdf.
11. World Intellectual Property Organization, "World Intellectual Property Indicators 2014," 12, www.wipo.int/edocs/pubdocs/en/wipo_pub_941_2014.pdf.

Chapter 2

1. Amazon's market cap reached $273.4 billion versus Walmart's $204.9 billion on January 28, 2016, http://quotes.wsj.com/WMT, http://quotes.wsj.com/AMZN.
2. Brad Molen, "Amazon Fire Phone Review: A Unique Device, but You're Better Off Waiting for the Sequel, *Engadget*, July 22, 2014, www.engadget.com/2014/07/22/amazon-fire-phone-review/.
3. Austin Carr, "The Real Story behind Jeff Bezos's Fire Phone Debacle and What It Means for Amazon's Future," *Fast Company*, February 2015, www.fastcompany.com/3039887/under-fire
4. "When Stuff Sucks #makeitright," Three, www.three.co.uk/makeitright. The advertisement for Hutchison's Three mobile service can be viewed there.
5. Pete Pachal, "How Kodak Squandered Every Single Digital Opportunity It Had," Mashable, January 20, 2012, http://mashable.com/2012/01/20/kodak-digital-missteps/#UQGV2CTkjZqy.
6. Jennifer Valentino-DeVries, "From Hype to Disaster: Segway's Timeline," *Wall Street Journal* Digits blog, September 27, 2010, http://blogs.wsj.com/digits/2010/09/27/from-hype-to-disaster-segways-timeline/.
7. "Segway Inc.," Wikipedia, last modified November 25, 2015, https://en.wikipedia.org/wiki/Segway_Inc.
8. Bloomberg News, "Segway Bought by Xiaomi-Backed China Transporter Startup Ninebot," *Bloomberg News*, April 15, 2015, www.bloomberg.com/news/articles/2015-04-15/xiaomi-backed-startup-says-it-plans-to-buy-u-s-rival-segway.
9. Nick Bilton, "Why Google Glass Broke," *New York Times*, February 4, 2015, www.nytimes.com/2015/02/05/style/why-google-glass-broke.html?_r=0.
10. Thomas C. Frohlich, "Worst Product Flops of All Time," 24/7 Wall Street, March 3, 2014, http://247wallst.com/special-report/2014/03/03/worst-product-flops-of-all-time/#ixzz3inYE1gyy.

Chapter 4

1. Ellen Byron, "Gillette's Latest Innovation in Razors: The 11-Cent Blade," *Wall Street Journal*, October 1, 2015, www.wsj.com/articles/SB10001424052748704789404575524273890970954.
2. Procter & Gamble Product Innovation Factsheet for the Gillette Guard, www.pg.com/en_US/downloads/innovation/factsheet_final_Gillette_Guard.pdf.
3. Mae Anderson, "Going into Homes to Make a Product People Like," Yahoo News, November 28, 2015, http://news.yahoo.com/going-homes-product-people-151614434--finance.html.
4. "Shaving Statistics," Statistic Brain Research Institute, August 18, 2012, www.statisticbrain.com/shaving-statistics/.
5. Ellen Byron, "Gillette's Latest Innovation in Razors: the 11-Cent Blade," *Wall Street Journal*, October 1, 2015, www.wsj.com/articles/SB10001424052748704789404575524273890970954.

6. Sarah Green Carmichael, "The Silent Killer of New Products: Lazy Pricing," *Harvard Business Review*, September 9, 2014, https://hbr.org/2014/09/the-silent-killer-of-new-products-lazy-pricing.

Chapter 6

1. "Where Does Microsoft Make Money?" Tanner Helland, updated 2013, www.tannerhelland.com/4993/microsoft-money-updated-2013.
2. Charles Miller, "Ryanair and EasyJet: The History of the Peanut Airlines," *BBC News*, June 20, 2013, www.bbc.com/news/business-22888304.
3. Ryanair home page, https://www.ryanair.com/gb/en/. Accessed January 28, 2016.
4. "Ryanair 2014 Annual Report," http://investor.ryanair.com/wp-content/uploads/2015/04/2014-Annual-Reports-Annual-Report.pdf.

Chapter 7

1. "History of the Michelin Group," www.michelin.com/eng/michelin-group/profile/history-of-the-michelin-group/.
2. Georg Tacke, David Vidal, and Annette Ehrhardt, "The Key to Higher Profits: Pricing Power," Simon-Kucher & Partners, April 2013, www.nelsonpricing.com.ar/biblioteca_pricing/2013_04_The_key_to_higher_profits_Tacke_G.pdf.
3. Amy Konary, "The New Software Landscape: Monetizing and Protecting Emerging Business," *IDC Analyst Connection,* November 2014, www.arxan.com/wp-content/uploads/assets1/pdf/IDC_1801.pdf.
4. Nick Wingfield, "How's My Driving? The Insurer Knows," *New York Times*, June 10, 2015, http://bits.blogs.nytimes.com/2015/06/10/hows-my-driving-the-insurer-knows/.
5. Kevin Smith, "Netflix Shares Surge after It Crushes Earnings Estimates," *Business Insider,* January 23, 2013, www.businessinsider.com/netflix-q4-2012-earnings-2013-1; and Frank Pallotta and Brian Stelter, "Netflix Nears 70 Million Subscribers, but Stock Falls," *CNN Money*, October 14, 2015, http://money.cnn.com/2015/10/14/media/netflix-third-quarter-earnings/.
6. International Federation of the Phonographic Industry, "IFPI Digital Music Report 2015: Charting the Path to Sustainable Growth," www.ifpi.org/downloads/Digital-Music-Report-2015.pdf.
7. "Price the Customer, Not the Service," TheoryBiz.com, http://theorybiz.com/implementing-value-pricing/price-the-customer-not-the-service/601-price-the-customer-not-the-service-2.html. Accessed January 26, 2016.
8. Patrick Rishe, "Dynamic Pricing: The Future of Ticket Pricing in Sports," *Forbes*, January 6, 2012, www.forbes.com/sites/prishe/2012/01/06/dynamic-pricing-the-future-of-ticket-pricing-in-sports/.

9. Stephanie Clifford, "Shopper Alert: Price May Drop for You Alone," *New York Times*, August 9, 2012, http://www.nytimes.com/2012/08/10/business/supermarkets-try-customizing-prices-for-shoppers.html.

10. Nicola Harrison, "Retailers Will Adopt Airline-Style Flexible Pricing, Predicts Kingfisher Boss Ian Cheshire," *RetailWeek*, October 22, 2013, www.retail-week.com/technology/retailers-will-adopt-airline-style-flexible-pricing-predicts-kingfisher-boss-cheshire/5054128.article.

11. Constance L. Hays, "Variable Price Coke Machine Being Tested," *New York Times*, October 28, 1999, www.nytimes.com/1999/10/28/business/variable-price-coke-machine-being-tested.html.

12. Auction History, National Auctioneers Association, www.auctioneers.org/consumers/auction-history. Accessed January 25, 2016.

13. Google financial table, https://investor.google.com/financial/tables.html. Accessed January 28, 2016.

14. Marco Iansiti and Karim R. Lakhani, "Digital Ubiquity: How Connections, Sensors, and Data Are Revolutionizing Business," *Harvard Business Review*, November 2014, https://hbr.org/2014/11/digital-ubiquity-how-connections-sensors-and-data-are-revolutionizing-business.

15. Vineet Kumar, "Making 'Freemium' Work," *Harvard Business Review*, May 2014, https://hbr.org/2014/05/making-freemium-work.

16. "Mobile Retention Benchmarks 2013–2014," Tapstream, September 29, 2014, http://blog.tapstream.com/mobile-retention-benchmarks-2013-2014/.

17. Eugene Kim, "The Inside Story of How $1 Billion Evernote Went from Silicon Valley Darling to Deep Trouble," *Business Insider*, October 3, 2015, www.businessinsider.com/evernote-is-in-deep-trouble-2015-10?op=1.

Chapter 8

1. Hermann Simon, *Confessions of the Pricing Man: How Price Affects Everything* (Switzerland: Springer, 2015).

2. Mike Isaac and Katie Benner, "LivingSocial Offers a Cautionary Tale to Today's Unicorns," *New York Times*, November 20, 2015, www.nytimes.com/2015/11/22/technology/livingsocial-once-a-unicorn-is-losing-its-magic.html?_r=1.

3. Andrew Frye and Dakin Campbell, "Buffett Says Pricing Power More Important Than Good Management," *Bloomberg Business*, February 17, 2011, www.bloomberg.com/news/articles/2011-02-18/buffett-says-pricing-power-more-important-than-good-management.

4. Geroge Tacke, David Vidal, and Jan Haemer, "Simon-Kucher Global Pricing Study 2014," September 2014, https://www.simon-kucher.com/en-us/news/72-percent-all-new-products-flop.

Chapter 9

1. "Cox Automotive Launches Dealshield Purchase Guarantee," Manheim, http://press .manheim.com/2014-09-11-Cox-Automotive-Launches-Dealshield-Purchase-Guarantee.
2. DealShield home page, www.dealshield.com.
3. "Oracle Crystal Ball—Overview," www.oracle.com/us/products/applications/crystalball/overview/index.html. Accessed January 28, 2016.

Chapter 10

1. Adobe Creative Cloud website, https://www.adobe.com/creativecloud.html. Accessed January 28, 2016.
2. Mini U.S. home page, www.miniusa.com/content/miniusa/en.html. Accessed January 28, 2016.

Chapter 11

1. Rebecca L. Waber, Baba Shiv, Ziv Carmon, and Dan Ariely, "Commercial Features of Placebo and Therapeutic Efficacy," *Journal of the American Medical Association* 299 (March 5, 2008): 1016–1017. doi:10.1001/jama.299.9.1016.
2. Jennifer Aaker, "Dimensions of Brand Personality," *Journal of Marketing Research* 34 (August 1997): 347–356, https://www.gsb.stanford.edu/faculty-research/publications/dimensions-brand-personality.
3. Kimberly Palmer, "Why Shoppers Love to Hate Rebates," *US News and World Report*, January 18, 2008, http://money.usnews.com/money/personal-finance/articles/2008/01/18/why-shoppers-love-to-hate-rebates.

Chapter 12

1. Daisuke Wakabayashi, "Glimmers Emerge on Apple Watch Sales, and They're Not Pretty," *Wall Street Journal Digits blog*, July 31, 2015, http://blogs.wsj.com/digits/2015/07/31/glimmers-emerge-on-apple-watch-sales-and-theyre-not-pretty/.
2. David Pogue, "The Apple Watch: Half Computer, Half Jewelry, Mostly Magical," Yahoo Tech, April 24, 2015, https://www.yahoo.com/tech/the-apple-watch-half-computer-half-jewelry-115815015484.html.
3. Joanna Stern, "What the Apple Watch Does Best: Make You Look Good," *Wall Street Journal*, April 8, 2015, www.wsj.com/articles/apple-watch-review-what-the-apple-watch-does-bestmake-you-look-good-1428494694.

Chapter 13

1. "Porsche, Reliant on SUVs for Sales These Days, Reminds Consumers of Performance Roots at Le Mans," Bloomberg report found on the Auto News website, June 16, 2014, www.autonews.com/article/20140616/RETAIL03/140619904/porsche-reliant-on-suvs-for-sales-these-days-reminds-consumers-of.

2. Based on data from Exane BNP Paribas, as cited by Matthew Curtin, "Minding the Margins at BMW, Audi, Mercedes and Porsche," *Wall Street Journal*, March 13, 2015, http://blogs.wsj.com/corporate-intelligence/2015/03/13/minding-the-margins-at-bmw-audi-mercedes-and-porsche/.

3. Porsche AG press release No. 2/16; January 11, 2016.

4. Adam Bryant, "In Sports or Business, Always Prepare for the Next Play," November 10, 2012, *New York Times*, www.nytimes.com/2012/11/11/business/jeff-weiner-of-linkedin-on-the-next-play-philosophy.html.

5. "VOC and Pricing Strategies for Superior Value Capture," presented at the Professional Pricing Society in Chicago in 2012, Ralf Drews - CEO & President Dräger Safety. http://pps.pricingsociety.com/content/CHI2012Keynote_Drews.

6. Maya Kosoff, "19 Quotes That Illustrate the Unrelenting Genius of Controversial Multibillionaire Uber CEO Travis Kalanick," *Business Insider*, June 1, 2015, www.businessinsider.com/travis-kalanick-uber-ceo-quotes-2015-5.

7. Liyan Chen, "At $68 Billion Valuation, Uber Will Be Bigger Than GM, Ford, and Honda," *Forbes*, December 4, 2015, www.forbes.com/sites/liyanchen/2015/12/04/at-68-billion-valuation-uber-will-be-bigger-than-gm-ford-and-honda/#1bbf7ff45858.

8. Conversation between Madhavan Ramanujam and Bill Gurley, September 2015.

9. "Person of the Year: The Short List, No. 6, Travis Kalanick," *Time*, time.com/time-person-of-the-year-2015-runner-up-travis-kalanick/.

10. "Trend Report: Making History, and Still Lookin' Good!" *Swarovski Magazine* 41 (2015), http://crystals.swarovski.com/magazine/2015/issue41/Milestones.en.php.

11. Photo of Marilyn Monroe on Swarovski Facebook page, August 5, 2013, https://www.facebook.com/Swarovski/photos/a.10151780259079462.1073741859.106921954461/10151780259254462/.

12. Swarovski Corporate Fact Sheet 2014, www.swarovskigroup.com/S/aboutus/Swarovski_Fact_Sheet_2014_EN_2.pdf.

13. Deborah Gage, "The Venture Capital Secret: 3 Out of 4 Start-Ups Fail," *Wall Street Journal,* updated September 20, 2012, www.wsj.com/articles/SB10000872396390443720204578004980476429190#articleTabs_comments%3D%26articleTabs%3Darticle. The article cites research from Harvard Business School of more than 2,000 companies backed by at least $1 million in venture capital from 2004 to 2010.

14. Dan Siroker, "Optimizely Raises $58 Million to Optimize the World," Optimizely blog, October 13, 2015, https://blog.optimizely.com/2015/10/13/optimizely-series-c-funding/.

15. http://www.prnewswire.com/news-releases/optimizely-raises-58m-reports-triple-digit-revenue-growth-300157690.html.

16. Laurie Segall, "The Secret to Winning a Presidential Campaign," CNN Money, July 30, 2015, http://money.cnn.com/2015/07/29/technology/optimizely-presidential-candidates/.

17. Conversation between Madhavan Ramanujam and Dan Siroker, July 2015.

18. "Cost to Develop and Win Marketing Approval for a New Drug Is $2.6 Billion," Tufts Center for the Study of Drug Development, November 18, 2014, http://csdd.tufts.edu/news/complete_story/pr_tufts_csdd_2014_cost_study. The $2.6 billion figure includes the out-of-pocket costs (about $1.4 billion) for a drug as well as the returns that investors give up (about $1.2 billion) in the 10-plus years in which a drug is under development (returns that they could get by investing the money elsewhere).

INDEX

A

A/B tests, 146, 194, 195
Adobe, 80, 130, 131
Adoption:
  and freemium pricing, 89–90
  of InMail, 171–172
  unrealistic assumptions about, 117
Alternative metric pricing, 88–89
Amazon, 183
  behavioral pricing at, 143–144
  feature shocks at, 16–19, 45
  market capitalization for, 16,
    220n.1
  pricing strategy of, 102
Amazon Web Services, 143
Anchors, price, 136–138,
  140–141
Anchoring tactics, 140–141
Apple, 16
  customer segmentation at, 59
  image of innovator for, 33
  monetization models at, 85
  price integrity at, 150
  product flops by, 6
  promotions at, 105
Apple Watch, 150
Appliances, feature shocks with, 20
Arch Deluxe, 29
Ariba, 102
Ariely, Dan, 136, 141–142
Asus, 22
Auctions, 82, 87–88
Audi, 165
Audi Q7, 22

Automobile manufacturers. *See also specific*
  companies
  holistic product development by, 168
  product innovation by, 3–7
Autotrader.com, 25–26
Average response trap, 49

B

B2B2C business, at Swarovski, 189
B2B settings, *see* Business-to-business
  settings
B2C (business-to-consumer) settings, 104.
  See also specific companies
Barriers to entry, low prices as, 102
Behavioral pricing, 135–147
  avoiding monetization failures
    with, 12–13
  defined, 135–136
  Internet start-up company example,
    137–140
  and tipping at Uber, 187–188
Behavioral pricing tactics, 140–145
  anchoring, 140–141
  compromise effect, 140
  pennies-a-day pricing, 143–144
  psychological thresholds in,
    144–145
  signaling quality with price, 141–142
  testing, 145–146
  upfront costs in, 142–143
Benefit statements:
  clear, 127–130
  in SaaS company example, 123
  segment-specific, 130–132

Benefit statements: (*Continued*)
  of SmugMug, 123–124, 126
  in value communications, 121
Beta-testing, at LinkedIn, 174
Big-bang approach, 211, 215–216
BMW, 154, 165
BMW 7 Series, 154
Breakthrough products, 103, 194–195
Brevity, of benefits statements, 130
Budget, for monetization process,
    210, 217
Buffett, Warren, 106
Build-your-own questions, 48
Bundles:
  premiums for, 75
  sizes of, 74
Bundling, 67–78
  avoiding monetization failures with, 12
  checklist before, 76
  key principles of, 71–73
  at Microsoft, 70–71
  at Optimizely, 198–199
  pizza and breadstick example, 68–70
  successful, 67–68
  tips on engaging in, 73–75
  and unbundling as strategy, 76–77
  unnecessary, 75
Business cases for new products, 111–120
  avoiding monetization failures with, 12
  building, 116–118
  ingredients of, 117
  as living documents, 111, 116–117, 168
  at Manheim, 112–114
  at Porsche, 168
  willingness-to-pay information in, 9,
    114–116
Business Insider, 91
Business-to-business (B2B) settings:
  anchoring in, 141
  behavioral pricing in, 137
  compromise effect in, 140
  "design the product around the price"
    approach in, 174–182
  price endings in, 104

Business-to-consumer (B2C) settings, 104.
    See also specific companies
Buy-in, on pricing strategies, 98
Buying centers, 178

C
Cable television industry, feature shocks in,
    20
Cameras, digital, 24–25
Cannibalization:
  in auto industry, 168
  in building of business case, 117
  product configuration to prevent, 64, 65
Capacity, pricing and, 86, 103
Carbonite, 129
Car clinics, 167
Car ownership, Uber as alternative to,
    186–187
Cars.com, 25
Chevrolet Cruze, 6
China:
  automobile market in, 168
  product innovation in, 11
Class Pass, 89
Clinical development team, 203–204
Cloud computing, behavioral pricing for,
    143–144
Coca-Cola:
  dynamic pricing at, 86
  undead products at, 29
Coke Classic, 29
Communication:
  about bundle pricing, 75
  about value of new products, *see* Value
    communications
Company(-ies):
  benefits of bundling for, 74
  impact of new product on, 118, 168
  tailoring monetization of innovations to,
    216
Competition:
  matching features with, 176
  on MOCA, 128–129
  price undercutting by, 153–154

products of, in CPM process, 179
reactions to new products by, 105, 106, 118, 156
selection of monetization model based on, 92–93
and subscription models, 85
war-gaming reactions to repricing by, 156
Compromise effect, 140
Concessions, price, 141
Construction industry, 82
Consumer needs, Swarovski's understanding of, 192
Consumer product companies, undeads for, 28–29
Contract prices, 144
Control, in product innovation mindset, 34–35
Controlled A/B tests, 146
Convenience, of product configuration, 76
Core benefits, messages about, 130
Core offerings, 15, 64–66
Corporate culture, *see* Organizational culture
Corporate strategy, changing, 182
Costco, 91
Cost-plus pricing, 35, 192
Cox Enterprises, 26, 112
CPM, *see* Customer Process Monitoring
Cross-functional teams:
    to analyze sales volume, 156–157
    creating, 209–210
    for deal deconstructions, 155
    importance of, 215
    at LinkedIn, 174
    at Porsche, 170
    roles and responsibilities of, 211–212
    value communications by, 126–127
    in willingness-to-pay talks, 49
Cross-selling, 76, 84
Crystal Ball, 117
Culture, organizational, *see* Organizational culture

Customer(s):
    benefits of product configuration and bundling for, 74
    designing products for "average," 53
    irrationality of, *see* Behavioral pricing
    monetization model based on preferences of, 91–92
    performance of, 89, 128
    perspectives of, in current product innovation mindset, 34–35
    segmentation based on size of, 54–55, 57
    testing pricing tactics with, 145–146
    willingness-to-pay talks with, 45–46
Customer lifetime value, 143, 151
Customer Process Monitoring (CPM):
    institutionalization of, 178–180
    making CPM stick at Dräger, 181–182
    phases of, 178–179
    in product development process, 180–181
Customer research:
    at Dräger Safety, Inc., 177, 178
    messy information from, 216–217
    at Optimizely, 197
    at Porsche, 165–167, 169
    at Swarovski, 190, 192
Customer segments:
    bundling based on, 75
    creating variations of products for, 180
    describing, 61
    market sizing to evaluate, 60–61
    number of, 60
    polarization in, 166
    in pricing strategy, 98
    product configurations for, 64–67, 73–74, 198–199
    selective pursuit of, 192
    tailoring benefit statements for, 130–132
Customer segmentation, 53–62
    avoiding monetization failures with, 12
    by best-in-class companies, 58–60
    at Dräger Safety, Inc., 179
    golden rule of, 58
    and leader/filler/killer classification, 72

Customer segmentation (*Continued*)
  paper company example, 54–57
  principles for conducting, 60–61
  tracking, 155
  typical pitfalls with, 57–58
  at Uber, 187
  and undeads, 29
Customer segments:
  fences between, 60, 64, 65
  observable characteristics of, 57, 61
Custom Solutions unit (Swarovski),
  191–193

D

Daredevil (television series), 84
Davis, Miles, 33
Deal deconstructions, 155
Deal escalation, tracking, 154–155
DealShield Purchase Guarantee, 114
Decision makers, 178–179, 202
Decision making, business case based on,
  112, 118
Demand curve, *see* Price elasticity
Demographics, segmentation based on, 54,
  57
"Design the product around the price"
  approach, 163–206
  benefits of, 35–36
  current product development vs.,
  8–9
  at Dräger Safety, Inc., 174–182
  implementation of, 207–218
  at LinkedIn, 170–174
  at Optimizely, 194–200
  pharmaceutical company example,
  200–206
  at Porsche, 164–170
  at Swarovski, 188–193
  at Uber, 182–188
Digital cameras, 24–25
Digital device component makers, 21
Direct questions, in willingness-to-pay talks,
  45–48
Documents, pricing strategy, 99–106

Dodge Dart:
  monetization and product development
  mindset around, 34
  as product innovation failure, 5–7, 9
  sales of, 219n.6
Dollar Shave Club, 84
Doorbusters, 143
Dräger Safety, Inc., 174–182
  changing product development process
  at, 176–177
  "design the product around the price"
  approach at, 164, 174–175
  institutionalization of CPM process at,
  178–180
  limitations of previous product
  development process at, 175–176
  making monetization process stick at,
  181–182
  monetization strategy of, 9
  sales and marketing messages at, 180–181
Dräger Tube, 175
Drews, Ralf, 175–179, 181, 182
Dropbox, 73, 89–90
Drucker, Peter, 121
Dynamic Perspective (feature), 16, 17
Dynamic pricing, 85–87
  advantages of, 86
  described, 85–86
  determining suitability of, 86–87
  at Uber, 82–83, 183–185

E

Early adopters, pricing strategy catering to,
  103, 169
eBay, 87
EC2 (Elastic Compute Cloud), 143–144
The Economist (magazine), 141
eee PC (product), 22
Elastic Compute Cloud (EC2), 143–144
Elasticity, price, *see* Price elasticity
Electronics, feature shocks with, 20
Enercon, 80
Engineering cultures, monetization failures
  in, 15

Escalated deals, number of, 154–155
Evernote, 91
Every Day Low Price promotion, 105
Executives:
 as drivers of monetization approach, 169–170, 217
 goal allocations by, 100–101
 and hidden gems, 26
 pricing patience for, 155
 response to change by, 182
 view of volume, price, and profit by, 101
Expert judgment workshops, 46

F
Facebook, 43, 102
Failure(s). *See also* New product Monetization failures
 in current product innovation mindset, 35
 new product, 7–9
 in product innovation, 33–34
Fashion sector, Swarovski in, 189–191
Fast Company, 17
Features:
 benefits vs., 127
 at Dräger Safety, Inc, 179
 leader/filler/killer classification for, 71–72
 matching competitors, 176
 at Porsche, 166–168
 in product configurations, 64–66
 value analysis for, 166–168
 and value communications, 121, 124, 125
 WTP and prioritization of, 43–45
Feature shocks, 16–20
 at Amazon, 16–19
 building business cases to avoid, 116
 causes of, 19–20
 company culture leading to, 15
 defined, 11
 at Dräger Safety, Inc., 176
 other monetization failures vs., 31
 product configurations to avoid, 64

responses to, 19
 warning signs of, 18–19
 willingness-to-pay talks to avoid, 41, 44, 45
Fences, between customer segments, 60, 64, 65
Fiat Chrysler:
 monetization and product development mindset in, 34
 monetization strategy of, 9
 product innovation at Porsche vs., 3–7
Fillers (features), 71, 72
Firefly service, 17
Fire Phone, 16–19, 45
"First principles," 8
Fitness clubs, 89
Fixed costs, freemium pricing and, 89–90
Fleet Solutions, 81
Focus groups, 145–146
Forecasts, sales, 36, 114–115, 158
4G networks, 23
Freed, Andrew, 173, 174
Freemium pricing, 90–91
 advantages of, 90
 business case for, 114–115
 described, 90
 determining suitability of, 90–91
 at Optimizely, 196
Fuzzy front end, of innovation, 175, 176

G
Garmin, 59
G/B/B strategies, *see* Good, better, best strategies
General Electric, 83, 88
Gillette, 39–40
Global Pricing Study, 157–158, 217
Goal Allocation Exercise, 100
Goals:
 bundling to advance, 76
 of LinkedIn, 170–171
 for pricing strategies, 99–101
 selecting pricing strategy based on, 97
 setting, for new products, 214

Goal trade-offs:
  in business case, 117
  in pricing strategies, 99–101
Gold, Josh, 173, 174
Good, better, best (G/B/B) strategies,
    72–74, 198, 199
Goods, price elasticities for, 109
"Good enough" mindset, 24
Google:
  monetization model of, 82, 85, 87, 88, 92
  undeads at, 28
Google AdWords, 87, 88
Google Glass, 28
Google Maps, 186
Groupon, 103
Guard (product), 40
Gurley, Bill, 183–188
Gut-check, 173
Gut feeling, pricing based on, 191

H
Hard bundling, 74
Harvard Business Review, 10
Harvard Business School, 10, 194, 224n.13
Hidden gems, 24–27
  building business cases to avoid, 115
  company culture leading to, 15
  defined, 11
  examples of, 24–25
  other monetization failures vs., 31
  warning signs of, 26–27
  willingness-to-pay talks to avoid, 41
High-level pricing strategies, 97–98
Honda Civic, 6, 7, 219n.6

I
Implementation, monetization model,
    92–93
Implementing "design the product around
    the price" approach, 207–218
  difficulty with, 182
  jump-start method of, 208–209
  organizational culture for, 213–214
  pilot program for, 209–210

  pitfalls with, 214–217
  and scaling up program, 211–213
India, Gillette in, 39–40
Information:
  from customer research, 216–217
  from willingness-to-pay talks, 44–45
Inhaled insulin, 29
InMail, 171–172
Innovation:
  customers' interest in, 129
  fuzzy front end of, 175, 176
  in monetization models, 82–83
  product, see Product innovation
Innovation process:
  assessing your, 208–209
  managers of, 181
Innovation teams, 126, 209
Inside-out thinking, 18–19, 42
Institutionalization, of CPM process,
    178–180
Integration value, 75
Integrity, price, see Price integrity
Internal gut feeling, pricing based on, 191
Internet companies:
  behavioral pricing at, 137–140
  willingness-to-pay talks at, 41–44
  willingness-to-pay talks for, 45
Inverse correlations, 75
iPhone, 6, 59, 142

J
Jayaswal, Vishaal, 112–113
Jewelry sector, Swarovski in,
    189–191
Jobs, Steve, 33, 142
Jump-Start and Pilot phase, 208–210
Jump-start method, 208–209

K
Kahneman, Daniel, 136
Kalanick, Travis, 182, 185, 187, 188
Kamen, Dean, 27, 28, 30
Kargruber, Christoph, 189–191, 193
Keighley, Jim, 40

Key performance indicators (KPIs), 154, 205, 212
Killers (features), 71, 72, 76
Kindle, 16
Kindle Fire, 16
Kodak, 24–26
Koomen, Pete, 194, 195
KPIs, *see* Key performance indicators

L

Land and expand strategies:
  with freemium pricing, 90–91
  at Optimizely, 196
  product configurations for, 74
  selecting, 101–103
Land-grab scenarios, 85
Language:
  about dynamic pricing, 184–185
  for willingness-to-pay talks, 50
Leaders (features), 71, 72
LinkedIn, 170–174
  benefits statements of, 130
  "design the product around the price" approach at, 163–164
  future of product development for, 174
  goals of, 170–171
  members-first principle at, 170–172
  monetization model of, 90
  monetization process at, 173–174
  successful product innovation at, 9
LivingSocial, 102
Lotus 1-2-3 software, 70
Lowballing, 214
Lufthansa, 77

M

MacAskill, Chris, 124
MacAskill, Don, 124
McDonald's, 29, 67
Mach 3 razor, 40
Manheim:
  business case for new products at, 111–114
  monetization model of, 87

Marchionne, Sergio, 6–7
Market(s):
  entering new, 39–40
  identifying target, 178
  increasing share in, 101–103
  pricing strategy and position in, 97, 98
  seller, 88
Market access team, 204
Market analysis, 201
Marketing:
  to customer segments, 61
  at Dräger Safety, Inc., 180–181
Marketing teams:
  clinical development, market access, and, 203–204
  innovation, R&D, and, 126
  involving, in product innovation, 215
Market leaders, 98
Marketplaces, two-sided, 87
Market research:
  for pilot tests, 210
  at Porsche, 165–166
  by salespeople, 175–176
  willingness-to-pay talks vs., 50
Market simulation models, 168
Market sizing, 61
Marketwatch, 6
The Matrix, 217–218
Matrix of competitive advantages (MOCA), 128–129, 132
Matrix pricing model, 94, 95
Maximization pricing strategy, 101
Members-first principle, 170–172
Membership economy, 84
Mercedes, 157, 165
Mercedes CLS, 166
Mercedes S-Class, 166
Mercedes SL, 157
Metromile, 83
Mettler Toledo, 59
Michelin, 80–82, 88, 89, 92
Microsoft, 29, 70–71

Mindset. *See also* Monetization and product development mindset
  changing, 182, 193
  "good enough," 24
Mini Cooper Countryman, 131
Minivations, 20–24
  building business cases to avoid, 115–116
  causes of, 24
  company culture leading to, 15
  defined, 11
  examples of, 21–23
  and Optimizely pricing model, 196
  other monetization failures vs., 31
  product configurations to avoid, 64
  sales volumes of, 156
  warning signs of, 23–24
  willingness-to-pay talks to avoid, 41
Mixed bundling, 69, 74, 75
Mobile phone cases, Swarovski crystals on, 191–192
MOCA (matrix of competitive advantages), 128–129, 132
Modeling, in LinkedIn monetization process, 173–174
Monetization and product development mindset, 33–36
  "design the product around the price" approach, 35–36
  and innovation failures, 33–34
  myths and misconceptions with prevailing, 34–35
  at Porsche, 5
Monetization hero, 210
Monetization models, 79–96
  alternative metric pricing, 88–89
  defined, 79
  dynamic pricing, 85–87
  freemium pricing, 90–91
  importance of, 80
  innovation in, 82–83
  market-based pricing, 87–88
  of Michelin, 80–82
  price-setting based on, 104
  and price structures, 93–95

  selecting your, 91–93
  subscription, 83–85
Monetization of innovations:
  budget for, 210, 217
  in guiding philosophy of Porsche, 169–170
  importance of, 7
  at LinkedIn, 173–174
  making new process stick, 181–182, 213–214
  rates of successful, 10–11
  scaling up new programs for, 211–213, 215–216
  at Swarovski, 193
  tailoring of, to your company, 216
Monetization task force, 195–196
Monetization team, 211, 215
Monsanto, 89
Monte Carlo simulations, 117
Most–least questions, 47
Multiproduct companies, scaling up at, 211–213

N
Negotiations, sales, 140, 141
Netflix, 82, 83, 93, 194
New Coke, 29
New markets, entering, 39–40
New product(s). *See also* Product innovation
  business cases for, *see* Business cases for new products
  causes of failure for, 7–9
  communicating value of, *see* Value communications
  failure rate for, vii, 10
  impact on company of, 117, 168
  price optimization for, 107–109
  pricing strategies for, 101
  repricing, *see* Price integrity
New product monetization failures, 15–32
  avoiding, 32
  building business cases to avoid, 114–116
  categories of, 11–12
  and company culture, 15

comparing types of, 31
and current product innovation
mindset, 35
feature shocks, 16–20
hidden gems, 24–27
minivations, 20–24
undeads, 27–32
Newspaper industry, hidden gems in,
25, 26
New York Times, 90, 103
Noah's Ark (product), 22
No/maybe/yes cultures, 214

O
Observable characteristics, of customer
segments, 57, 61
Office suite (Microsoft), 70–71
Online advertising, 82
Online music services, 85
Online offers, A/B tests of, 146
Online subscription company, price
thresholds for, 144–145
OpenTable, 91, 183
Optimal price, 101, 157
Optimizely, 194–200
breakthrough innovations at, 194–195
bundling decision at, 198–199
"design the product around the price"
approach at, 164
expanding product portfolio at, 197–198
monetization hero at, 210
monetization strategy of, 9
selecting pricing metrics at, 196–197,
199–200
WTP talks at, 195–196
Organizational culture:
changing, 182, 202
for "design the product around the price"
approach, 213–214
and new product monetization failures,
15, 30
of Porsche, 164
Osbourne, Ozzy, 53–54
Outcomes, tracking, 154–155

Outcomes-based services, 88
Overall willingness to pay, 44

P
Products, 74, 196. *See also* Product
configuration
Paid pilots (LinkedIn monetization process),
174
Paper company:
customer segmentation at, 54–57
product configuration at, 64–66
Park Assist system, 23
"Pay as you go" model, 80, 88–89
Penetration pricing strategy, 101–103,
185–189
Pennies-a-day pricing, 143–144
Per-user pricing, 196
Pharmaceutical company, 200–206
cooperation between teams at,
203–204
"customer value–driven new product"
approach at, 202–206
definition of success at, 205–206
"design the product around the price"
approach at, 164
early stages of product development at,
203
input from local teams at, 202
monetization strategy of, 9
R&D processes at, 200–201
risk reduction at, 204–205
Phase III testing, 203, 205
Phase II testing, 203
Playmobil, 22, 156
Porsche, 164–170, 224n.1
business case for new products at, 168
changing R&D approach at, 188
"design the product around the price"
approach at, 163–165, 169–170
early customer research at, 165–166
feature selection at, 166–168
guiding philosophy of, 169–170
monetization strategy of, 9
pricing strategy at, 103

Porsche (*Continued*)
  product innovation at Fiat Chrysler vs.,
    3–7
  skimming strategy of, 169
Porsche Boxster, 165
Porsche Cayenne:
  business case for, 168
  customer research about, 166, 167, 169
  executive involvement in development
    of, 169–170
  feature selection for, 166–168
  sales of, 165, 170
  skimming strategy for, 169
  as successful product innovation, 3–5, 8,
    9, 163
Porsche Macan, 170
Porsche 911, 3, 165, 166
Porsche Panamera, 163
  business case for, 168
  customer research about, 166, 167
  executive involvement in development
    of, 170
  feature selection for, 166–168
  sales of, 165, 170
  skimming strategy for, 103, 169
The Porsche Principle, 169–170
Positioning:
  of benefits statements, 129
  and bundling/product configuration, 76
  in market, 97, 98
  price, 166
  and value communications, 124
Post-launch phase, 153–157
  deal deconstructions in, 155
  high sales in, 156–157
  patience in, 155–156
  problems in, 153–154
  tracking monthly outcomes in,
    154–155
  war-gaming competition's reactions in,
    156
Practicality, of customer segmentation, 60
Predictably Irrational (Dan Ariely), 136
Premiums, for bundles, 75

Premium offerings:
  behavioral pricing for, 138, 139
  at LinkedIn, 171, 172
  product configurations with, 64
Pressure-tests, for business cases, 117
Price:
  in business case, 114–115
  customer segment valuing, 56, 73
  defined, 4
  optimal, 101, 157
  and sales volume/profit, 101
  signaling quality with, 141–142
Price anchors, 136–138, 140–141
Price concessions, 141
Price–demand relationship, *see* Price
    elasticity
Price differentiation, 104
Price elasticity:
  in business cases, 117
  and dynamic pricing, 86
  market simulation model to determine,
    168
  and price integrity, 151
  and price optimization, 106–109
  in sales forecasts, 158
  at Uber, 184–186
Price endings, 104
Price floors, 104
Price hikes, 102
Price increases, 104, 157
Price integrity, 149–159
  at Apple, 150
  avoiding monetization failures by
    maintaining, 13
  and feature shocks, 19
  and patience, 151–153
  and preparing for post-launch phase,
    153–157
  and price wars, 157–158
  and repricing too early, 149–150
Price low strategy, 185–186
Price optimization, 106–109, 216
Price point, 4
Price positioning, 166

Price ranges, from WTP talks, 167
Price reactions, 105–106
Price setting, 87, 103–104
Price structures, monetization models and, 93–95
Price-tier system, 94, 190–191
Price undercutting, 153–154
Price wars, 157–158
Pricing:
  alternative metric, 88–89
  avoiding monetization failures with, 12, 32
  behavioral, *see* Behavioral pricing
  communication about, 75
  dynamic, 83, 85–87
  for feature shocks vs. minivations, 21–22
  freemium, 90–91
  market-based, 87–88
  with mixed bundling, 75
  Optimizely's metrics for, 196–197, 199–200
  in product development, 8–9, 33
  rational, 140
  for undeads, 28
  value, 136
Pricing board, 193
Pricing office, 193
Pricing power, 106
Pricing strategies, 97–110
  avoiding monetization failures with, 12
  "business as usual," 21–22
  creating pricing strategy documents, 99–106
  defined, 97
  high-level, 97–98
  of LinkedIn, 171–172
  and price elasticity, 106–109
  and price integrity, 151–153
  price reaction principles in, 105–106
  price-setting principles in, 103–104
  selecting, 101–103
  setting goals for, 99–101
  of Swarovski, 189–191
  of Uber, 183–188
  updating, 98–99
Pricing strategy documents, 99–106
Procter & Gamble, 29, 39–40
Product configurations, 63–67
  avoiding monetization failures with, 12
  key principles of, 71–73
  at Optimizely, 196
  successful, 64–67
  tips on engaging in, 73–75
Product development. *See also* Monetization and product development mindset
  changing early stages of, 203
  at Dräger Safety, Inc., 175–177
  and feature shocks, 19–20
  future of, 174, 188
  hidden gems in, 26
  pricing in, 8–9, 33
Product-driven cultures, 15
Product innovation, 3–13. *See also* Monetization of innovations
  causes of new product failures, 7–9
  customer input in, vii–viii
  failures in, 11, 33–34
  importance of successful, 9–11
  at Porsche vs. Fiat Chrysler, 3–7
  prevailing mindset about, 33–35
  and pricing pressure, 10–11
  rules for successful, 12–13
Product roadmaps, 44–45
Product valuation, 34, 35
Profit(s):
  and bundling, 67
  and minivations, 20–21
  at Porsche, 5, 165
  and price integrity, 151
  and sales volume/price, 101
  at Swarovski, 192
Promotional reactions, 105, 106
Psychological thresholds:
  in behavioral pricing, 137, 144–145
  and bundling/product configuration, 74, 76

Purchase probability questions, 47
Purchase simulations, 46, 47

Q
Qualitative discussions, in WTP talks,
    49–50
Qualitative research, in CPM, 179
Quality:
    customer segment valuing, 56, 73
    price as signal of, 141–142
    repricing and perception of, 149–151
Quantitative studies, at LinkedIn, 173–174
Quantitative surveys, in CPM, 179
Questions, in willingness-to-pay talks,
    45–50

R
R&D, *see* Research and development
Repricing. *See also* Price integrity
    early, 149–150
    war-gaming competition's reactions to,
    156
Research. *See also* Customer research
    market, 50, 165–166, 175–176, 210
    qualitative, 179
Research and development (R&D):
    cost of, 10
    customer-value driven approach to, 206
    at Dräger Safety, Inc., 175–178
    early-stage, 209
    global, 10–11
    at pharmaceutical companies, 200–201, 205
    sales/marketing teams and, 126
    signs of feature shocks from, 18–19
Resistance, organizational, 213
Retailers, behavioral pricing by, 143
Revenue(s):
    from behavioral pricing, 138
    estimating new product, vii
    at LinkedIn, 164, 172, 173
    at Optimizely, 194, 197
    at Porsche, 165
Revenue models, 12
Risk assumptions, 117

Risk-averse cultures, 15
Ryanair, 76–77

S
SaaS companies, *see* Software as a service
    companies
Sales:
    bundling/product configuration and, 76
    and G/B/B strategies, 73
    of Porsche Cayenne and Panamera, 165
    of X-zone 5000 gas detector, 178
Sales campaigns, at Dräger Safety, Inc.,
    180–181
Sales-driven companies, 182
Sales forecasts, 36, 114–115, 158
Sales negotiations, 140, 141
Sales team(s):
    and feature shocks, 19
    and hidden gems, 26
    innovation and, 126–127
    and minivations, 23
    in product innovation, 215
    R&D and, 126–127, 175–176
    tracking performance of, 154–155
    and undeads, 29
Sales volume (volume):
    in business case, 114–116
    higher than expected, 156–157
    nonprice actions for improving, 155–156
    in post-launch phase, 153–154,
        156–157
    and profit/price, 101
    repricing in response to, 149
Samsung, 102, 191–192
Sasson, Steven, 24–25
Satisfaction, customer, 67–68
Scale and Stick phase, 211–214
Scaling up monetization programs,
    211–213, 215–216
Scenario planning, 92
Scope creep, 176
Segmentation schemes, number of, 58.
    See also Customer segmentation
Segway PT, 27–28, 30

Seller markets, 88

Selling stories, creating, 180–181

Semiconductor companies, 20

Service companies, product configurations for, 66–67

Simon-Kucher & Partners, viii, 9–11, 217

Simulations:
market simulation models, 168
Monte Carlo, 117
purchase scenario, 46, 47

Siri, 16, 19

Siroker, Dan, 194, 195

Skimming pricing strategy, 103, 169

"Smell test," at LinkedIn, 173

SmugMug, 123–126

Software:
bundling of, 70–71, 75
as hidden gem, 24–25
at Optimizely, 194–195

Software as a service (SaaS) companies. *See also* Optimizely
bundling at, 199
business case for, 114–115
monetization model of, 82
pricing models of, 196
value communications at, 122–124

Software industry:
behavioral pricing in, 143
monetization models in, 82, 85, 88
pricing models in, 196

Southwest Airlines, 76

Speed, customer segment valuing, 56

Sporting events, dynamic pricing for, 86

Spotify, 85

Square, 92

Stage gates, 216

Start-ups:
assessing market potential of new products at, 164
behavioral pricing at, 137–140
failure rate for, 10, 194
scaling up at, 211

Static business cases, 116–117

Strategic decisions, about promotions, 105

Subscription economy, 84

Subscription model, 83–85
advantages of, 84
combinations of other models with, 91
described, 83–84
determining suitability of, 85
at Netflix, 82

Successful product innovation:
importance of, 9–11
rules for, 12–13

Supermarkets, dynamic pricing at, 86

Supply, for Uber, 183–184

Surcharges, 76–77

Surge pricing, 184–185

Swarovski, 188–193
completing monetization journey at, 193
"design the product around the price" approach at, 164, 191–193
evolution of, 188–189
monetization strategy of, 9
pricing strategy at, 189–191

Swarovski, Daniel, 188–189

Synergies, in product configuration, 76

T

Technology companies, feature shocks at, 19–20

Telecommunications companies:
minivations for, 23
monetization models for, 89
price integrity at, 156

Tesco, 86

Testing (product):
bundling decision for, 198–199
pricing model for, 196–197, 199

Tests:
A/B, 146, 194, 195
of behavioral pricing tactics, 145–146

Thaler, Richard, 136

Tier-based models:
pricing, 94, 190–191
product configuration and bundling, 72–74

Time frame, in pricing strategy, 97

Timing, of customer segmentation, 57

TK (ton-kilometer) monetization model, 81–82

Toyota Corolla, 6, 7, 219n.6

Trade-offs, goal, 99–101, 117

Travel industry, monetization models in, 86

Tversky, Amos, 136

Two-sided marketplaces, 87

U

Uber, 182–188

    "design the product around the price" approach at, 164

    dynamic pricing at, 183–185

    future of product development at, 188

    monetization model of, 9, 83, 85–86

    penetration pricing at, 185–189

    pricing strategy of, 102, 183–188

    success of, 182–183

Unbundling, 76–77

Undeads, 27–32

    building business cases to avoid, 114–115

    causes of, 30, 32

    company culture leading to, 15

    defined, 11

    examples of, 27–29

    and implementing "design the product around the price" approach, 213–214

    other monetization failures vs., 31

    product configuration to avoid, 64

    warning signs of, 29–30

    willingness-to-pay talks to avoid, 41

United States:

    failure rate for start-ups in, 194

    product innovation in, 11

    view of innovator in, 33

Unstructured conversation, in WTP talks, 49

Upselling, 74, 84

V

Valeo, 23

Value:

    adding, 155–156

    from benefit statements, 127

    in business case, 114–116

    customers' perceptions of, 89

    in entry-level products, 74, 137

    and price, 4, 191

    repricing and perception of, 149–151

    in willingness-to-pay talks, 46, 47

Value analysis, for features, 166–168

Value communications, 121–133

    avoiding monetization failures with, 12

    creating, 127–132

    difficulties with, 126–127

    at pharmaceutical company, 201

    refining, 132

    SaaS company example, 122–124

    at SmugMug, 123–126

    by Uber, 184–185

Value differentiation, 204

Value proposition:

    in current product innovation mindset, 35

    and feature shocks, 18–19

    for minivations, 21

    in selection of monetization model, 92

Value-selling spreadsheets, 122–123

Value story, 127

Volkswagen, 22–23

Volume, *see* Sales volume

W

Wall Street Journal, 84, 90, 124, 150

Walmart, 16, 105, 220n.1

Walt Disney Company, 194

War-gaming competitive reactions, 156

"Why" questions, 49

Wiedeking, Wendelin, 3

Willingness to pay (WTP):

    behavioral pricing and, 136

    in business cases, 9, 114–116

    customer segmentation based on, 53, 56, 58–60

    defined, 39

    at Dräger Safety, Inc., 175, 179

    overall, 44

    price integrity and, 151

in pricing strategy selection, 101, 103
prioritizing features based on, 43–45
product configuration/bundling based
    on, 64–65, 69
selecting features based on, 167–168
at Swarovski, 190
Willingness-to-pay (WTP) talks, 39–51
avoiding monetization failures with, 12, 30
benefits of early, 41–44
in business cases for new products, 114–115
at Gillette, 39–40
methods of conducting, 47–48
necessary information from, 44–45
at Optimizely, 195–196
optimizing price based on, 216
at Porsche, 167
tips for having, 45–46, 48–50

WTP, *see* Willingness to pay
WTP talks, *see* Willingness-to-pay talks

X
Xerox, 80
X-zone 5000 gas detector, 175
    pilot testing CPM with, 181
    product development process for,
        177–178
    variations of, 180
    WTP analysis for, 179

Y
Yes/maybe/no cultures, 214

Z
Zune, 29